The Typographic Medium

History and Foundations of Information Science
Edited by Michael Buckland, Jonathan Furner, and Markus Krajewski

The Typographic Medium

Kate Brideau

The MIT Press   Cambridge, Massachusetts   London, England

The MIT Press would like to thank the anonymous peer reviewers who provided comments on drafts of this book. The generous work of academic experts is essential for establishing the authority and quality of our publications. We acknowledge with gratitude the contributions of these otherwise uncredited readers. ·

This book was set in Arnhem Pro Blond and Berthold Akzidenz Grotesk by The MIT Press. Printed and bound in the United States of America.

Library of Congress Cataloging-in-Publication Data

Names: Brideau, Kate, author.
Title: The typographic medium / Kate Brideau.
Description: Cambridge, Massachusetts : The MIT Press, [2021] | Series: History and foundations of information science | Includes bibliographical references and index.
Identifiers: LCCN 2020037099 | ISBN 9780262045858 (hardcover)
Subjects: LCSH: Graphic design (Typography) | Graphic design (Typography)—History. | Type and type-founding. | Type and type-founding—History.
Classification: LCC Z246 .B7375 2021 | DDC 686.2/2—dc23

LC record available at https://lccn.loc.gov/2020037099

10   9   8   7   6   5   4   3   2   1

For Beth & Darcy

Contents

Preface and Acknowledgments

The illustrations that appear throughout this book were drawn by hand—perhaps an odd choice for a text about a medium that is mass produced. However, this is inspired in part by the aesthetic of Gerrit Noordzij's books (*The Stroke* and *Letterletter*), and to a lesser extent by other calligraphic teachers like Edward Johnston (*Writing & Illuminating & Lettering*). The basic principle behind the use of calligraphy in typographic education is that drawing these characters by hand allows one to become physically familiar with the nature of these shapes and the possibilities they contain. A similar principle guides this book's illustrations as well. Producing these drawings allows for a closer study of forms—since the eye and hand together slow down the act of observation; the drawing hand produces a different kind of thought. Further, this process provides me a personal, albeit amateur, glimpse into the significant amount of detail and labor involved in typographic design. The results of that drawing are illustrations of type, not type itself—just as in chapter 7 the illustration of the brain is not a brain itself. As such, the majority of the creativity in these illustrations belongs to others, but any technical errors are my own.

At the start of each chapter, you'll find a diagram of typographic anatomy referenced in that chapter. Typography has its own (relatively settled) vocabulary, full of stems, eyes, and tails; and rather than having a single anatomical glossary at the back of the book, these diagrams are intended to offer greater ease of access. You may find by the later chapters that the specialist language of typography has become familiar to you (if you aren't familiar with it already). The combination of these diagrams with a quote to start each chapter is a modest nod to the sociologist and information designer W. E. B. Du Bois—who began each chapter of his book *The Souls of Black Folk* with a few lines of poetry by mostly White European men, and a few meters of music from Black spirituals (in the last chapter, both pieces come from a spiritual). That book was the first to show me that the structure of a text can communicate ideas of its own (for Du Bois's information designs, see *W. E. B. Du Bois's Data Portraits*).

I am a generalist at heart, and this book is the result of at least four years of writing nested within a decade of mostly failed writing, and fifteen years of research. So, there are a lot of endnotes. And while some merely attribute information to original sources you might want to look up yourself, many add explanations, expansions, and intersections with a diverse range of fields of study. So, I encourage you to pay attention to them; some are hiding interesting ideas.

Finally, there are all sorts of type puns in this book, and in every case, they are intended (though generally not doubled up like this).

Given how long this book has been in the works, many people and institutions have contributed to its completion. I'm grateful first of all to the editors and reviewers at the MIT Press who saw the value in this book, as well as its flaws—in particular, Michael Buckland, Jonathan Furner, Markus Krajewski, Gita Manaktala, Judith Feldmann, and Emily Gutheinz. My own writing has benefited from the opportunity to teach critical thinking and writing in the NYU College of Arts and Sciences' Expository Writing Program, and in the Department of Management Communication at NYU's Stern School of Business. My primary intellectual home, however, has been NYU's Department of Media, Culture, and Communication (MCC), and there my life is made manageable by the staff, particularly the department's rock Darrell Carter, and my friend and hero Rebecca Brown. For their support of this book's design, I'm particularly grateful to MCC's Lisa Gitelman, Rod Benson, Tracy Figueroa, and Dani Resto. Rodrigo Novaes Maltez and the team at the Flusser Archive at Universität der Künste Berlin introduced me early in this process to Flusser's unpublished essay, "On Typography," and allowed me the time to gain a fuller view of a philosopher whose work is woven throughout this book (and all my thoughts), even when not named. Every two years since 2012 (with the sad exception of 2020), I have made a pilgrimage to the St. Bride Library in London, and am indebted to Bob Richardson, Heather Jardine, and the rest of the library's volunteers for their help, expertise, and good humor. Since 2013, I've taken every opportunity to bring my students to the Woodside Press in Brooklyn, and am grateful to Andy Birsh and Davin Kuntze for those years of technological inspiration and tours.

Some of the ideas in this book have been developed through teaching, and I am grateful to all the students who have studied with me—in particular, Jacob Ford, Marcha Johnson, Isabella Reyes, and Austin Snyder, who spent a semester poking at the more speculative edges of typographic shape with me. I've benefited from numerous conversations on typography and technology with Mara Mills, Charles Berret, Alex Galloway, Tom Mullaney, Marita Sturken, Dorothea von Mücke, and Lisa Gitelman (whom I've already mentioned, but am particularly indebted to for sending me down a road of research lined with flatware, chess pieces, and intellectual property law). Fergal Hogan provided me with a home and friendship during the most productive and formative three months of this book's writing; Beza Merid's enthusiasm encouraged this book's moments of typographic trickery; Paul Melton and Scott Selberg are founts I return to perpetually; and Jamie Berthe, Brett Gary, Andrew Fischer Hurt, Seth Reiser, Ryan Sarni, and Adam White have all influenced how my intellectual work and life have been balanced through the completion of this book. Finally, to my family: this is what I've been doing for the past decade; you're under no obligation to read it.

ascender · bowl · crossbar · counter · descender · ear · nose · loop · serifs · Sloped axis · stem

Source: author.

1 Introduction

To see what is in front of one's nose needs a constant struggle.
—George Orwell[1]

There's a story in type history that goes like this: In the second half of the eighteenth century, there was a dramatic divide among type aficionados, between those who loved the work of John Baskerville and those who hated it. Baskerville's typeface (1754) was a modification of a Dutch-inspired face designed by William Caslon about thirty years earlier. In England, Caslon's type was supremely popular, while many decried Baskerville as a typeface so sharp and light that it hurt the reader's eyes. Likewise, in the United States, where Caslon was the typeface chosen for John Dunlap's 1776 printing of the Declaration of Independence, Baskerville had few champions. One of those champions, however, was Benjamin Franklin. A printer himself, one day Franklin was debating the quality of Baskerville's work with an avowed admirer of Caslon. As the two men argued, Franklin picked up a type specimen, tore off its identification, and handed the page to the other man. He told him to point out all that was terrible about Baskerville. The man took the printed sheet and began to identify everything that was wrong and ugly and offensive about this face. Franklin then revealed to the man that the specimen he had been critiquing was not Baskerville at all, but rather the man's beloved Caslon.

This story is told rather frequently in texts about type.[2] This could be because it captures a moment when typographic history intersects with recognizable historical events or figures. It could be that the story is humorous, or that it reflects how worked up people can get about typefaces.[3] However, what I find significant about this story is that it reflects just how little we understand about this medium that carries so much of our information on a daily basis. What sets Caslon apart from Baskerville is a number of minute differences in shape, and what is peculiar about those differences is that they can inspire strong reactions and at the same time be completely overlooked.

Comparing two characters drawn from Caslon and Baskerville (figure 1.1), we can begin to see some of the details that set these two faces apart. Notice the e's: sharper in Baskerville and rounder in Caslon. In its bowled characters, Caslon has a slight slope—notice on the d that the top of the bowl flares as it meets the stem, whereas in Baskerville the bowl meets the stem with *two* narrow strokes. In general, the counters in Baskerville are more open than in Caslon, and the serifs are horizontal and more delicate.[4] One can also see that the noses of the e's have different arcs, and so on. Overall Baskerville's details create greater contrast between the black and white of the page, while Caslon integrates figure and ground more intimately. While these differences may be easy to overlook, they are representative of the details that set apart most of the many thousands of typefaces that exist.

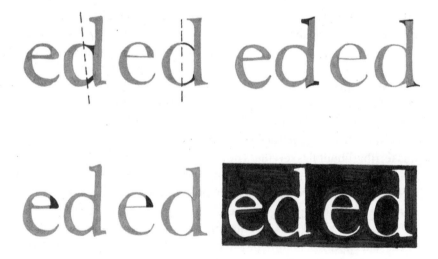

Figure 1.1
Four comparisons of Caslon (William Caslon, 1725; "ed" on the left in each) and Baskerville (John Baskerville, 1754; "ed" on the right in each), showing a few of the minor ways characters in these two related typefaces differ from one another. *Source*: author.

These minor differences in shape are an indication that typography is stranger and more complicated than we may assume. Our daily use of the medium, and the ease with which we consume information through it (as you are doing now), makes it appear simple at first. And one could argue that our ability to successfully make use of the medium means there is no reason to interrogate it further. One could argue that these detailed iterations of shape are inconsequential to our ability to signify—to paraphrase the Swiss linguist Ferdinand de Saussure, regardless of how it's produced, a t is a t until it is no longer recognizable as such.[5] But even if differences in typographic shape have no effect on signification (which, after Roland Barthes, is debatable), it is nonetheless important to understand the detailed operation of typography precisely because of how much of our daily information is carried through this medium.[6] We access vast amounts of our species' knowledge through media, and a vast amount of that mediated knowledge through typography. Not only in books, magazines, newspapers, and posters, typography is found on every screen you view—from the wristwatch-sized to multistory IMAX movie screens. It does important work in labeling of all sorts, and wayfinding signage through streets, airports, and buildings. Increasingly it's worn as a fashion statement and plays a critical role in the now widespread social practice of branding.[7] It is everywhere in daily life, and like most things that are this dominant in society, we have been encouraged to overlook type, in order to ensure it works smoothly. This book, on the other hand, encourages you to pay attention to the typographic medium, to see its vast expanse, to see that it is not letters.

Though I will expand upon this in the next two chapters, the simplest reason typography is not letters is because a letter is a pure abstraction, a linguistic concept with no physical form.[8] We can embody a letter in a physical form, or character, for instance translating the concept "A" into one of its characters: A, a, or a. And typography, then, involves more detailed levels of physical instantiation—A, but also A, and A, and **A**, and so on. As we'll see, what is unique in the materiality of type varies depending on who you ask and what technological period you're looking at. For the Czech-born media theorist Vilém Flusser, what was revolutionary about typography is that it treats letters like three-dimensional objects—manipulable types, rather than fixed Platonic ideals. Alternatively, for the literary scholar Walter Ong, typography introduces writing with preexisting characters—unlike handwriting, in which characters do not exist prior to being created on the page.[9] What seems to transcend these views, however, is that the typographic medium has a physical (or at the very least visual) manifestation—something that letters lack.

The typographic medium has a long and steady history: accompanying humanity from eleventh-century China and fourteenth-century Korea, and independently from fifteenth-century European mass production, through industrial printing and typewriters, phototypesetting, dry transfer, to digital printers and twenty-first-century networked screens. Going on one millennium now (or six hundred years, depending on your measure), typography remains a medium at the center of our daily lives.[10] And beyond persisting, it is also proliferating. While one can debate the necessity of continuing to design these shapes, there is no end in sight to typography's population growth and diversification.[11] Whatever happens to print in the future, typography continues. It would make sense, then, to have a better understanding of this formidable medium. At some point, we must realize that the typographic medium is vast and old and variable and growing.

Typography, like many media, is something we are assured will work best if we don't look at it too closely. Typographic characters, with all their variety and detail, are everywhere. Yet our common sense tells us that this variety and detail are inconsequential. Until we cannot read it, we have no reason to pay attention to the formal ways in which this medium is working. But perhaps paying attention to typography can be a model for also turning our attention to the rest of what is in front of our noses. Perhaps if we pay attention, we will begin to notice just how much of our world is designed, and perhaps we can then ask why it is designed in this way or that. Who is this designed for? What values does it convey through its design?[12] In what ways is this design informing our behavior, or expectations, or common sense? Perhaps too, taking typography seriously can be a lesson in getting beyond surface attention more generally, of being critically aware—an exercise in not accepting the world at face value.[13] Whether one takes up a position of skepticism, of questioning, of resisting defaults, the constant struggle to see what's in front of one's nose that Orwell writes about is an effective counterforce to comfort and habit—to think not of oneself (and one's comfort), but for oneself.[14] This will require a certain kind of seeing.

Typographic Shapes

To see the typographic medium as it is, we have to interrupt the automatic response that sees this:

A

and equates it with a variety of linguistic and social concepts—the first letter of the alphabet, the highest grade one can earn, the first in a list, an indefinite article, and so on. What you see above is a shape, and though it is a shape that may evoke all the associations listed, in and of itself it has particular features that set it apart from, and into conversation with, countless other shapes. Both W and W signify the same letter; linguistically, they are identical. But as typographic shapes, their identity ends. The typographic medium is populated by a vast number of these non-identical shapes, and the possible expansion of that population appears to be infinite.[15] As we'll explore in more depth in the next two chapters, being able to see this diversity of shape requires that we set linguistic concerns largely aside, because they obscure too much of the medium. If the essence of typography were linguistic, then the formal variety found in W and W and all their other variants would be unnecessary. These are shapes, and their variety is at the heart of what the typographic medium is.

To see the typographic medium, then, will first require that we pay attention to the scope of the medium—both the small differences in shape that distinguish characters from one another, and also the many hundreds of thousands of varieties that make up the entire medium. Typography has been studied from a number of directions before—there is a large literature on the history and techniques of typographic design,[16] a historically robust literature on bibliography,[17] and a conceptually rich literature on how the materiality of the text contributes to the production of meaning.[18] But a study of typography as a medium is a different sort of task. Well-known media texts like Walter Ong's *Orality and Literacy*, Harold Innis's *Empire and Communications*, and especially Marshall McLuhan's *Gutenberg Galaxy* understand movable type printing as a paradigm shift in culture, notably bringing about a move away from the oral to the visual.[19] There are also more technical histories and mechanical descriptions of various typographic technologies (as well as a growing number of documentaries that explore the influence of shifting technologies on design work).[20] As we'll see, the history of typographic technologies is particularly important for understanding this medium, and one can't discount typography's wider social and semantic connections. However, typographic detail is conspicuously absent from much of the above literatures, besides some engagement in that first category of technical works written for, and often by, typographers themselves.

This book offers an unconventional view of typography. While it references some of the more conventional means of understanding its history, formal patterns, and classification, much of what is discussed in the following pages doesn't often make it into books on type. For instance, intellectual property and the theories behind the early work of computer scientists occupy a considerable amount of space in this book. From the population of typefaces, this book discusses some canonical faces, alongside experimental type, and recently designed faces that may never take off.[21] But this is not meant to be a survey of the most important episodes of type history; it is meant to provide a sense of the breadth and depth of the medium as a whole. It is meant to capture the medium's sense of possibility.[22]

On one hand, the shapes populating the typographic medium are conservative—the roman forms developed by Nicolas Jenson in the 1470s do not look radically different from those designed today (see figure 1.2).[23] There are relatively minor differences between the first romans and those we favor now, differences not unlike those between Baskerville and Caslon. On the other hand, some shapes in this medium bear no resemblance to

Figure 1.2
Jenson's Roman (Nicolas Jenson, 1470). *Source*: author.

the Latin alphabet in our mind's eye (or to any other script). The radical designs push the limits of the set of typographic shapes further and further out, while the conservative forms find a way to hold it all together. But this combination of the conservative and the radical also makes defining the set of typographic shapes challenging. The majority conservative shapes might lead us to believe we can define the typographic medium according to its function; we might be tempted to conclude that the typographic shape is alphanumerical. However, the radical shapes make it clear that *all* typographic shapes (including the conservative ones) are best defined formally rather than functionally. That is, the ways in which experimental typefaces exceed their linguistic functions is only an exaggerated version of what takes place in all typographic shapes—as we saw in the two W's above, they are particular shapes, not generic linguistic concepts. So the search to understand the typographic medium will be best served by studying its forms.

As we'll see in the next chapter, isolating typographic form from its linguistic function is possible, but not always simple—form and function have a complicated relationship in the typographic medium. Not only does linguistic function lead our attention away from typographic forms, but the nature of the relationship between form and function also varies among typefaces. Consider three roughly contemporaneous examples, Bell Centennial, Data 70, and Meander, shown in figures 1.3, 1.4, and 1.6.

In 1976, Matthew Carter started designing a typeface for the publication of AT&T's phonebooks. That typeface, Bell Centennial, has designs that are deeply informed by their functional requirements. Because they were designed for phonebooks, the shapes in this typeface had to be clearly and unambiguously legible at small sizes, and in tight columns. But they also needed to take into account the means of production for these books. Phonebooks aren't printed to be enduring documents; they are printed with cheap ink, on newsprint paper, using fast presses. The degree of ink-spread resulting from that combination of factors is significant, so Carter designed this typeface to anticipate that spread. Ink is most likely to bleed, to spread beyond its intended boundaries, wherever strokes meet. Because of this, Bell Centennial's characters have notches cut out of them anywhere two or more strokes meet. This results in an awkward set of shapes in design, but a normal set of shapes in the printed book (see figure 1.3). For Bell Centennial to work, it had to be functional on the page, and this first required being functional on the press. In this way, its designed forms are a direct reflection of its functional constraints.[24]

FGHIJKL

FGHIJKL

Figure 1.3
Bell Centennial (Matthew Carter, 1976) prepares for the effects of ink-spread, by cutting
out notches anywhere strokes meet. *Source*: author.

A typeface like Data 70 (Robert Newman, 1970) takes that same kind of intimate form–function relationship and transforms it into a style, something more purely formal (see figure 1.4). This typeface was designed for Letraset, a firm specializing in dry-transfer type. Because dry-transfer type involves shapes that are screenprinted onto (and then rubbed off of) clear plastic sheets, the technology grants designers more flexibility of form than metal type does.[25] In this respect, Robert Newman was designing with fewer technological constraints than Carter was. However, Data 70 is based on shapes with a close connection to functional constraints—MICR typefaces. MICR, or magnetic ink character recognition, is used to automate reading and sorting of documents in industries that process large amounts of paperwork—banks, for example. The magnetic ink is read by a scanner (ill-suited for ambiguity), but also must be legible for humans, and so an MICR typeface takes on unconventional shapes (which will be explored in chapter 5). Data 70 took some of the unconventional details of MICR faces and divorced them from their functional requirements. This typeface does not need bulbous tabs on its sides, though it borrows these from MICR's functionally determined forms. In fact, Data 70 likely would not have worked well as an (early) MICR or OCR (optical character recognition) typeface—there is ambiguity in some of its forms, characters that can easily be confused for one another. The 2 looks remarkably like the Z, the I like the l, the 5 like the S; and the & and 8, and B and 6 are a bit too close to one another for comfort (see figure 1.5).[26] Though based on functionally constrained designs, Data 70's peculiar shapes serve only a formal aesthetic.

Finally, Maxim Zhukov's 1972 experimental typeface, Meander, presents a close interaction between form and function, but with an alternative view of what "function" might mean in relation to typography. Like a number of the typefaces that will appear in the coming chapters, Meander emerges out of particular constraints and out of a desire for something systematic. Drawing on a long tradition of grid-based design, Zhukov designed his multiscript forms out of a grid with sixteen units, and eliminated superfluous features like serifs, but allowed for (and even

Figure 1.4
Data 70 (Robert Newman, 1970).
Source: author.

Figure 1.5
The ambiguity between these pairs of characters would likely be avoided in a typeface designed for MICR or OCR scanners.
Source: author.

added) curves (see figure 1.6).[27] Beyond wanting to explore the forms possible in the constraints of his grid, Zhukov was interested in systematizing the design of typographic forms. A type family is a collection of different weights (bold, light, etc.) and styles (extended, condensed, etc.) all governed by a single overarching design principle. Varying weights are often constructed in unsystematic ways, individually adjusting strokewidth and the resulting character proportions. But Meander constructs its type family by systematically constructing each character out of a set of seven stripes—the heaviest weight will be seven-stripes thick, the lightest, one-stripe—but the basic contour of each character never changes.[28] Like Bell Centennial, the forms in this typeface are reflections of their function, but rather than being read or produced, that function is actually the systematic creation of forms. In these three examples we can see form being nearly dictated by function (and function in turn being reliant on those forms); functional details becoming merely formal; and forms that redefine what their functions can be. Needless to say, these are only three examples of how form and function interact in the typographic medium.

While keeping one eye on the complex relationship of forms to various functions, exploring the limits of the set of typographic shapes is at the heart of developing a rich understanding of the medium. One might explore those limits using a reductive method, an expansive method, or a relational method; all three of these possibilities will be explored in this book. Using a reductive method would involve boiling the set of typographic shapes down to a basic, skeletal definition for each character. Every variation of A, or of ∂, would be reduced to its barest necessities, and this irreducible core would serve as one part of the definition of the class of typographic shapes. This is akin to the existential journey twentieth-century minimalist painters took in trying to define their medium. Was the essence of painting primary colors? Straight lines? The flat surface of

Figure 1.6
Meander (Maxim Zhukov, 1972). *Source*: author.

the canvas? What, they asked through their practice, is left of painting when all that is extraneous is eliminated?[29] And, whether or not it can be answered, that same question can be asked of an A (as we'll see in chapter 4).

Using an expansive method would involve pushing our expectations of the typographic medium outward in an attempt to locate the outer limit of the category. Here, one would experiment with our expectations of what an S could be, without losing that which makes it an S. This is akin to the Dadaist project, which showed that our basic expectations of what constitutes "art" are not in fact the limit of what can be called, or can function as, art. And recognizing that false limit, Dadaists and some type designers (as we'll see in chapter 5) have sought to find the new limit of their field.

Finally, using a relational method would involve neither a single irreducible core nor a single outer limit, but rather a multitude of similarities among the various inhabitants of the category of typographic shapes. The g in Arnhem (Fred Smeijers, 1998) shares a similar ear to the g in Bodoni (Giambattista Bodoni, 1788), which shares a similar loop with the g in Baskerville, and so on (see figure 1.7). This kind of method is

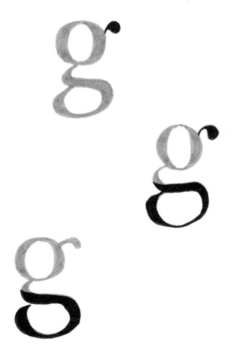

Figure 1.7
In a relational exploration of typographic shape one would look for similarities across characters and typefaces. From the top: Arnhem (Fred Smeijers, 1998), Bodoni (Giambattista Bodoni, 1788), Baskerville (John Baskerville, 1754).
Source: author.

perhaps most famously illustrated in Ludwig Wittgenstein's definition of what constitutes a "game." Because there is no single definition that will capture every variant of game, Wittgenstein argues for the use of family resemblance instead.[30] A child shares the deep brown eyes of her mother, the height of her father, and the freckles of her grandfather, and yet no one feature will define either the child or their whole family as a category. In chapter 6 we will see that this relational method suits an understanding of typography best, as it allows for more variety of shape while still revealing key shared features throughout the medium.

The Typographic Medium

Seeing typography will first mean paying attention to countless relational forms, but, as we'll see in chapter 7, typographic shapes are not just forms—they're functional forms. So, seeing typography will also require setting aside our assumptions and associations in order to see *the medium itself*. Rather than being considered merely a design element in "print media" or "digital media," typography is being seen here as a medium, able to transcend the life and death of particular technologies.

As a medium, typography is a third thing. It stands between two things (world and mind, author and reader, text and scanner, input and output, encoding and decoding, etc.). And as a third thing, no medium is identical with either end of the experience it mediates, and neither are the experiences on either end of that mediated chain identical to one another. This is not a value judgment—I am not casting media as manipulative or adulterating—it is merely to note that any medium, including typography, employs a "mode of presentation" that affects in some way the information communicated through it.

This idea of a mode of presentation is borrowed from Gottlob Frege, a philosopher of language, who can help us see what it means to be a third thing between us and the world.[31] More commonly referred to in his circles as the "sense," the mode of presentation is a property of certain words. A name like "Venus" or "the morning star" refers to a particular thing (the planet between Earth and Mercury), but these names also have different senses, which are distinct from their referent.[32] The mode of presentation is an idea embedded in Frege's logical project, a project with little relation to the study of media, but in writing on this idea he constructs an analogy that suggests a possible expansion of the concept's reach. Imagining a person with a telescope pointed at the moon, Frege explains that the mode of presentation is not the moon itself; nor is it the subjective "retinal image" one sees while looking into the telescope. Instead, the mode of presentation is akin to the "real image" that exists *inside* the telescope.[33] It is objective, but not an object in the world; and it is accessible to any individual, but is not itself a subjective view. Recognizing the telescope as a medium, we could then say that, in this apparent no man's land between the object and the subject, the mode of presentation *belongs to the medium itself.* It would be there in the telescope whether there is someone looking or not. Where typography is concerned, the mode of presentation would be distinct from the message being carried by type, but also different from the impression a particular design makes on a subjective viewer (see figure 1.8). The typographic design is not simply clothing in which we dress up a message; the design is an integral part of the medium's operation. It belongs to the medium itself.

It is easy to think of media, whether typography or telescopes, as being defined by its relationship to us, to humanity. As media producers and consumers ourselves, the content in and interpretation of media are both relatable. And so, it is comfortable to think about media as tools with which *we create* content, and through which that content becomes available for *our* interpretation. But media involve more than such a purely human definition will allow. In Frege's analogy, the mode of presentation exists before and independently of perception, and so to understand it is to bracket both content (because it is more than this) and interpretation (because it is prior to this).

Beyond human definitions, media possess their own operational logics and internal patterns—a mode of presentation that belongs to the medium itself. The German media philosopher Wolfgang Ernst argues that media only exist as themselves when they are operating.[34] We can study the uses to which these media have been put, or the content they have been used to produce, but this doesn't necessarily get us any closer to understanding the medium—this only gets us closer to understanding ourselves. Ernst's particular brand of media archaeology suggests that media have, as a significant part of their existence, their own autonomous operations.[35] While there may be human involvement at some point in the medium's process, the operations can be said to take place within the device or among devices, and are often beyond the capabilities of human beings. For instance, he argues that when we hit the keys on a computer keyboard a process of transubstantiation takes place. Symbols that have

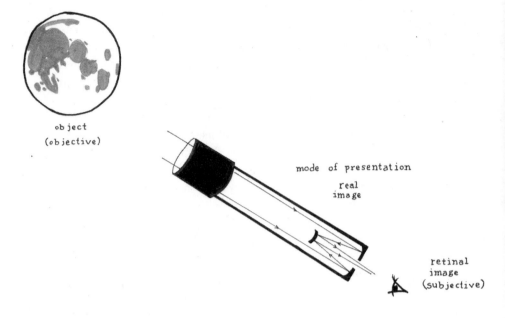

object
(objective)

mode of presentation
real
image

retinal
image
(subjective)

[content]

typographic
shape

[interpretation]

Figure 1.8
In Gottlob Frege's philosophy, the sense, or mode of presentation, is akin to the "real image" that exists inside a telescope pointed at the moon. The typographic medium's mode of presentation (embodied in its shapes) similarly belongs to the medium itself: in excess of the content fed into the medium, and prior to the subjective interpretation of any reader. *Source*: author.

semantic value in our minds lose this content and are transformed into signals; they lose meaning and gain indexicality—the ability to be an indication of where they came from.[36] Similarly, OCR scanners are described by Ernst as having a "cold gaze," indifferent to the semantic content of a text. Media like these record at a subsemantic level that is largely inaccessible to us without the aid of these media.[37]

Because media work at this subsemantic level, Ernst is interested in studying enumeration (the work media does) rather than narrative (tied to meaning). He seeks to liberate the idea of "telling" from its hermeneutic (i.e., interpretive) connotations. Drawing on the etymology of "to tell"—an etymology in both English and German—he argues that the original purpose of telling was to count or account for, and for him it is only by understanding this counting that media is understood.[38] It may be easy to see how Ernst's media archaeology applies to the cold gaze of a late typographic technology like the OCR scanner; but he also sees a valuable subsemantic quality in movable type printing itself. He notes that in Gutenberg's technique, even empty spaces or absences count.[39] That is, a block of text is constructed by the combination of individual units of type, *and also* by the empty spaces that are part of the calculation of the page as a whole (the pieces of metal, wood, etc. that are used to space out pieces and lines of type and keep them in place—known as leading and furniture). Flusser, who we met earlier, similarly sees this quality of quantification in typographic technologies. Not only in the development of movable type printing, but also in the typewriter, Flusser sees the breaking down of narrative lines—the transformation of letters into calculable bits. Flusser sees typographic technology as helping humanity adapt to an atomic age. Less computational than Ernst's view, Flusser sees the stuttering typewriter bridging the gap between creation and calculation. He argues it is "a programmed instrument that reaches into the swirl of particles and packages them into texts"—acting outside human capability.[40]

Perhaps difficult to see, media have operations that belong to themselves. They have a life of their own—and typography as a medium should be understood in this light. We could view typography simply as an extension of human faculties. Certainly, like writing, it *could* be viewed as an extension of our memory—a means of creating a record of the human species' collective memory.[41] Or, as Flusser argues, we *could* identify typography as an extension of humanity's ability (and willingness) to manipulate the natural world. Not merely a means of recording our speech, metal type shows us that the "types" (i.e., the Platonic ideals) that form reality are not fixed but manipulable.[42] Once we were made aware that types are malleable, we could imagine changing the world through the manipulation of those types. This, Flusser argues, is how humans arrived at Enlightenment thinking. Or further still, as Marshall McLuhan argues, we *could* view movable type printing as a development of our subjective point of view. Placing knowledge, ideas, the world into our hands in the form of portable and affordable books made each individual reader the center of their own worldview.[43] However, if we understand typography only in these ways, it remains a tool working for us, or upon us.[44] If, on the other hand, we view typography as a medium with its own mode of presentation, its own operational logic beyond human capability (perhaps quantification as Ernst and Flusser suggest, perhaps something else), it can be understood as a far more complicated beast.[45] To understand typography as having capabilities beyond us requires a certain suspension of our own point of view, of our sense of human importance, and of the automatic assumptions we often make. To see what is in front of our noses, we will have to bracket certain assumptions and biases.

On Seeing in Front of One's Nose

The idea of bracketing I propose bears some resemblance to the phenomenological bracketing (or *epoché*) that the philosopher Edmund Husserl wrote about. Early in the twentieth century, Husserl wanted to refashion philosophy as a science, to throw away the abstract theories that formed the basis of modern philosophy and turn instead "to the things themselves."[46] This project would require a new way of thinking; in particular, it required a bracketing of any judgments concerning existence. Husserl's thinking was this: the basis of this new science, phenomenology, was to be subjective experience—not ideas, assumptions, or even the sorts of propositions upon which natural scientists build their work. He wanted to use the experience of a thing as the basis for knowing that thing. And so, he argued that whether or not a thing exists should be of no concern. An illusion can provide us with just as valid an *experience* (identical mental states, or *intentions*) as an actual thing can, and so whether or not the thing exists is irrelevant. What remains once we bracket questions about the existence of a thing is consciousness, and this forms the terrain from which Husserl's science would grow.[47]

Husserl is careful to distinguish this process of bracketing from a mere denial of fact. He writes, "I am *not negating* this 'world' as though I were a sophist; I am *not doubting its factual being* as though I were a skeptic."[48] Instead, he sets aside "the world which is continually given to me beforehand as existing,"[49] until his new science has established, through experience, that this world is fact. Certainly, some aspects of Husserl's bracketing are of no use here. First of all, questions of typography's existence, or more broadly ontological concerns, are not what stand in the way of knowing it. The shift to digital type does raise some interesting questions about what type *is* these days, and has led to some counterintuitive conclusions in the US copyright debates regarding typeface; but these existential issues will be addressed in future chapters, since they in fact tend to *aid* in knowing type. Second, the subjective experience of type is of little concern. While what you experience or feel when you see a particular typeface might be of interest to some designers, or those with branding concerns, it can't open up a broader understanding of the medium as a whole.[50] What is useful in Husserl's philosophy of bracketing is the idea of getting a clearer picture by facing the thing, rather than our assumptions about the thing. Even further, Husserl's concept of bracketing encourages us to interrogate what we assume we *know*. He distinguishes his own proposed bracketing from that found in scientific positivism, where scientists were merely meant to set aside personal views in the interest of objectivity. He argues it is not only bias *but also fact* that needs to be bracketed (keeping in mind that parentheses are distinct from rejection). He believed we should be open to the possibility that things could be different from how we've *known* them to be.

Later in the twentieth century, the political theorist Hannah Arendt, schooled in the phenomenological tradition, proposed a more grounded version of this bracketing, aimed at grave and consequential subjects. In *The Origins of Totalitarianism*, she argues that comprehension requires "the unpremeditated, attentive facing up to, and resisting of, reality—whatever it may be."[51] Facing up to reality is bold enough, but to do so without the comfort of premeditation, without assuming what's been taken as given, is far more unsettling. Her political theory is opposed to orthodoxy, common sense, the cliché, and all else that is without thought. And so, in *Origins* (and in *Eichmann in Jerusalem*) she brackets the simple equation of totalitarianism with evil, and, without rejection or denial, arrives at a far more nuanced understanding of the specific nature of that evil, the perpetrators, and the victims.[52] Typography has little to do with totalitarianism (though it does make an appearance in the politics of the Third Reich, and in the complexities of world domination).[53] However, this same kind of uncomfortable bracketing will be necessary for comprehending the typographic medium. As in both philosophers' work, it will require a temporary suspension of what seems to come naturally. But more importantly, bracketing our assumptions—whether about typography or totalitarianism—is what allows us to face that which we've been taught to ignore.

Ultimately, the bracketing required to comprehend typography reveals a mess. Our linguistic concepts and taxonomical systems have helped us to contain the countless individual characters that populate the typographic medium, and so bracketing these leaves us with an undifferentiated sea of shapes. But opening the medium up in this way can also reveal social, political, and cultural histories; technologies; philosophies; questions about design ethics, about the nature of shape and pattern; and so on. At the very least it can open up more awareness of the media in our daily surroundings. This sea of shapes should make us curious about what is being communicated through *them*.

The different methods this book will explore for comprehending typography's sea of shapes (in chapters 4–6) all pose the question: how far can these shapes be pushed before they are no longer part of the category of typographic shapes? In the reductive method, the question is how far can these shapes be boiled down. In the expansive method, it is how far can these shapes stray from that boiled down skeleton. And in the relational method, the question is whether one can design a typographic shape that bears no resemblance to any other typographic shape. The other basic question that this sea of shapes raises is: why are there so many? While individual typefaces have specific reasons for being—from aesthetic ideals to cost-saving and technological requirements—the question here is why the typographic medium needs to be so expansive. As we'll see, typography's existence exceeds both linguistics and aesthetic taste. It is instead, as the designer Laszlo Moholy-Nagy argued, "a tool of communication," a complicated practice that involves, *but is not limited to*, linguistics and aesthetics.[54]

At a basic level, we could understand communication as the mathematician Claude Shannon defined it. "The fundamental problem of communication," he writes, "is that of representing at one point either exactly or approximately a message selected at another point. Frequently the messages have *meaning*."[55] This is an understanding of communication as transmission. Communication in this tradition involves (1) representation (2) at a distance from a starting point. But the message being represented is not necessarily synonymous with linguistic content or an author's ideas—often cited as typography's primary responsibility. Furthermore, there is also nothing in this definition that limits communication to humanity—this kind of communication is practiced not only by other species of flora and fauna, but also (increasingly) by inanimate objects and machines. As John Durham Peters notes in his history of the idea of communication, when communication came to be viewed as information exchange this recast it as "a site for exploring posthuman couplings with aliens, animals, and machines."[56] If that which is selecting a message "at another point" need not be a human actor, could it be typography itself?

Perhaps most importantly from the perspective of typography, in Shannon's definition meaning is not a necessary consideration; it is an afterthought of the transmission. He continues his definition: "These semantic aspects of communication are irrelevant to the engineering problem. The significant aspect is that the actual message is one *selected from a set* of possible messages."[57] Because the designer/engineer doesn't know, when designing a communication system, what message will be selected for transmission, communication needs to be able to handle any message that is chosen (from a set of possibilities). And being one from a set of possible messages—its meaning (or lack of meaning) is irrelevant to that communication system. If typography communicates, it does not need to contain meaning in order to do so. It simply needs to embody information at one point and represent it at another. But "simply" is misleading, because communication is never a simple process. Exact communication is a greater problem than approximate communication, and it is likely there will always be some sort of gap between the source of the message and its end point.[58] While Shannon pioneered ways of eliminating noise from transmissions, this communication gap is still possible at the technical level and *probable* at the level of content analysis.

The transmission view of communication is admittedly limited given its disregard for the social aspects of content analysis, and the gaps this introduces into the efficacy of communication. The map of communication that cultural theorist Stuart Hall draws (in considering how televisual messages communicate) indicates a few points at which this gap can occur (see figure 1.9). Developing a theory of communication that is both formal and social, Hall notes that miscommunication occurs when there

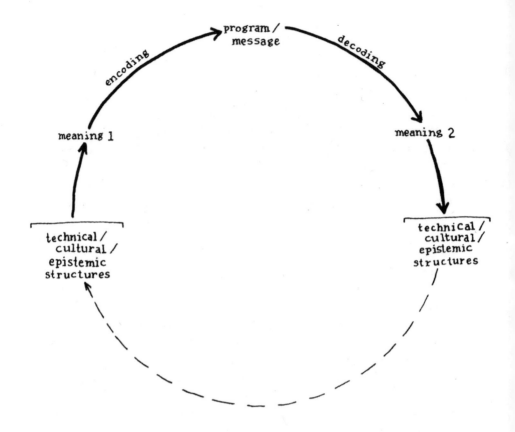

Figure 1.9
In Stuart Hall's theory, communication is developed first from technical and institutional structures of the industry, as well as from sociocultural and political knowledge. Meaning is then encoded into a (televisual) program or message. That message is then decoded by viewers, who similarly draw upon sociocultural and political knowledge (and the meaning they decode can then contribute to the technical/sociocultural foundation for future messages). It is in asymmetry between the encoding and decoding that communication gaps occur. For Hall the sources of asymmetry are the relative positions of the encoder and decoder, and the identity or nonidentity of the code itself. *Source*: author, based on Hall's diagram.

is asymmetry between the codes involved in the broadcaster's encoding, and those involved in the audience's decoding. Unconcerned with the "noise in the channel"—the sort of technical failures that would interest Shannon—Hall instead sees a hegemonic power play involved in connotative communication gaps.[59] He argues that messages are polysemic—they have multiple possible meanings—but are *not* pluralistic—not all those meanings are seen as equally valid.[60] This means that exact communication is not only unlikely at the level of content (given polysemy) but also undesirable, since it would mean the absolute dominance of the encoder's hegemonic message over the audience members' ability to participate in the creation of multiple meanings.

Hall reveals that communication is not quite as simple as the transmission view suggests, but also that exact communication may not be what is most desirable. In visual communication especially (film, photography, etc.), he notes that apparent transparency can actually lead to its own form of misunderstanding. This occurs, he writes, "not because we as viewers cannot literally decode the sign . . . but because we are tempted, by its very 'naturalisation' to 'misread' the image for the thing it signifies."[61] Seeing becomes believing. The naturalized appearance not only allows for the successful communication of the *dominant* message but also obscures that message's hegemonic interests—it keeps us from seeing that the image was encoded or constructed. We'll see in the next chapter that because conservative typographic shapes are so transparent, because they so neatly meet our expectations, we are prone to confuse them with letters, and to assume that this is all the information they communicate. But typographic design and layout are processes of encoding.

Given the communication gap (in technique and content), communication systems often build in redundancies, to cut down on the noise that gets in the way of accurate signal transmission. Even in less technical terms, a speaker might express a single idea in multiple ways to increase the probability that the intended message will reach its audience. Considering conservative typographic shapes, perhaps the numerous and often minor shifts in typographic form are such redundancies. Or perhaps the set of typographic shapes is working something out within itself, aspiring to bridge the communication gap between two things. From the vantage point of radical typographic shapes, the medium's variability might be a guard against hegemony, introducing more pluralism into the medium's polymorphism.

At this point, I can't say with certainty what purpose the apparent redundancy and excess of typographic shapes serve in communication, but what is certain is that the typographic medium encodes—it collects, stores, and gives shape to information; and this giving shape matters. Friedrich Nietzsche argues as much at the level of technology—"our writing tools," he writes in a letter, "are also working on our thoughts."[62] The German media theorist Friedrich Kittler writes about Nietzsche's use, late in life, of a Hansen Writing Ball typewriter (*skrivekugle* in Danish), and links this to his style of writing—shifting from lengthy argument to brief aphorisms.[63] As we've seen, Flusser similarly saw the influence of the typewriter's mechanics on the writer, but also argues that the overall *topography* of a means of recording information encourages certain dominant forms of thinking. Prehistoric images, writing, and what he called "technical images" each arranged information in a different way, and this in turn favored different kinds of thought. The prehistoric image is spread out across a plain and so inspired fluid, cyclical forms of thinking. Writing strings images out in a line and so introduces historical thought. And the technical image would inspire a new form of quantized thought.[64] Nietzsche's analysis is at the level of the tool, Flusser's is at the level of the spatial arrangement of symbolic elements; but what about the level of the specific shape that information takes?

It may not be possible, at least today, to determine what difference it makes to information whether the crossbar of an e is horizontal or slanted, but it doesn't follow from this that such differences *don't* matter. We can see in other visualizations of information that how something is made visible can affect how we know that thing. As Johanna Drucker notes, "*Most information visualizations are acts of interpretation masquerading as presentation.*"[65] How one graphs economic information, for instance, is a reflection of and influences how one conceives of the nature of the economy. Susan Buck-Morss has illustrated this by comparing the neat, simplified graphs of classical economics, when the field was working to establish itself as an empirical science (late eighteenth to early nineteenth century), with the more complex webs that are used in the global economics of today.[66] Or consider the ways in which we map cities. In his map of the London Underground, which would influence countless subway maps after it, Harry Beck found that a *reduction* of spatial information actually facilitated navigation. Still today, those of us who navigate major cities likely think of large portions of them as nodes linked by lines, rather than as rich and multidimensional spaces.

Typography is a medium that visualizes and communicates information; it gives information form. It is worth considering to what extent the design and operations of the typographic medium affect the ways we perceive, consume, recall, and pass on information. But this is a question that can be addressed only once we bracket linguistic function and face the medium's own operational logic—embodied in the full diversity of typographic forms. This book is a step in that direction. It is meant to illustrate the philosophical depth and formal diversity of the typographic medium, before returning to the question of how this formal medium participates in communication (how it functions). Along the way, it should become clear that the typographic medium affects everything from human history, political and social ideals, cultural patterns, and technological constraints, to our willingness to imagine something new. Let's begin by exploring the particular tension that exists between function and form in the typographic medium.

serifs B

Source: author.

2 The Battle of Form and Function

In our new art we have ended the conflict between "being" and "seeming."
—Jan Tschichold[1]

The fundamental contradiction of typography is the relationship between form and function. Typography is a visual medium whose revolutionary force emerges from its ability to create an efficient, standardized, and mass-produced visual record of humanity and its accumulated knowledge. But at the same time, it functions most effectively on the page when its forms (the visual parts of that record) are overlooked. This fundamental contradiction has been articulated in a number of ways throughout the history of type—for instance, in questions about the proper role of the designer or punchcutter: are they artists inventing forms or functionary craftspeople? It is also present in the question of typography's proper role—does it aim at beauty, utility, neutral communication, or personal and political expression? The type cast for Gutenberg's press and the typesetting of his forty-two-line Bible (ca. 1450) remain among the most beautiful examples of typographic form. And yet they were intended to mimic the work of scribes, to blend in with existing books. They elide their own formal possibilities to ensure that these new books would meet the functional expectations of medieval readers. Since then, function has generally been viewed as a more pressing concern for Latin typography than form, despite the fact that form is more fundamental to typography's existence.[2]

Though a fundamental undercurrent in typography since its beginnings, the contradiction of form and function became an open discussion in the modernist design of the long twentieth century. It was the architect Louis Sullivan who declared in 1896 that form should be guided (if not determined) by function. For Sullivan, it was a law governing all things—natural and artificial—that "form ever follows function," and there was no good reason for the arts to resist this law.[3] His view was in line not only with the functional interests of architecture broadly, but also with his historical moment, when the functional possibilities of new building materials encouraged divergence from traditional forms. It was also in line with other aesthetic theories of this period, which largely sought purity in design by limiting forms to necessity. Turned into a slogan, Sullivan's law is in harmony with Adolf Loos's equation of "Ornament and Crime" and with Ludwig Mies van der Rohe's belief that "less is more," and it is a concept embraced by Walter Gropius in developing the pedagogical philosophy of the Bauhaus.[4] There, Gropius and the other founding faculty sought to unite the formal with the practical, endowing students not with a particular aesthetic style but with fundamental principles and practices to guide their arts. As the school embraced technology as part of its mission, they stressed clarity of communication, and the idea that new materials will suggest new forms for themselves.[5] The so-called New Typography that emerged in this period was, in part, a response to the new technological reality experienced in early twentieth-century Europe—a response that adopted a view of form and function in line with engineers, the producers of that new technology. As Jan Tschichold noted, the engineer produced "pure constructional forms that correspond to the functions of the objects."[6] This was the ideal for modernist designers in typography and beyond.

In this modernist vain, the supremacy of function over form meant that windows, chairs, or Q's have certain formal requirements based not on the fickleness of taste or style, but rather on the function each serves. The early twentieth-century consensus regarding typography appears to be that its function is communication. Bauhaus designers interpreted the demands of this communicative function as an invitation to explore new shapes, layouts, and materials. Beyond the near-religious belief in the sans serif as the most functional of all typographic forms, New Typographers used accent colors, varying sizes of type, and asymmetrical layouts to create visual hierarchies of information.[7] And designers like Laszlo Moholy-Nagy and Piet Zwart used the (relatively) new medium of photography to add more clarity of communication to their typographic work.[8]

However, another aesthetic interpretation of the primacy of communicative function over form was developing roots in England at the same time. This more utilitarian aesthetic was perhaps most influentially articulated in Beatrice Warde's concept of invisibility. Form following function did not mean experimentation for Warde, but rather required the transparency of form altogether. In her famous speech from 1932, "The Crystal Goblet, or Printing Should Be Invisible," she argues that the best type is that which draws no attention to itself. "Type well used," she writes, "is invisible as type."[9] This is because books are meant to be read, and print is meant to transfer ideas from one mind to another. Type that draws attention to itself draws that attention from those ideas, and interrupts the ease of reading, thereby undermining the function of type. Using a crystal wine glass and a window as metaphors, Warde determines that typography is meant to be looked *through* rather than *at*. Her contemporary, and fellow utilitarian, Stanley Morison echoes these ideas in his "First Principles of Typography." Under this philosophy, because type is a service art, because it is meant to reach the most people with the most ease, it should meet the reader's expectations even at the cost of formal considerations. Morison, for instance, identifies Caslon as a "feeble" typeface, but still recommends its use because the people like it.[10]

As a utilitarian position, this way of thinking about type's form and function makes practical sense. And transparency continues to be a powerful concept in typographic theory today (particularly for book type).[11] But transparency is a dangerous concept that requires vigilance on the part of anyone attempting to understand the complex medium that is typography.[12] In her work on literacy and alphabet books, Patricia Crain writes, "the alphabet functions best when it dissolves, disappearing into text; only then does it become fully legible. But I've had to keep an eye on it, and so I've brought it back continually into a realm where its operations are visible."[13] The same is true of typography. Despite Warde's practical aims, it isn't the case that good type is synonymous with transparent type. It is function that asks for transparency, not form, and so to see the typographic medium (which is both function *and* form), we have to make a conscious effort to reconsider the value of forms.

Consider two aesthetically divergent typefaces like Morison's Times New Roman (1931), and Zuzana Licko and Rudy VanderLans's Variex (1988; see figure 2.1). Times New Roman is a typeface that is both legible and readable, and can carry information efficiently to readers; and this is valuable.[14] But a typeface like Variex is also legible (if less readable), and can carry information to readers while also making the familiar suddenly unfamiliar. Variex conveys information, but also prevents the reader from taking its forms for granted. It invites the viewer to consider what a character is, what typography is, perhaps even what language is, and this is abcdefghij

abcdefghij

valuable as well.[15] The great weakness of Warde's theory is that it not only devalues faces like Variex for not being transparent, but also ignores the subtle beauty and detail in a face like Times New Roman by assuming, erroneously, that it is transparent.

Warde's valorization of function over form is problematic because she employs an understanding of transparency as destructive—for her typography is meant to sacrifice itself for the message. In a book about Victorian shop windows, Isobel Armstrong elaborates a definition of transparency that captures this sort of destructive quality. She writes, "Transparency is something that eliminates itself in the process of vision. It does away with obstruction by not declaring itself as a presence. But the paradox of this self-obliterating state is that we would not call it transparent but for the presence of physical matter, however invisible—its visible invisibility is what is important about transparency."[16] Here the transparent thing is described as obliterated, eliminated, obstructed, but this is all self-inflicted. It is not an external force that causes the invisibility; rather it is some property (or set of properties) of the thing itself that denies its existence. The self-obliterating quality is not the most important quality of the transparent thing—it is rather the visible invisibility that is a necessary quality. Without it and its materiality, there would be nothing to call transparent in the first place. If we consider typography as a transparent thing, its necessary visible invisibility would be its forms and whatever materials are used to manifest those forms. And its contingent, self-obliterating property is its linguistic function. When we read type, we fail to see type.

It is important to note that in this definition both form and function are parts of the typographic medium—one is just more necessary to the medium than the other. And so, we can't resolve this problem of destructive transparency by getting rid of either property. This was something the Bauhaus designers and New Typographers realized—in order for form to get in line with function, the form itself had to become communicative. And, given that today the typographic medium's longevity seems tied to its continued usefulness for communication, it is unlikely that the design ideal of transparency will disappear anytime soon. Perhaps, then, transparency needs to be understood in a different way.

For this, I propose using the definition of transparency offered by György Kepes. A former studio assistant to Moholy-Nagy, Kepes was a designer and influential educator who emerged from the Bauhaus tradition. But his theories exceed the figure of the prewar engineer that Bauhaus designers valorized, and instead build on postwar scientific fields like cybernetics, in which nature and machine mix in more radical and social ways. On transparency, he writes:

> If one sees two or more figures overlapping one another, and each of them claims for itself the common overlapped part, then one is confronted with a contradiction of spatial dimensions. To resolve this contradiction one must assume the presence of a new optical quality. The figures are endowed with transparency: that is, they are able to interpenetrate without an optical destruction of each other. Transparency however implies more than an optical characteristic; it implies a broader spatial order. Transparency means a simultaneous perception of different spatial locations. Space not only recedes but fluctuates in a continuous activity. The position of the transparent figures has equivocal meaning as one sees each figure now as the closer, now as the further one.[17]

Transparency here is clearly a perceptual state. The transparent thing isn't denying its existence or declaring itself transparent. All it declares is an equal claim to a single space at the same time as something else. Transparency, then, is the sense our minds make of this spatial contradiction. Furthermore, the relationship between the competing properties—for instance, form and function—is dynamic in Kepes's view. So even if, for instance, function obscures form, taking the closer space, it is not a relationship of obliteration or invisibility; it is temporary and easily reversible. We can, in this more dynamic view, read without seeing the type, and can then also bracket the linguistic function in order to see the shapes. In the overlapping part, form and function are equivocal. Typography's value is not defined by its ability to serve linguistic functions at the expense of its visual properties, and yet typography also cannot be form alone.

The equivocal status of form and function—their contradiction—is a concept that needs to be lived with in order to understand what typography is, and how it stores and carries information. It isn't, however, an easy contradiction to come to terms with. Spread out through the history of typographic theory, there are examples like Warde's, of misjudging the relationship of form and function; but a more condensed picture of this misunderstanding (and its consequences) can be seen in US legal history. Where intellectual property law meets typography, we find function being allowed to obliterate form. Because decision-makers have found it difficult to hold both form and function together in their minds in the same space when considering typefaces, US type designers have not had the same access to adequate intellectual property (IP) protection as other artists have.[18] Without protection, a type foundry can invest thousands in the design, production, and promotion of a typeface only to have a competitor copy that design *after* its popularity has slowly been established, and sell it, sometimes under the same name, with no legal repercussions.[19] This risk would seem to undercut the monetary incentive structure that IP protection relies on in the United States. And if the goal of the patents and copyright clause of the US Constitution is to use this incentive structure to encourage creativity and innovation in the arts and sciences, where else does the resistance to protecting typefaces come from, but from the entanglement of form and function?[20]

Form, Function, and Intellectual Property

In US legal circles, it's commonly believed that typeface design is one of the arts that belongs in intellectual property's "negative space"— that, for various reasons, it not only doesn't need IP protection, but is stronger without it.[21] Some have likened typographic characters to bricks—copyrighting them, they argue, would ultimately be a limit on the other forms of creative arts that make use of those building blocks. However, others maintain that the lack of copyright protection leaves designers open to piracy and economic deprivation.[22] Certain forms of IP protection are available to typography as a field. It is not uncommon, for instance, for typographic technologies to receive patents; in fact the fourth patent ever issued in the United States was granted to the printer

Francis Bailey for a "method . . . for forming Punches."[23] The thornier issue for IP protection has been the design of typefaces themselves. It is notable that the first *design* patent issued in the United States was for a typeface by George Bruce. In the text of his patent application, his justification for why this protection should be granted, he makes an important distinction that is worth quoting at length. The 1842 patent reads:

> It is difficult to find much in Printers Types that is new in a design if we regard only their characteristic lines, but if we look at the ways in which the figures are varied while the characteristic lines are retained, we find the same variety that would be expected in the portraits of a person painted by many different artists in different positions. The characters called Roman, Italic, Gothic, Black, Script, &c. and numerous Border Pieces have been for ages regularly produced by the Typefounders, who have executed therein various Styles, with more or less of design, by which the Types of one Typefounder could be distinguished from those of another. To produce a facsimile of an alphabet of types by the method followed by Typefounders who form the original of each type in steel, may indeed be pronounced impossible. Each one therefore produced originals, which were his own exclusive property, and without a patent, he enjoyed them safely, there being no method known until lately by which types could be copied or reproduced.[24]

Bruce distinguishes the characteristic lines of an alphabetic character from the detailed designs of an individual typeface. With the generic alphabet in mind, there may be no perceptible difference between one foundry's type and another, and so no sense of originality. But by drawing a comparison to portrait painting—another well-established art form, marked by the originality of the artist—Bruce claims that a typeface can be recognized as belonging to a particular artist.[25]

The core issues that Bruce raises in this passage have followed typefaces for well over a century as their creators have sought out protections, and each issue emerges in various ways from a confusion of form and function. First is the issue of type's relationship to technology. Many in favor of protection, including Bruce, raise concerns whenever a new technological development makes it easier to copy. As the above passage suggests, it was the introduction of a means of copying type exactly that required protection where before there was none. In 1838, electroplating made it possible to create perfect copies of existing type. And copying technologies have continued to develop. In 1884, Linn Boyd Benton invented a punchcutting machine that made the copying (and revival) of typefaces easier, once again raising questions about the need for protection.[26] And in the 1970s and beyond, questions about protection have been raised as phototype and digital type (particularly vector-based programs) each made copying easier still. When the courts have wrestled with the relation of type to its technologies, however, they have generally failed to see a clear distinction between the forms being copied and the function of the print and typographic technologies involved.

Second is the issue of originality—if most typefaces are variations on the same basic set of shapes, one might ask: at what point does a variation become something original? While some legal traditions recognize originality by the observable trace of an author's style, which Bruce identifies, others have foregrounded the intellectual labor exerted, and the United States has more or less settled on the idea of a "modicum of creativity" and "independent creation."[27] A former US register of copyrights, Ralph Oman, has characterized the criteria of originality as falling somewhere between novelty and mere variation.[28] Though some design patents have been issued, when considering originality, both copyright and patent inspectors have historically found it difficult to focus on the details of typographic form and rule out mere variation.

The final persistent issue that Bruce's patent raises is that of a typeface's relationship to the alphabet. The core theoretical question raised throughout this IP debate concerns the separability of *a typeface* from *the alphabet* (or form from function): Is it possible to copyright the variable forms of typography without also copyrighting the "characteristic lines"? And if not, what possible risks do the alphabet and free expression face? In these three points, the question of whether or not to protect typefaces quickly becomes a question about the very nature of typography—what it is, and what it isn't—particularly in relation to form and function.[29]

On Typography and Technology

The courts in America have struggled to accurately capture the relationship of typeface design to typographic technologies, generally viewing the design as a minor element embedded in technology. In *Goudy v. Hansen*, for instance, the prolific type designer, Frederic Goudy, found his patent infringement case thrown out in part because the judges struggled to articulate the relationship between metal type and the imprints they produce.

The patent application Goudy submitted illustrated the imprint, rather than the metal type, and the court's decision found that "the disclosure in [the patent] does not constitute subject-matter patentable under the patent law."[30] In this case, the court understood the patent application to be for metal type, but the application itself (its "disclosure") illustrated the imprint, and given this confusion, the judges addressed both in their decisions. Judge Hale found neither to be patentable—the metal type because it lacked anything inventive, and the imprint because it was merely an illustration of "the letters of the alphabet and the Arabic numerals," which, he continues, "have been known to the world for many generations of men."[31] The implication being that these shapes are so familiar, they also show no invention.

Judge Bingham concurred with Hale's decision, but elaborated on the relationship between the design of the forms and the functional technologies in which they're used. Using the earlier case *Clark v. Bousfield*, he compared the typeface's role in printing to the mechanical impression of a pattern onto tin pails. In the 1869 *Clark* case, the Supreme Court decided that a design being imprinted on a pail was not subject to its own patent, because it was merely a part of a larger mechanical process that formed these tin pails. Viewing movable type printing in the same way, Bingham understood type (and by extension the typeface) to be merely a part of the machines used to print. What both of these judges seem to have misunderstood, and what the dissenting judge in *Goudy* pointed out, was that there is only one design that applies to the punches, matrices, type, and page, and it is *that design* for which type designers were seeking patents.[32]

To address the question of what relation the (potentially) patentable typeface has to its technologies, the dissenting Judge Brown related this to another case involving metal dies. *Byers v. F. T. Pearce Co.* found that a patent for dies would also apply to the blanks struck from them. He wrote, "There was but one design; but it was both for the stock ornament and for the die which was used to strike up the ornament from metal."[33] Applied to typography, that would mean that Goudy's application for a single patent could be applied to both the typeface and the metal type that produces it. If the courts see a typeface as merely parts belonging to the presses that use them, then they likely belong either to already patented technologies or to the public domain. If, however, they see typefaces as designs (for both imprint and metal type) that are independent of presses, they should be subject to the same protections as any other work of art or design.

That being said, when the courts have divorced the design of a typeface from the technologies that produce or use it, it hasn't always resulted in protection from copying. The decision in *Keystone Type Foundry v. Portland Publishing Co.*—an unfair competition case—found that typeface design was not simply a part of typographic technology, but this worked against the designer's interests. In this case, Keystone spent considerable time and money developing, producing, and marketing a typeface called Caslon Bold. Portland Publishing Co. copied, cast, and sold Caslon Bold type under the same name, and yet was found to be justified in their actions.[34] The court argued that Portland Publishing was justified because (1) it didn't attempt to deceive consumers into believing that its cheaper product was Keystone's; (2) it used a different (cheaper) means of casting the type; and (3) since Keystone was a foundry, and not a design firm, Portland was not encroaching on its business by copying a *design*. Because the underlying means of production were different (and because Keystone was a type *foundry*), the copying of design was not seen to be a problem.

Such a decision suggests that a typeface can legally be copied so long as the means of production differs—an argument that was reinforced in the digital era by *Adobe v. Southern Software Inc.*[35] In this software copyright infringement case, Paul King (a.k.a. Southern Software Inc.) was found to have taken several of Adobe's font programs, altered them slightly using already existing font-editing software, and resold the programs as his own. The courts ruled in favor of Adobe, finding that King's copying was illegal, because the difference between his programs and Adobe's was *not significant enough*. While this is a victory for the protection of digital font-generating programs (the means of production), the court still ended up ruling *against* the protection of typeface design. The *Adobe* court based their decision on the precedents that font-generating software could be copyrighted (following the Copyright Office's 1980 decision to register computer code as literature) and that typefaces could not (following the 1978 decision in *Eltra v. Ringer*), and concluded that simply because a computer program produced something that is not copyrightable, this does not mean that the code itself cannot be protected. The Copyright Office's decision to register the computer programs underlying digital typefaces, but not "typeface as typeface," led to some confounding logic concerning not only technology but also originality.[36]

The decision in this case draws upon the Copyright Office's "Final Regulation" on the copyrighting of digital typefaces from 1992, which states that "the creation of scalable font output programs to produce harmonious fonts consisting of hundreds of characters typically involves many decisions in drafting the instructions that drive the printer."[37] The Copyright Office decided to offer protection to font-generating software because their construction required creative decisions. Yet somehow, this reasoning does not extend to the decisions made in the design of a typeface itself. It would seem that, if you can find a different way of describing a design in code, you can copy that design exactly—the formal design is seen as subordinate to the functioning technology that underlies it.[38]

This is where the issue stands today. A type designer in the United States can trademark a name, may be able to obtain a design patent, and can copyright the computer code producing their digital typeface (unless they are using preexisting font-generating software),[39] but cannot copyright their designs.[40] There appear to be two main reasons for this peculiar state that makes the underlying computer program copyrightable, while still restricting the protection of a typeface design. The practical (and thoroughly unsatisfying) reason is simply that US governing bodies are in a long-term stasis on this point. The Copyright Office does not register typefaces because they view it as Congress's responsibility to change the Copyright Act. But Congress and the courts have tended to defer to the precedent set out by the Copyright Office's past actions.[41] The second, and more conceptual, reason seems to be that these decision-making bodies find it difficult to define originality in the field of typography, and to separate any given typeface from the alphabet itself. As the above examples illustrate form being subordinated to technological function, the following legal examples will consider form's subordination to linguistic function.

On Originality

Both copyright and patent protections hinge on the criteria of originality. Any work eligible for IP protection has to first of all be original work by an author or inventor. Typography's key hurdle where originality is concerned (besides its relationship to the alphabet, which we will discuss in a moment) is that tens of thousands of typefaces exist in the Latin sphere alone, most based on relatively few basic shapes. In the early 1970s the then Register of Copyrights, Barbara Ringer, opened up a public comment period on the issue of whether to extend protection to "Original Typeface Designs." In her prompt she asked "whether a typeface design can, by its nature, incorporate the degree of originality and creativity necessary to support a copyright."[42] She was concerned that digital technologies were leaving typeface designs vulnerable to easy piracy, but was not yet convinced that originality to the degree required by copyright was even possible in type design.

As we saw in the introduction with Caslon and Baskerville, many type-faces are distinguished by minute differences, begging the question: how much of a difference needs to exist between two original faces, and what kind of differences?[43] A 1905 patent decision rejecting an application from Julius Schmohl found that originality in typeface design needs to involve more difference than simply combining existing elements.[44] The US Patent Office found that "there can be no invention in the application of an irregular outline to letters of one style when this has already been done upon letters of style not widely different unless some new effect of orna-mentation is secured."[45] In addition to requiring more difference than mere recombination (an outline by one designer applied to a typeface by another), this decision also suggests certain standards about the obvious-ness of the differences between faces. The decision is a rejection based on the vague measure of being "not widely different," suggesting that certain quantities and kinds of difference are more likely to qualify as original.[46]

The Schmohl decision shows a preference in the courts for the in-troduction of ornamentation as a sign of originality where typefaces are concerned. This is echoed in other rulings against the patentability of individual typefaces. In *American Type Founders v. Damon & Peets*, for in-stance, the Circuit Court decided that ATF's claim of patent infringement had no bearing, because the typeface in question "shows no such peculiar configuration or ornamentation in the type as would authorize a design patent."[47] The idea that a "peculiar configuration" or the addition of or-namentation would be the measure of originality suggests an insufficient understanding of the creativity and artistry of type design. The addition of ornamentation may make it easier to spot the differences between one typeface and another, but the majority of variation in the typographic medium is not based on ornamentation at all. As the designer Hermann Zapf frequently argued, the art of designing (good) type requires years of study, practice, and creativity.[48] While the work may be more obvious in ornamentation, the hard work and originality of design is present even when a typeface seems to disappear into its alphanumerical characters. Reaching back to our previous example, though Times New Roman may disappear from our conscious view when we read it, it is able to do so *only because* of countless small and creative decisions made by Morison. Text typefaces like Times New Roman, or display typefaces like DIN 1451

(Linotype, 1930s), may not shout their originality, but they possess originality all the same.

In 1983, a committee at the annual meeting of ATypI (Association Typographique Internationale) met to discuss the US copyright problem and defined originality in such a way as to reflect the labor and artistry that Zapf refers to.[49] According to Edward Gottschall's report on the meeting, a typeface could be identified as original "if its distinctive features, which establish its aesthetic value, exhibit the result of an individual's creative activity, exceeding in its level of creative design the average skill of type designers and the work of an ordinary craftsman."[50] The committee's definition suggests that we should see originality in the high level of skill being employed in the crafting of distinctive features.[51] And given the skill required, the committee makes no assumption that originality might be entirely beyond the natural capabilities of typography, as Ringer did.

If "by its very nature" typography seems incapable of establishing sufficient originality, to counter this view it would be necessary to show the ways in which designers make conscious decisions—that is, to show that the functioning of the alphabet does not dictate the forms of typefaces. Though often ignored by the US courts, one piece of evidence for this is the existence of copying itself. That is, if a typeface were not original, were not uniquely formed to be more than just *any* typeface, why would piracy be an issue at all? As the dissenting Judge Brown argued in *Goudy v. Hansen*, "The fact that the design has been infringed is sufficient to establish its utility as a design."[52] If one typeface is as good as any other, as the characteristic lines would suggest, why would copyists choose to copy a particular face? A designer will tell you these are particular forms; the legal system seems to see primarily letters.

On Typography and the Alphabet

We saw the issue of separability raised in the decision of *Goudy v. Hansen*—in Judge Hale's statement that Goudy's diagram showed only characters that had been known to "generations of men."[53] Judge Hale clearly did not see Goudy's design as separable from the characteristic lines of the alphabet (or perhaps even from the concept of the alphabet). The issue of separability also lies at the heart of the only major US court case to deal explicitly with the *copyright* of typeface design: *Eltra v. Ringer* (1978). Eltra Corporation (which merged with Mergenthaler Linotype in 1963) commissioned a typeface from a "well-known designer" (reportedly

Hermann Zapf) for $11,000. When it applied for copyright, it was predictably denied, because the typeface had "no elements, either alone or in combination, which can be separately identified as a 'work of art.'"[54] Eltra Corp. then attempted to compel the Register of Copyrights (Barbara Ringer) to register the typeface as a "work of art." The case was dismissed by a US district court, and that decision was upheld in appeals.[55] The court of appeals found that the "type face design for which registration was sought could not exist independently as a work of art and thus was not entitled to copyright protection as a 'work of art.'"[56] What the decision reveals is the importance of the distinction between art and utility where copyright is concerned, and the related question of whether form and function can be separated, where typography is concerned.

The *Eltra* court's decision hinges on what was then §202.10(c) of Copyright Office regulations, which reads: "If the sole intrinsic function of an article is its utility, the fact that the article is unique and attractively shaped will not qualify it as a work of art. However, if the shape of a utilitarian article incorporates features, such as artistic sculpture, carving, or pictorial representation, which can be identified separately and are capable of existing independently as a work of art, such features will be eligible for registration."[57] If the artistic qualities of an item (form) can be separated from the utilitarian qualities (function), then those artistic qualities can be copyrighted; and the courts have gradually established what separation means, beginning with the 1954 case of *Mazer v. Stein.*

The *Mazer* case concerned a lamp with a figurine attached to its base, and established the idea of physical separability between the (noncopyrightable) utility of the lamp and the (copyrightable) artistry of the figurine. The ability to separate these two qualities became more nuanced in *Kielstein-Cord v. Accessories by Pearl*, a 1980 case concerning the design of a belt buckle. In this instance, the utility of the buckle and the artistry of its design could not be *physically* separated, yet the court found that the utility of the buckle was secondary in importance to the decorative qualities, and so the design was conceptually separable, and therefore copyrightable.[58] In *Brandir International v. Cascada Pacific Lumber* (1987), a test for separability was codified. According to the Denicola test (proposed by law professor Robert C. Denicola), if the aesthetic and the functional are merged together in an object, it cannot be copyrighted, but if "the designer's artistic judgment [is] exercised independently of functional influences, conceptual separability exists."[59] Assuming we're dealing with conceptual separability rather than physical where typography is concerned, copyrightability should depend on whether the designer has clearly made decisions that are independent of the simple signifying function of alphanumerical characters. However, the definition of separability has been refined once more, this time distancing the definition from the designer's intention or process.

In the recent Supreme Court decision of *Star Athletica LLC v. Varsity Brands Inc.* (2017), the Roberts Court set out two requirements for determining when artistic elements of objects can be recognized separately. Justice Clarence Thomas writing the decision argues that such an artistic element would be eligible for copyright protection only if it "(1) can be perceived as a two- or three-dimensional work of art separate from the useful article, and (2) would qualify as a protectable pictorial, graphic, or sculptural work—either on its own or fixed in some other tangible medium of expression—if it were imagined separately from the useful article into which it is incorporated."[60] The clarity with which Thomas spelled out the test for separability—apparently throwing out other tests, like Denicola—is potentially significant from the perspective of typefaces, since it refocuses attention on the artistic elements themselves.

Since no typefaces have been eligible for copyright, it would appear that the Copyright Office, the US Courts, and Congress have decided that there is no separability between a typeface design and the alphabet. Shortly before the *Eltra* decision, the House of Representatives took up a reform of the Copyright Act, and briefly considered the issues of separability and of typeface copyright (in part at the urging of Ringer). The House bill maintains that even if a design is produced with aesthetic rather than functional concerns, "only elements, if any, which can be identified separately from the useful article as such are copyrightable."[61] The design of a typeface would have to be able to be identified separately from its signifying function. When the House of Representatives took up the issue of typefaces, they determined that such separation isn't possible. In full, the House bill's statement on typeface reads:

> The Committee has considered, but chosen to defer, the possibility of protecting the design of typefaces. A "typeface" can be defined as a set of letters, numbers, or other symbolic characters, whose forms are related by repeating design elements consistently applied in a notational system and are intended to be embodied in articles whose intrinsic utilitarian function is for use in composing text or other cognizable combinations of characters. The Committee does not regard

the design of typeface, as thus defined, to be a copyrightable "pictorial, graphic, or sculptural work" within the meaning of this bill and the application of the dividing line in section 101.[62]

Using logic that IP attorney Gloria Phares has correctly identified as circular, the House of Representatives defines typeface, and then denies it protection based on that definition.[63] One could ask any number of questions about the soundness of this definition—for example, to what extent does the embodiment of design apply to digital type? Or, does the idea of consistent application of repeated elements leave room for hybrid typefaces like Dead History (P. Scott Makela, 1990), or random typefaces like Beowolf (Erik van Blokland and Just van Rossum, 1989)? But even as a working definition, the real trouble arises from the idea that typefaces have an "intrinsic utilitarian function" of composing texts. It is on this basis that Congress refuses copyright to typefaces; but the function of typographic forms is not as simple as Congress makes it seem. And according to the *Star Athletica* decision, the specifics of a useful item's function may not even be relevant to the question of separability.

Thomas's definition of separability requires a design element be perceived as a work of art, and be able to be imagined as a protectable work if it were separated from its functional item (and where necessary, affixed to something else, like a canvas). If we assume that a typeface design, as shapes, has perceptible pictorial or graphic qualities, the House's assertion of an intrinsic function would suggest that a typeface design fails on the second point—the function being intrinsic to the artistic forms, there would be nothing left of the useful item if we imagined the typeface design removed.[64] However, in response to a similar argument made in *Star Athletica*, Thomas writes, "the separability inquiry focuses on the extracted feature and not on any aspects of the useful article remaining after the imaginary extraction. The statute does not require the imagined remainder to be a fully functioning useful article at all."[65] Assuming the separability of typographic design, the statute wouldn't require us to consider what's left of the linguistic function after separation. Ignoring the linguistic function is, in a way, what IP attorney Terrence Carroll proposed when he reworked the House's definition of a typeface in his proposal for an amendment to the Copyright Act of 1976.

Writing before the *Star Athletica* decision, Carroll argues that "typeface" should be added as a special category of pictorial, graphic, or sculptural works subject to copyright. The definition he then proposes is simply the first clause of the House of Representative's definition: "a set of letters, numbers, or other symbolic characters, whose forms are related by repeating design elements consistently applied in a notational system."[66] He leaves behind the idea of a typeface having an intrinsic (linguistic) utility. But even with such a legal redefinition, the separation between these two is admittedly difficult to conceptualize. This is not because they aren't separable, but because the alphabet is a concept that has attached itself to a set of shapes. Legal scholar Jacqueline Lipton offers a useful variation on the theme of *Mazer* that might help facilitate the conceptual shift from seeing letters to seeing designs.

If *Mazer* found that a figurine attached to the base of a lamp could be copyrighted (according to its separability, and dependent upon its originality), Lipton asks us to imagine the base of the lamp adorned with a character from the alphabet instead. Would this character then be copyrightable? Or consider alphabetic characters used to decorate a child's bedroom door—are these not primarily artistic, standing independently from their possible utility in constructing a text? She argues that if "a lamp base or door sign would otherwise be copyrightable—assuming sufficient originality in the design—it seems bad policy to deny copyright protection merely because the article also happens to incorporate communicative text."[67] The designer's artistic work is recognized in this example, which suggests there are instances where copyright could be possible without risk to the alphabet and its place in the public domain.

Rudy VanderLans, cofounder of Emigre Fonts, has argued that typography has two aspects: one artistic and one functional. Writing in 1997, at the tail end of deconstructivist design, he notes that some typefaces are purely artistic, even openly rebelling against signification.[68] At the time, Jon Wozencroft and Neville Brody's magazine *Fuse* was full of such typefaces, and we will explore some of these examples in chapter 5. The existence of such peculiar typefaces (throughout the history of type) has led several commentators on this copyright debate to take a relativist position. Even those like Carroll and Lipton, who argue in favor of the extension of copyright to typefaces, argue that it depends on the typeface.[69] Lipton argues that there are likely many typefaces that aren't artistic "because they are the most obvious ways of expressing given letter forms." She suggests that one compare "the letter 'A' in the Times New Roman or Arial fonts . . . with a more unusual font like Magneto."[70] The latter is seen as more artistic than the neutral Times or Arial, and she later takes this line of thinking further, raising pictorial typefaces like a pair of Christmas-themed fonts, or a novelty font called Putty Peeps (Richard Moore, 2008).[71] Carroll makes a similar comparison, again using Times New Roman as the neutral base, but taking San Francisco (Susan Kare, 1984) as the obviously artistic typeface.[72]

The error that Carroll and Lipton make is the same one Beatrice Warde made decades earlier. Yes, the designed aspects in typefaces like Magneto (Leslie Cabarga, 1995) or San Francisco are more obvious, but that does not mean that design is absent from Times New Roman. Far from being the most obvious expression of its letters, Times New Roman is a historically specific typeface designed with specific intentions: to meet the requirements of newspaper publishing, while also capturing a sense of the refinement of book type that had been championed by William Morris and his small press movement. In his design of Times New Roman, Morison was influenced by recent typefaces like Ionic (Vincent Figgins, 1821) and Century (Linn Boyd Benton, 1894), and many of his design decisions were informed by early twentieth-century studies of legibility.[73] Morison himself acknowledges some of the typeface's specificity when he compares its disappointing qualities to the ideals set out by Morris decades earlier. He writes, "As a new face, it should, by the grace of God, have been broad and open, generous and ample; instead by the vice of Mammon and the money of the machine, it is bigoted and narrow, mean and puritan."[74] Times New Roman is neither a typeface just like any other nor a set of obvious shapes. Contemporary commentators like Carroll and Lipton likely turn to it as an example of an unremarkable typeface only because it has become ubiquitous in our eyes. Ubiquity, however, is not the same as being without design, or without artistry.

Arial (Robin Nicholas and Patricia Saunders, 1982), Lipton's example of sans-serif neutrality, has achieved similar ubiquity. While Times New Roman built up its reputation for decades before becoming the default for early word-processing software, Arial's ubiquity was established specifically through its presence in computer technology (its availability in word-processing software, operating systems, and eventually web standards).[75] The only reason Arial might be said to be obvious is the fact that it is an uncomfortably close approximation of the already existing shapes of Helvetica (Max Miedinger and Eduard Hofmann, 1957). Arial was designed for IBM to share the dimensions of Helvetica, so that it could be used as a replacement when the more well-known sans serif wasn't available; and Arial ended up sharing a number of Helvetica's shapes as well. Based as it is on Helvetica, it is not the best candidate to make the case for copyright; but based as it is on the supremely designed (some would say overdesigned) shapes of Helvetica, it is also not an obvious expression of anything other than perhaps Helvetica. What this relativist view of typeface copyrightability misses is the fact that all typographic shapes are abstract forms, and only alphanumerical characters after that. There should be no confusion between *a typeface* and *the alphabet*, if for no other reason than that *the alphabet* doesn't exist as anything other than an idea. This fact is made abundantly clear in the font Hypnopaedia, designed by Zuzana Licko in 1997 as a commentary on the problematic logic behind America's copyright debate (see figure 2.2).

Hypnopaedia takes forms from existing Emigre typefaces and rotates and repeats them to produce patterns—clearly distancing these typographic forms from their signifying potential. In Licko's own words, "It is [the] inability to distinguish between the ornamental design of letter forms and the alphabetic characters they represent, which has resulted in

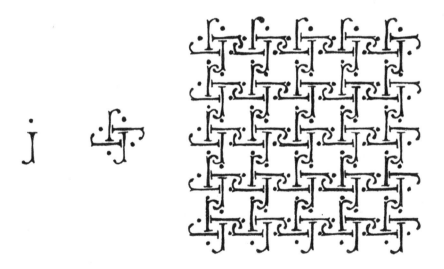

Figure 2.2
Hypnopaedia (Zuzana Licko, 1997). *Source*: author.

the lack of US copyright protection for letter form designs. By turning letter designs into texture, the Hypnopaedia pattern illustrations allow us to make this distinction and appreciate letter shapes on a different level."[76] Hypnopaedia draws attention to typographic forms by detaching them from their normal function, and in the process illustrates the absurdity of the slippery slope argument that copyright protection of typefaces could somehow lead to copyrighting the alphabet. What's more, the fact that Hypnopaedia is able to accomplish this simply by altering the orientation and context of these shapes illustrates just how separable aesthetic form and linguistic function can be in typography. That such a gimmick is required to see this speaks to a general ignorance about the amount of work and creativity involved in designing a quality typeface, as well as to the laziness with which we all read past what is in front of us. In inviting us to "appreciate letter shapes on a different level," Licko is not necessarily suggesting we deny these forms their linguistic function, but that we see they can have different functions as well. Though potentially equivocal, as Kepes's definition of transparency would suggest, these shapes are not equivalent to their linguistic functions, and can be admired simply as beautiful and creative forms.

Functional Forms

The copyright debate over typefaces raises the question of what a typeface is—is it a set of forms, or is it the alphabet, a tool for linguistic function? The persistence of this debate suggests the extent to which linguistic function can obscure form in typography—leading some to worry that its protection could endanger the freedom to use the alphabet itself. If considered carefully, however, we can see that the means of production do not determine the shapes produced, even if (as we'll see in the next chapter) typographic technologies place certain limitations on what shapes are possible. One can also see that well-designed typefaces are full of originality, that is, full of small design decisions that set a typeface apart from its peers, as well as apart from the characteristic lines of the alphabet. And, perhaps most importantly, we can see that the alphabet is not an embodied thing, and so will never be able to be copyrighted, no matter how many typefaces may receive that protection.[77] In response to Ringer, "by its very nature" a typeface exists essentially outside of language, and it merely offers itself up to language for use. Typographic shapes are functional forms—like the belt buckle in the *Kielstein-Cord* case, they are formal first. But to be fair, the relation of form and function in typography is more complex than in a belt buckle. More like chess pieces, their function is also communicated by their forms.

In perhaps the most explicit example of chess forms indicating function, the Bauhaus sculptor Josef Hartwig designed a set in 1924 in which each piece is a representation of the moves it is able to make. The bishop is a cross, indicating its diagonal moves; the knight is L-shaped, indicating its possibilities; and so on (see figure 2.3).[78] But a set like this is rare. Generally, chess pieces look more like the set John Jaques designed in the 1840s. Known as the Staunton set, it codified many of the conventions of chess design (and is likely the set you carry around in your

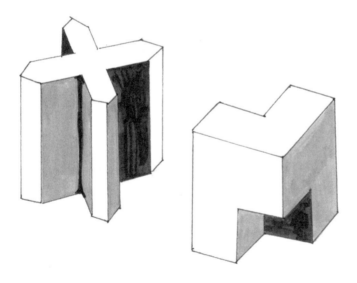

Figure 2.3
The bishop and knight from Josef Hartwig's chess pieces (1924) represent their possible directions of travel. *Source*: author.

mind's eye; see figure 2.4). The Staunton set comprises pieces that bear varying degrees of representational similarity to a king, queen, bishop, etc. However, it is not because of this representational quality that their forms are able to communicate function. Long before the Staunton set, certain formal standards were established—the king and queen were to be the tallest pieces and the pawns the smallest, with the knight, bishop, and rook in between. Usually, the king and queen would be adorned with crowns, the pawns would have no more than a knob for adornment, and the knight, bishop, and rook would be set apart from one another by their various adornments.[79] Reaching back even further, among the first Indian and Persian sets were purely abstract lathed forms, differentiated (and so communicating their function) using only height, width, and sometimes color.[80]

These general formal constraints are one reason that so many variations in chess forms have been possible—if you can be sure that the tallest piece is the king, it matters little what that king actually looks like. Technological developments and new materials (especially plastic resins) have further encouraged diversity in chess design—allowing sets to capture everything from popular culture to social status and global

Figure 2.4
The bishop and knight from the Staunton set, which has become the standard chess design. *Source*: author.

politics. In that diversity we find tall elegant pieces, like the Selenus set, which are more beautiful than they are useful (given their tendency to be knocked over). We find the pure abstraction of early lathed sets, and the modernist abstraction of Hartwig's or Marcel Duchamp's sets. And in some digital chess fonts we find forms reduced to no more than a few, indicative lines (see figure 2.5).[81] Though a player may be able to use the standard Staunton set with less thought in the same way one might find it easier to read a "transparent" typeface, there is no reason chess pieces need to look a certain way.

A pawn indicates its function not because it takes the form of "a pawn" any more than an A functions by taking on a form like this: A. Rather, a pawn indicates its function by being the smallest, least adorned piece on the board (and by being one of eight identical pieces in the set). In chess sets, the specific design of the queen can vary freely, as long as it is clear to the player which piece is the queen—all the form must do is indicate a function that is distinct from other pieces. So (and as we'll see in typography as well), form indicates what the function will be, not the other way around. Certainly, these chess pieces exist in a centuries-old history of game development, and in that way the function precedes any individual

Figure 2.5
Knights from a Selenus set, Marcel Duchamp's chess set, and Chess Millennia font (Armando Marroquin). *Source*: author.

chess piece's design. However, when we are setting out a board, or making use of a piece in a game, the function of each chess piece is indicated by the form, and critically, by its relationship to other forms on the board. The king and queen can only be the tallest pieces (and so indicate their functions), in relation to other pieces.

The particular relation of form and function in chess pieces and typographic shapes challenges commonsense assumptions of the causal relationship between form and function in a way similar to D'Arcy Thompson's work on biological morphology. In exploring how biological forms come to be, Thompson rejected then-existing views on the causal relation between form and function. A femur, he argues, is not formed *to bear weight*—that is, the biological system has not determined that a femur will be shaped as it is because this is the best form for bearing weight. Instead, a femur's shape emerges *by bearing weight*.[82] Of course, the presence of human actors complicates this idea in typography and chess, but the parallel for typography would be: a Q functions not because it has taken a particular "Q"-signifying form; rather, a Q functions by having been accepted as (i.e., by functioning as) a "Q."

If it seems as though function is once again at the fore in our Kepesian model of transparency—that the limits of function are what determine possible forms—this is no accident. Any Q functions as a Q as long as it is accepted as a Q. But as we explore the nature of typographic shape more closely, we will see that this acceptance as a Q depends not on linguistic concepts but, as with chess, on a relation of forms. And so, the two aspects of typography, making an equal claim to the same space at the same time, will fluctuate in our understanding of the medium. A typographic shape is formed to perform a particular function, but its ability to function also depends on its formal characteristics, and more importantly the relational characteristics of that form. This entangling of form and function is integral to the typographic medium, but also presents challenges for those trying to study it. As it has been for the US courts, it is easy for us to be distracted in this entanglement by typography's linguistic function. But in the next chapter we'll see that shape is primary to what typography is—not only existentially, but historically and technologically, as well.

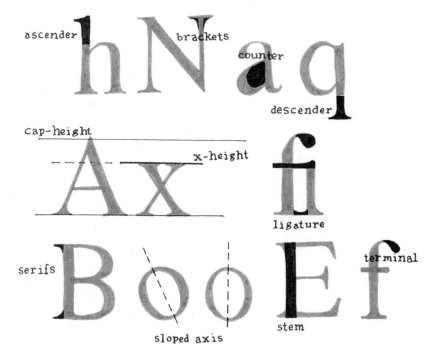

ascender   brackets

counter

descender

cap-height

x-height

ligature

serifs

sloped axis

stem

terminal

Source: author.

3 Typography Is Shape

Letters are things, not pictures of things.
—Eric Gill[1]

According to the typographers Phil Baines and Andrew Haslam, typography is "the mechanical notation and arrangement of language." For Alan Bartram, letters "can be transformed visually without any loss of their essential character. The changes reflect new societies, new technologies, new preferences, new functions; but within these changes the symbols are constant, always themselves." As much as Robert Bringhurst's famous *Elements of Typographic Style* provides a view of the immense amount of designed detail involved in typographic work, he still writes that the "typographer's one essential act is to interpret and communicate the text." For Karen Cheng, "Type is the visual manifestation of language." And for J. Abbot Miller and Ellen Lupton, typography (and writing), when viewed from a deconstructivist vantage point, involves "the intrusion of visual form into verbal content, the invasion of 'ideas' by graphic marks, gaps, and differences."[2] The solid, unchanging essence of typography is frequently portrayed as linguistic.

The position that typographic design is a visual intrusion into, or mere variation of, a verbal core is one that needs to be challenged. It is not that typography is unrelated to language; the particular set of shapes that have been cast and recast throughout the history of type are primarily linguistic shapes. But linguistic communication does not serve as the stable core of the medium around which shapes change—the linguistic describes but one use to which we put this medium. The shapes, constantly churning as they may be, are in fact the core of the medium. Why then, do we have this backwards?

From an early age, those of us who use the Latin alphabet are taught that this:

A

is the first letter of that alphabet, and (in English literacy training) "is for" something like "apple" or "aardvark." We are taught to ignore the differences in appearance between A, A, A, A, etc., and to more or less equate A and a, or B and b. The Dutch calligrapher and teacher of typographers, Gerrit Noordzij, criticizes this pedagogical method as teaching comprehension at the expense of perception.[3] And he is likely right. The flexibility of our reading brains is impressive, but without conscious effort our attention to visual detail tends to be lacking.[4]

So, while we may be tempted to listen to our common sense that equates a typographic shape with a letter of the alphabet, we should in fact question where that common sense comes from. We have an automatic association of typographic shapes with letters, but this is not necessarily evidence of an essential link between the two. Rather, it may merely be evidence of successful learning and of the flexibility of our brains. This is an instance where the commonsense explanation for what typography is leads us astray.

The distinction that needs to be drawn is between a practical definition of typographic shapes and a definition of necessity (one that looks for the necessary features of the medium rather than its behavior).[5] In his highly influential *Course on General Linguistics*, Ferdinand de Saussure argues that "the values of the letters are purely negative and differential. So the same individual may write t in . . . variant forms. . . . The one essential thing is that his *t* should be distinct from his *l*, his *d*, etc."[6] This is no doubt true from the perspective of use—if the goal is to elicit the concept (or signified) "t," then this t will do just as well as:

t　т　t　ₗ　t　✗　t　τ　t　t　†　ₜ　**t.**

However, this view favors the concept of "t" above its manifestations. The concept is a reduction of, or abstraction from the complexity of the t's that actually exist. As Friedrich Nietzsche argues, all concepts are formed from the equation of unequal things. And so, as part of his broader project of revaluing values, he argues that we should question what is behind such a mistaken equation.[7] What is the motivation? What is lost?

For Saussure's equation t = **t** = t, the question is, what is lost if we accept the concept "t" as dominant over the reality of all the extant t's? At the very least, the answer is: nearly six hundred years of typographic history. But we also lose a clear understanding of what the typographic medium is—it has many more moving parts than Saussure's equation will allow. So, although his theory makes a significant amount of sense in light of our lived experience, this view cannot get us closer to a rich understanding of how typography operates. In order to use a semiotic theory like Saussure's to understand typography, one either needs to stretch that theory far beyond the ground on which it stands, or one has to ignore the rich variation of shape that serves as the driving force for the typographic medium.[8]

We can see a large amount of diversity in the above line of t's, even in just this handful of examples. So even if common sense tells us we should identify t as a letter, the sensory data of the variability of t's should make it clear to us that these are primarily shapes. But we don't have to rely on visual information alone to recognize typography as shape—if we look to typographic history, we see that shape is ultimately what made Johannes Gutenberg's method of movable type printing so revolutionary.

A Technology of Shapes

Movable type printing was developed in China in the eleventh century, and in Korea at the end of the fourteenth. Though Korean type was cast metal, and both systems involved movable pieces of type (as opposed to earlier blockprinting) hundreds of years before Gutenberg's work, these earlier methods didn't have the influence that Gutenberg's technique would have. Nor did these East Asian methods of printing have a direct influence on the development of European movable type.[9] First in Europe, and then globally, mass-produced movable type printing would fuel countless major and minor revolutions. Due to its relationship to movable type printing, typography has also often been depicted as a revolutionary force. Writing as type personified, Frederic Goudy muses, "Cold, rigid, implacable I may be, yet the first impress of my face brought the Divine Word to countless thousands. . . . I am the leaden army that conquers the world. I AM TYPE."[10] Providing a less dramatic riff on this metaphor of type as a revolutionary army, Michael Middleton's 1943 treatise on the use of typography in British Labour Party publications sought to use design to win elections and create party unity. Here the soldiers of lead are to be armed with "dignified" design and sent out to compete with other printed matter to further the party's political aims.[11]

This image of type as a leaden army is often attributed to an anonymous seventeenth-century printer, who wrote, "with twenty-five soldiers of lead I have conquered the world."[12] The path traveled by this conquering army has been traced by contemporary scholars, winding through social structures, labor practices, and artistic endeavors. Transforming labor practices, movable type printing has been credited with bringing diverse classes of people together in the divided labor of mass-producing books. It contributed to the efficacy of the Protestant Reformation, circulating revolutionary ideas while also putting the words of the Christian God into the hands of the lay population. By providing new ways of collecting, organizing, and searching data, it contributed to the Copernican Revolution in science. And it was an active participant in both the standardization of languages and the vernacularization of texts, which aided the formation of the collective memory (and collective forgetting) that makes modern nations possible.[13]

In addition to rearranging the structures of power and knowledge, by Marshall McLuhan's account, Gutenberg's method of printing introduced new *kinds* of knowledge and of thinking. Culture shifted from the oral to the visual, from the tribal to the individual, from the simultaneous and superficial to the sequential and historical, and from direct experience to ever-increasing abstraction.[14] As referenced in the introduction, Vilém Flusser similarly argues that typography introduced a break from the dominant philosophy of Platonism—a way of thinking that saw theoretical work as work done at a distance from ideal and immutable forms. Typography introduced the idea that forms were tangible and mutable, and this, Flusser argues, served as the basis for modern science and philosophy.[15] Typography introduced the idea that we could reshape the world. But bearing all of these grand effects in mind, what was it about Gutenberg's typographic technology that made it so revolutionary?

As Flusser recognizes, in developing his method for movable type printing, Gutenberg actually invented very little. The arts of printing and metal casting already had considerable histories by the middle of the fifteenth century, so Gutenberg merely had to come up with the optimal mixtures of ink and of metals to make his process successful. The press itself, which was built for Gutenberg by Konrad Saspoch, was based on other platen presses of the day, used for pressing grapes. Though modifications had to be made throughout, none of this was particularly new. Flusser argues that Gutenberg's revolution was in "handling the letters as if they were three-dimensional objects (as if they were 'realities' and not symbols)."[16] Although Flusser is making a philosophical claim, he's not far off from identifying the technological innovation at the heart of movable type printing. The revolution in Gutenberg's print shop emerged from the mold used for casting type.[17]

The mass production of pieces of metal type involves a process of cutting metal punches, which are in turn used to create metal matrices, from which countless individual and identical pieces of type can be cast. During casting, a matrix is held in a wooden type mold, into which a molten alloy of lead, tin, and antimony is poured. If a single mold is used to cast (i.e., to hold the matrices for) every character in a font, this means that the mold needs to have a certain amount of flexibility. What makes Gutenberg's type mold such a revolutionary force is the particular amount of flexibility it achieves.

Because movable type printing involves making a uniform impress from multiple individual pieces of type arranged on the bed of a printing press, the pieces of type have to be of uniform size in two dimensions. To create a level printing surface, the pieces of type have to be of uniform depth—each type face rising a uniform distance from the print bed. And to create a line of text that is evenly spaced from the lines above and below it, the piece of metal on which each character appears has to be of the same height. The third dimension, however, requires variability. There are significant differences in the widths of our characters (e.g., between l and m), and so the mold for casting type has to be variable in one dimension and fixed in the other two (see figure 3.1). Above all the other necessary factors, it was this mold and the ability to cast individual yet uniform pieces of type that made Gutenberg's method of printing revolutionary. The key to movable type printing was the introduction of individual shapes that were both uniform and variable.

The type mold is the key to making Gutenberg's method work, and it is also what makes movable type printing economically and then socially revolutionary—the shapes it creates introduce a level of efficiency unheard of in mid-fifteenth-century book making. In pretypographic Europe, scribes produced books by hand, a means of production that was labor intensive and time consuming. This in turn meant that books were scarce and expensive, and so their contents belonged to a privileged few. Periodically scribes were able to increase their efficiency by cutting down

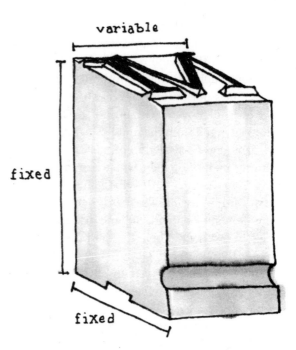

variable

fixed

fixed

Figure 3.1
The success of
movable type printing
depended on pieces
of type that were fixed
in two dimensions,
but variable in the third
to allow for the varying
widths of characters.
Source: author.

on the number of pen strokes it took to create a single character, but books remained rare objects. What made Gutenberg's method a significantly more efficient means of creating documents was the elimination of pen strokes altogether. Typography replaced multiple strokes with individual shapes, all imprinting the page at once.[18] Even in a typographic tradition like the Chinese, where the stroke remains a central factor, efficiency is achieved through the singular impress replacing the gradual movement of the pen or brush.

In Chinese typography, the stroke-count remained a key measure by which characters were ordered and stored (not only in type cases, but in some Chinese typewriters as well). And in the development of divisible type—type that divides certain Chinese characters into constituent (and reusable) parts to cut down on the number of pieces needed for a font—the stroke posed both a challenge and an opportunity for design. Two Frenchmen, Jean-Pierre Guillaume Pauthier and Marcellin

Legrand, attempted to base their divisible type not on the stroke but on the radical—a collection of strokes usually used for taxonomical purposes. As a result, their divisible type, though workable, failed to capture the ways in which strokes vary depending on the radical's position in a character.[19] In both the East and the West, the stroke is eliminated in typographic production; even when the stroke retains a role, typography replaced the analog *motion* of the calligrapher's pen with the digital impress of the typographic shape.

In addition to defining the first revolutionary spark of movable type printing, shape is also the driving force for the rest of typographic history. The type designer Erik Spiekermann has said that "the history of type is a history of technical constraints." What is elided in this declaration is what it is, exactly, that technology is constraining.[20] One can certainly divide typographic history into broad technological periods. After the ceramic, wooden, and sand-cast metal type of Song Dynasty China and fourteenth-century Korea, the first four hundred years of Western movable type would largely follow the spread of Gutenberg's method of printing. After the sack of Mainz in 1460, Gutenberg's techniques were carried by printers first trained in Mainz to other European cities, and eventually to other continents. Sometimes spread by colonial forces, sometimes by individual business interests, the technology of movable type printing remained largely unchanged until the end of the eighteenth century. Industrialization radically transformed typographic printing, as it did so much of late-eighteenth- and nineteenth-century society. This second period of typographic technology sees the development of rotary presses, Linn Boyd Benton's punchcutting machine, and perhaps most notably from a typographic perspective, Otmar Mergenthaler's Linotype, and Tolbert Lanston's Monotype (industrial typecasting machines). This period is followed in the second half of the twentieth century by the popularization of phototypesetting machines, followed quickly by digital printers, personal computers, the phenomenon of "desktop publishing," and mobile devices. What is important to see, however, when sketching out such a technological history is that within each of these periods, there are countless variations of shape. The technological history of typography, then, is actually a history of shapes constrained, or informed, by the technologies in which they first appear.[21]

In the first four hundred years we can observe a gradual progression from calligraphic influence to an exploration of the capacities of metal itself (see figure 3.2). As noted, Gutenberg's type imitated the work of the Northern European scribes around him. His books were to look no different from those produced by hand; they were merely to be more efficient to produce. When print moved from Germany to Italy, its next major center, the typefaces that were cut there by Johann von Speyer, Conrad Sweynheym and Arnold Panartz, and Nicolas Jenson were imitating the local Carolingian style of calligraphy. The shapes produced under the influence of the pen had minimal contrast between thick and thin strokes, a slope to curved characters, and serifs that stayed close to the body.

As the experimentation with typographic shape continued through this first period, punchcutters worked on refining their art, creating shapes that were more delicate, more balanced between upper and lower cases, and between the figure and ground. This is a common pattern in

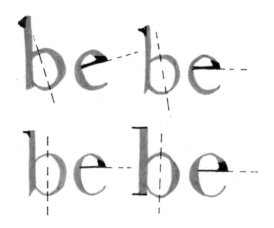

Figure 3.2
The first four hundred years of typeface design have often been traced through three features: (1) the straightening of the axis of bowled characters; (2) the straightening of the crossbar on the e, and (3) the thinning of the serif, eventually losing its bracket entirely. These four steps align with the often-used categories for classifying serifed typefaces: Humanist, or Venetian (top left), Old Style, or Garalde (top right), Transitional (bottom left), and Modern, or Didone (bottom right). *Source*: author.

the history of typography: the first stage of design that follows the intro-duction of a new technology imitates shapes from previous technologies. This, then, is followed by a stage of experimentation and innovation that draws on the particulars of the new technology at hand.[22] According to William Morris, the typeface that reflects the first triumph of the engi-neer over the calligrapher was Romain du Roi at the end of the seven-teenth century.[23] Though because this typeface was reserved for use by the French Imprimerie Royale, the Modern shape (that is, the shape di-vorced from the medieval scribe) was not fully developed until the late eighteenth century, right before industrial machines transformed the art again.

Though it took some time for it to find its own shapes, the technology of punchcutting exerts certain characteristic pressures on the shapes pro-duced with it. For instance, serifs and other details cannot be too delicate, due to the difficulty of cutting these forms, and the pressure of the press that will dull these thin pieces of metal. John Baskerville is said to have melted down and recast his type frequently in order to keep his nearly unbracketed serifs as sharp as possible.[24] But it makes far more practi-cal sense in this technology to design serifs that are stubbier, bracketed close to the character's stem (as William Caslon did). Another aesthetic pressure is exerted by the rectangle of metal on which each shape appears. This put a limit on the bounds of an individual shape—making it difficult to produce something like a script face (a face that mimics the fluid and connected lines of handwriting). It also restricts the variability of spac-ing that is possible between characters of different orientation. A closely kerned arrangement of inverted triangular characters like this:

VA

is far more difficult to achieve when the V and A are each segregated on their rigid rectangle of metal.

Each of the other typographic technologies also determine the range of shapes produced within them. This determination, to borrow from Raymond Williams, is not "the notion of an external cause which totally predicts or prefigures," but rather "a notion of determination as setting limits, exerting pressures."[25] The operative limits of the technology's own processes and materials limit the field of possible shapes that can be produced. Considering the shift from movable type printing to type-casting machines like the Linotype and Monotype, the basic material of the finished product remains the same—metal characters on rectangular supports—but the process changes markedly and exerts different pressures on shape.

The Linotype expanded the field of typographic printing through automation. It brought about a revolution in publishing, thanks to its combination of typesetting, type casting, and type sorting into a single machine. Before the Linotype, printers set each piece of type individually into lines of text, and after printing broke down a page and re-sorted those pieces of type into their appropriate compartments in type cases. The automation of casting and sorting saved a considerable amount of time in the production process, allowing for the growth of book publishing and the expansion of newspapers to more pages and multiple daily editions. Comparable to movable type printing, the keys to the Linotype's increase in efficiency are the matrices (or mats) that circulate through the machine, and from which a slug (or line-o-type) is cast. Indicative of their importance in the process, these matrices went through about sixty steps in their production, and through more than fifty examinations to ensure accuracy.[26] The matrix is the only piece involved in all three basic sections of the Linotype—setting, casting, and sorting. The extensive checks on the accuracy of mats ensures that they can move fluidly throughout each of these sections. But for the machine to be of a manageable scale, the matrices must also be economical in how they store information. To minimize the number of mats running through the machine, most are used for casting more than one typographic shape. On a typical Linotype matrix, there will be both a roman character and its italic equivalent. This efficient means of storing characters also exerts pressure on how these roman and italic shapes can be designed. Not only are Linotype characters confined to the rigidity of metal matrices, but the roman and the italic, normally of markedly different dimensions, are confined to the same piece of metal. To ensure pleasing lines of type, then, the roman and italic characters both have to be designed in such a way that the spacing between typographic shapes is equally harmonious.

The mats were also only capable of carrying type of a certain size range, generally up to 14 points, sometimes 24.[27] And the ascenders and descenders of characters were generally kept short, to better facilitate a wide variety of leading (the space between lines of text). In addition to being designed to fit the Linotype machine, these characters also had to fit the presses that would eventually print their faces. These rotary presses were faster than traditional movable type presses, and automated the inking process with rubber rollers. This meant that typographic shapes had to be designed in such a way as to limit ink-smearing and pooling.

The Linotype's influence on typographic shapes was also social and economic—for instance, the earliest clients for the machine were newspapers, and so the typefaces and styles designed were initially limited to the needs of that industry. The diversity of Linotype faces expanded, and the machine now provides a glimpse at the long-term effects that the pressures of a particular technology can have on the field of typographic shapes more broadly. Given the dominance of this technology in the industry, whether originally designed for the machine or not, those faces that were supported by the Linotype, those that had matrices cut for *this* machine, survive today as some of our most popular typefaces. In short, because these faces *could* be used in the dominant technology, they frequently *were*, and became standards, if not defaults, in the industry.[28] These frequently appearing faces, in turn, influence what designers and readers alike commonly expect a typographic shape to be.

Roughly concurrent with the Linotype's rise, experiments with incorporating photographic technologies into typesetting began in the late nineteenth century—though the first successful phototypesetting machines didn't appear until the 1930s, and one could argue that designers didn't take full advantage of the design possibilities in this particular technology until the 1960s. Some phototypesetters used matrices similar to those in the Linotype; others used strips or discs of photographic negatives. Whether controlled manually or by digital instructions, phototypesetting machines worked by projecting, with light and lenses, typographic shapes onto light-sensitive, bromide paper. A photographically produced page of text could then be converted into a plate for printing on rotary presses. Both the advantages and disadvantages of this typographic technology emerge from the replacement of metal with light as the medium producing the shapes on the page.[29]

Light is a far more flexible medium than metal, so phototypesetting overcomes the difficulties of creating fluid script faces, or of nestling characters close to one another as in the VA example above. One can see in a flowing script face like Matthew Carter's Snell Roundhand (1966), or in the dramatically overlapping characters in Herb Lubalin's Avant-Garde Gothic (1968; see figure 3.3) that this technology invited the production of wildly new typographic shapes. But as Adrian Frutiger notes, it also introduced new challenges or limitations. Each typographic form, he notes, "is exposed by a flash timed at a few millionths of a second and

Figure 3.3
Avant-Garde Gothic
(Herb Lubalin, 1968).
Source: author.

the intensity of the light must be very high. Proportionately less light penetrates through a small opening than through a large one, so it is necessary to thicken the i-dots and points in light faces."[30] Given the speed of exposure, and the difficulty of containing light, the edges of typographic shapes also had to be designed with the knowledge that light would seep out beyond the area a designer might intend.

Phototypesetters were quickly partnered with, and then superseded by, digital typesetters and printers beginning in the middle of the 1960s, by purely digital typefaces in the middle of the 1970s, and then by home computers with graphical user interfaces in the middle of the 1980s. Throughout these digital developments, common issues affecting designs were how to achieve an efficient storage of information, and most notably how to deal with the influence of the pixel. The primary challenge was how one could render a curved or diagonal shape out of squares—the puzzle of what typography is when it moves into digital technology was a puzzle of shape, rather than of signification. Computer displays use a raster that is governed by the machine's underlying binary logic. That is, a cell of the grid can either be on or off, with no in between. As frequently as grids had been used to design typefaces in the past, early digital type designers found that designing familiar typographic shapes *out of* a grid of pixels was no easy task. Significant amounts of detail had to be abandoned, counters had to be opened more widely, x-heights had to rise, and sans serifs frequently were favored over serifs. Comparable to the early days of movable type printing, delicacy was not an easy achievement in early digital typography.

Although one can sketch such a history of typographic shapes as I've just told, there is no teleological, narrative line for the history of these shapes. Benton's punchcutting machine from the nineteenth century allowed for the easy reproduction of typographic shapes from centuries before—increasing interest in historical typefaces and drawing these old shapes into new time. And even if typefaces like Romain du Roi, Bodoni (1790), or Futura (1927) indicate the triumph of the engineer over the calligrapher, still today designers are producing Old Style typefaces (faces that reveal the influence of the pen). What is important to understand is first of all that typography is not simply a technology—it is not equivalent to movable type printing but has in fact survived through numerous technological shifts. Second, the history of typography is littered with countless variations of shape; it is nearly six hundred to one thousand years of shaping and reshaping a particular class of forms. And finally, with a significant amount of variability, the shapes that populate the history and medium of typography are constrained by the technologies that make them.

A Preference for Latin Shapes

Beyond the specific limitations that each technology imposes on the delicacy of a serif, or the sharpness of an edge, most typographic technologies are also best at accommodating certain kinds of shapes. Traditionally, the typographic medium works most efficiently with typefaces made up of a manageable number of discrete shapes, able to sit within relatively uniform rectangular bounds. These are constraints imposed by typography's early technologies and have been carried on either by more contemporary technologies, or merely by convention and expectation. One can observe the influence of these pressures on the design of any typeface, but it is more pronounced when a set of shapes that doesn't fit neatly into this discrete, uniform, rectangular framework are introduced into one of these technologies—revealing the bias toward that which fits in, by being that which does not. Take as an example the challenges that have historically confronted the development of Arabic typography.

Generally speaking, the typographic history of the Arabic script is less voluminous than that of the Latin. The reasons for this are numerous and complex, including cultural and geopolitical factors. The earliest Arabic typefaces were designed by Western Europeans, rather than Arabic calligraphers or native speakers, thanks to the interests of European intellectuals and Christian missionaries.[31] Equally important for the slow development of Arabic typography is the religious significance of calligraphy in Islam. Calligraphy is part of the Islamic creation myth—it is the means by which God created the book of nature (i.e., the universe). The Aleph (first letter) was the first creation, a point from which drips the ink that Allah used to create the rest of the universe. Following from this, calligraphy here on Earth is to be a mirror of this heavenly writing—its proportions and forms, informed by strict and sacred traditions.[32] Such sacred and practiced calligraphy cannot easily be replaced by a secular machine. The first printed Qu'ran was produced in Venice around 1537, but the first edition produced by an Arabic press was not until 1924. Likewise, although there were presses established in the Middle East in the seventeenth century, the first Muslim press was not established until 1820, in Egypt.[33]

Setting these cultural, political, and religious issues aside, there are also formal reasons for the relatively slow development of Arabic typography; and these in turn reveal the formal biases of typographic technologies. In short, many of the technologies of typography are not well formed for the kinds of shapes that Arabic writing employs. Unlike some other non-Latin scripts, like Chinese, that wrestle with how to fit the production, storage, and retrieval of tens of thousands of characters into Western typographic technologies, the Arabic script is a relatively manageable system.[34] Arabic writing is phonetic, primarily consonantal, with vowel sounds indicated by diacritical marks. There are eighteen basic shapes that are elaborated with additional diacritical marks to produce the script's twenty-eight linguistic characters (not including the Lam-Aleph ligature). So rather than scale, the typographic difficulties arise from the nature of Arabic shapes, how they interact with one another.

The orientations of strokes in Latin and Arabic characters are opposites. In Latin, vertical strokes are traditionally thicker than horizontals, while in Arabic it is the horizontal that is weighted more heavily. In most styles of Arabic calligraphy, the shapes are more curved or fluid than Latin shapes are, and significant portions of the characters extend beneath the baseline.[35] In general, then, Latin characters are better suited to the confines and conventions of movable type's metal rectangle. The differences are not merely aesthetic, they also indicate a difference in how these shapes behave. Some of the challenges of fitting Arabic into typographic technologies came from the basic qualities of the shapes, but even more challenging is how Arabic characters are transformed by their interactions with one another.

Arabic writing is a heavily ligatured system, that is, the individual characters are linked to one another. Ligatures do exist in Latin typography as well, but are infrequent. Combinations of characters like ff or fi will sit together as a single shape on a single piece of type. But this is largely in the interest of readability; for instance, the ligatured fi is used to avoid the dot of an i from running into the terminal of an f preceding it. In Arabic, however, ligatures are not incidental, nor are they simply for readability—they are a basic part of the writing system. As Mourad Boutros has noted, if the basic unit in Latin writing is the letter, the basic unit in Arabic is the word, and this means that Arabic writing challenges the dominance of the discrete unit of type one has come to expect.[36] What's more, when combined, the characterforms change depending on where they appear in a word. In figure 3.4, the character "jiim" can be seen in three different forms at the beginning, middle, and end of a word.[37] This means that the twenty-eight linguistic characters that made for a manageable set quickly become one hundred and thirty.[38]

Arabic ligatures can vary. Most notably, the orientations of the ligatures are not uniform—sometimes these connections are horizontal (as they are in Latin), and sometimes they are vertical. This means not only that more variabilities need to be built into an Arabic typeface, but also that Western typography's basic grid isn't as useful here. The grid has held a privileged place in Western typographic history. In his typeface Fibonacci (1994), designer Tobias Frere-Jones argues that the grid is all that remains if you take a typeface and subtract the alphabet from it. According to the description accompanying Fibonacci's publication, the grid is "the essential 'grammar' of the system."[39] The British designer Anthony Froshaug argued that typography is itself a grid. The medium's vertical axis was originally provided by the type mold, its horizontal by the composing stick in which lines of text are collected from their cases. He writes, "To mention both typographic, and, in the same breath/sentence, grids, is strictly tautologous. The word typography means to write/print using standard elements; to use standard elements implies some modular relationship between such elements; since such relationship is two-dimensional, it implies the determination of dimensions which are both horizontal and vertical."[40] Froshaug identifies typography's modularity as the essence of the medium, but modularity cannot similarly be used to describe the traditional behavior of most Arabic characters.[41] The shapes of Arabic writing exceed such a grid in both their interactions and in their proportions. So, whereas Western typographers have frequently laid out ideal proportions within a grid, the tenth-century Arabic calligrapher Abu Ali Muhammad Ibn Muqlah laid out his proportions in a circle.[42]

Figure 3.4
The character jiim (top) takes on three different forms depending on where in a word it appears—beginning, middle, or end (remember that Arabic is read right to left). *Source*: author.

Typographic technologies are not built specifically for Latin *languages*, but they are built to accommodate shapes that behave as Latin shapes do. Other scripts, like Greek or Cyrillic, have typographic histories nearly as long as that of Latin, in part because their shapes behave in the same way as Latin shapes. To be sure, some of the prominence of Greek or Cyrillic typography is also attributable to geopolitical and scholarly reasons, just as Arabic typography's slower development is. Chinese and Korean characters also possess the discrete quality that makes Latin, Greek, Cyrillic, and Hebrew so amenable to typographic technologies—while China has an issue with scale (the number of those discrete characters required), all of these scripts can be found in the earliest history of typographic shapes in the East and West. One reason why an alphabet like Arabic moves more tentatively into the history of typography is because its shapes are more fluid, less discrete, and more variable. The technologies designed for typography were not well suited to the behavior of Arabic script.

It is certainly not impossible to translate Arabic writing into the technological logic of Western typography, but there has long been a negotiation at play in such a translation. The earliest Arabic typefaces either lacked accuracy or quality, designed as they were by people unfamiliar with the details of how Arabic calligraphy was produced, and for technology that was a poor replacement for the calligrapher's pen.[43] Newer typographic technologies have made designing successful Arabic type easier—phototypesetting, Letraset (dry transfer lettering), and now vector-based digital type allow for more flexibility in the kinds of forms that can be designed. And contemporary Arabic typefaces are being designed that are, at the very least, of equal beauty to any Latin typeface. Furthermore, these technologies (and perhaps the passage of time) have inspired less traditional Arabic typefaces as well. The Syrian designer Abdulkader Arnaout, for instance, explored new possibilities for Arabic forms starting in the 1960s. Still rooted in the calligraphic tradition, and eventually distributed by Letraset, his faces play with concepts of systematicity, modularity, and the communicative potential of shape. From cutout forms that are reminiscent of Saul Bass's movie posters, to an intensely angular architectural Kufic typeface (Ayat al-Kursi, 1965), Arnaout's work reaches outside of traditional typographic shapes to fully explore Arabic characters' potential in the typographic medium (see figure 3.5).[44]

As typographic technologies have become more flexible and more global, an increasing number of multiscript typefaces are being designed.

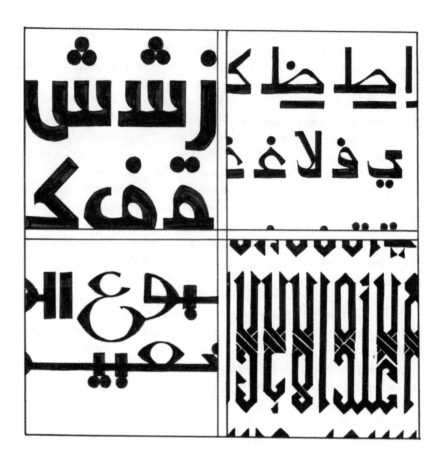

Figure 3.5
A sampling of typefaces designed by Abdulkader Arnaout. Clockwise from top left: Al-Khatt al-Arnaouti, Letraset S35920, Ayat al-Kursi, and Usbu'al-Funun. *Source*: author.

In this process, it's significant which script one designs first. The shapes of one will (for the purposes of achieving design harmony) influence those designed for the other. The Khatt Foundation, a center for Arabic typography in Amsterdam, has launched a series of typographic "matchmaking" projects, which bring designers and scholars together to design typefaces that span scripts. In their third such project, a team of designers produced Qandus, a type family for Northern Africa that brings together Arabic, Latin, and Tifinagh (used for Berber languages). According to Laura Meseguer, the designer of the Latin set of shapes, the project began with the Arabic—specifically with the nineteenth-century Moroccan Suffi calligraphy of Al-Qasim al-Qandusi.[45] One can see the influence of this Arabic starting point reflected in the forms of the Latin and Tifinagh sets as well (curvature, distribution of thick and thin strokes, and so on; see figure 3.6). We can imagine that a different type family would have been developed had Latin been the starting point, and a different set of shapes still if the starting point were Tifinagh.

Even in such multiscript projects, however, there remains a general pressure to bend the forms of a script to a (Western) technology. Recently, in their rollout of the universalizing Noto type family, Google came under fire for providing an Arabic typeface in the naskh style of calligraphy, and not in the nastaliq. The project's aim is to create a digital type family that will support every script currently encoded by Unicode. Given the importance of nastaliq to the Urdu language (used by over 100 million people), its omission was seen as a significant cultural oversight.[46] Google has since released a Noto Nastaliq Urdu, but their initial oversight speaks to

ق وﺲ Qandus ⵣⴰⵉⵏⴻⵙⴾ

Figure 3.6
Qandus (Kristyan Sarkis, Laura Mesegeur, and Juan Luis Blanco, 2017). *Source*: author.

the relative ease of digitally rendering the more angular naskh style than the elegant and swooping curves of nastaliq. If one is not careful, the biases of a technology will encourage the growth of certain shapes and the possible extinction of others.

The entire Noto project is itself a formal assumption being made by Google, as it has been made by others before them who have attempted to achieve universality through type. The assumption is that typography's conquering army can be a universalizing response to the tower of Babel—that is, that type can overcome the complexity introduced by the multiplicity of human languages. Within a single language one can see this universalizing potential, as when the fifteenth-century publications by William Caxton helped to create linguistic unity, standardizing the spelling and grammar of a variable and vernacular English language.[47] Across languages, polyglot Bibles were printed (e.g., by Arnao Guillén de Brocar in 1514, and Christophe Plantin in 1572), laying out the text of the Bible in multiple languages side by side. These publications offered a metaphorical unity, by using multiple languages simultaneously, to set the same text.[48] In these examples, typographic publications are seen as being able to bridge linguistic divides, not through formal unification, but simply by making the printed word more uniform and more available. In the modern era, the universalizing aspirations of some type designers were more explicitly expressed.

In part a contrary force to the cultural and political rise of nationalism in Europe, New Typography's various movements promoted ideals of universal design. Herbert Bayer, the head of typography at the Bauhaus, advocated for a universal typeface that would be able to set one language as beautifully as any other. One characteristic of such a face would be the elimination of uppercase characters, perhaps to nullify the capitalization practices that vary from one language to another (capitalizing all nouns in German, but only proper nouns in English, for instance).[49] As this reference to the uppercase suggests, Bayer's idea of a universal typeface was a Latin face (few other writing systems have multiple cases). Jan Tschichold's idea of a universal typeface to resist nationalism was, likewise, Latin. In his book *New Typography*, Tschichold explicitly identifies non-Latin writing systems as antithetical to typography's universalizing potential. At the time, the use of roman and blackletter type was being debated in Germany—blackletter generally being cast as nationalistic; and Tschichold classed Cyrillic, Arabic, Chinese, and Indian characters in with blackletter styles (Fraktur, Schwabacher, and Gothic) as similarly nationalistic. For Tschichold, the modernist's Latin, sans-serif typeface would transcend political and cultural borders, and the romanization of non-Latin scripts was inevitable.[50]

Today Google's Noto project aims at a similarly transnational end, but does so by working *with* diverse scripts, instead of against them. However, as evidenced by the protests raised over the inclusion of naskh rather than nastaliq, the project has faced scrutiny.[51] Even as more faces have been added, making the project as a whole more inclusive, the project's goal has a certain hubris and brute functionality to it. When creating a digital type family for every script (and providing these faces in as compact a digital file as possible), subtle differences between entire languages can be ignored (as in the commonly used Han Unification of Chinese, Japanese, and Korean in Unicode), and frequently small formal details, like diacritical marks, can be lost.[52] Each of these universalist theories not only make linguistic assumptions but attempt to utilize a medium of shapes for their *linguistic ends*; and the failure to achieve universality has followed accordingly.

In whatever guise it takes, the universalizing assumption in typography misses the fact that the differences in shape that exist across writing systems cannot simply be ignored. Yes, the relationship between the signifier and signified is arbitrary; but the parallels between the behavior of shapes in the Latin alphabet and the operational logic of dominant typographic technologies is not.[53] The typographic medium itself is built up around a set of shapes that are discrete, and that lose no vital linguistic information by being confined to individual rectangles of space. Typography is shape, and historically, it is a particular (albeit expanding) class of shape. It may be that Google will be successful in using typography to offer universal support to content, but many of the scripts being supported may well be changed in the process.

To the larger issue of establishing typography as shape, it is significant to note the root of the Google project's name—Noto. This approximate acronym stands for "No tofu," referring to the empty rectangle that appears on a digital screen in place of unsupported script. That is, if a program being used has no knowledge of a sign appearing in a text, like this ¢, that sign will be replaced by an empty rectangle (reminiscent of a block of tofu), indicating that something was there, but that the program has no way of displaying it. The missing sign is not replaced by another similar sign, in the way that some languages are transcribed from their original writing system into another by using approximations of pronunciation. Instead, the unsupported shape is replaced by a different (empty) shape. It is not the sound or the meaning that the program cannot support, but rather the desired shape (which in turn supports the sound and/or meaning). So, while multilingual typographic projects like Noto may be aimed at primarily linguistic ends, at refuting Babel, they are ultimately about adding to the store of shapes one can use in this particular typographic technology.

The Noto project is not about using typography to support every possible language, but rather every script. This means that shape is at the heart of this and other universalist ideals, and it is also what undermines such ideals. Different scripts use shapes that behave in different ways, and typography tends to favor some kinds of shapes over others. This is true in the meeting spaces between Latin and non-Latin scripts; it is also true at a broader (and less geopolitically thorny) level. If we consider how the reading brain processes typography, we can see evidence not only that typography is shape first, but also that it is a certain set of shapes.

Recounted in a simplified form, one theory of how the reading brain works is that it first takes characters in through the fovea of the retina—the center-most focal point in the eye. They are then processed by the visual cortex at the rear of the brain and then passed onto a specific area of the left occipitotemporal region. Although this region appears to contain neurons adapted to the recognition of letters (and not, for instance, of numerals), at this point in their processing, the shapes do not appear to have any linguistic content or meaning. The association with meaning, the link to language, occurs later in the processing and in different regions of the brain.[54] I will discuss the neurological process of reading further in chapter 7, but for now it is sufficient to recognize that the brain treats typographic (and written) characters as shapes first of all, and only after that as language.[55]

There is no doubt a risk involved in hewing too closely to the neuroscience of reading in an effort to understand typography, given that the brain seems to make no significant distinction (in recognizing characters) between handwriting and typography. However, the neural processing of characterforms does raise the idea that they are of a particular category of shape, as opposed to shape in general. The region of the brain where some neuroscientists believe typographic and written characters are processed, after they've moved through the visual cortex, is set among other visual processing areas—areas that are specified for particular classes of things: objects, faces, and so on. And because this area of the brain is used by readers regardless of which writing system they are reading, it appears that these characters are similarly a particular class of things.

It is important to understand that the neuroscience of reading is still being studied, and as such there are changing views and disagreements among scientists. As we'll explore more in chapter 7, the left occipitotemporal area of the brain is referred to by some as the visual word form area, while others challenge that label and even the centrality of this area to the reading process. However, given the similar pathways used to process different scripts, there do appear to be similarities between the kinds of shapes found in typography and writing across languages. To get a clearer picture of typographic shape, the following chapters will temporarily leave behind the context of the reading brain.

If we grant that shape is primary in the typographic medium, we should now consider what constitutes the category of typographic shapes. The next chapter will consider the possibility of defining the category of typographic shapes by locating the irreducible core of each character. Following that will be the possibility of locating the outer limit of typographic shapes—the point beyond which no shape can go and still remain a member of this category. And failing these, we will then consider a messier, but more inclusive, possibility of simply defining each included shape in relation to other included shapes.

ascender · bowl · brackets · counter · cap-height · x-height · crossbar · descender · serifs · sloped axis · stem · tail · thick & thin strokes

Source: author.

4 The Typographic Skeleton

The letter-craftsman must have a clear idea of the *skeletons* of his letters.
—Edward Johnston[1]

If we accept that the typographic medium is fundamentally shapes, that this is its essential feature and the basis of its operational logic, then the next question is: what kinds of shape are we dealing with exactly? For now, let's assume that there must be a limit to what counts as a typographic shape, or what constitutes this category, and let's try to locate this limit. To begin with, consider the possibility of an indivisible limit, a definition of shape based on the inability to reduce that definition any further. Do typographic shapes have irreducible skeletons on which each typeface drapes its particular details?

A philosophy that subscribes to the idea of a typographic skeleton is basically a depth model. The assumption is that if you dig down deep enough, you'll arrive at the heart of an issue, at the purest A, the purest f, the purest 3. In philosophical history, this assumption is related to Plato's ideal form and Kant's noumenon, but also to Marx's rational kernel and Freud's unconscious.[2] It also has parallels in other forms of art, related as it is to Leonardo da Vinci's *Vitruvian Man* and Malevich's *Black Square*. Like the *Vitruvian Man*, the premodernist typographic skeleton is a geometric ideal with perfect proportions, linked to some greater order or harmony. Later, and comparable to Malevich's *Square*, modernist attempts to locate pure characters stripped away all that could be considered excess. Perfect circles, equilateral polygons, and pure verticals and horizontals came to constitute the characters themselves. Here we'll look at these two skeletal movements in typographic history, as well as a more functional skeleton that arose with computer science, and its early attempts to define typographic characters within the computer's systematic way of operating, as a set of parameters and rules.

Early Ideals

The earliest Renaissance treatise on the perfect proportions for roman characters is attributed to Felice Feliciano, and was published sometime in the late 1450s. Produced primarily in Italy, the various treatises that followed Feliciano's all took ancient Roman inscriptions as their models, and sought to define the ideal proportions of these characters in relation to numerical and geometric principles.[3] According to Luca Pacioli in his 1509 study of characters, it is through the proportions of things like the human body that "God reveals the innermost secrets of nature."[4] The assumption was that the ancient Greeks and Romans had studied the proportions of the human body, and had then modeled their temple designs and lettering on those same proportions. This being said, the scholars studying these ancient inscriptions in the Renaissance period were unable to agree about which proportions were in fact ideal. Feliciano used a width-to-height ratio for strokes of 1:10; his friend and colleague Andrea Mantegna called for a ratio of 1:12; and Pacioli claimed 1:9 was ideal.[5]

These treatises did not focus in depth on things like serifs, the size of counters, or the slope of axes, which would become key concerns in later definitions of typographic shapes. Rather, their primary interests were in the proportions of the strokes to one another, and the relation of these characters to the perfect geometric forms of circles and squares. Frequently the ideal characters diagrammed in these treatises were set within a circle and square overlain upon one another (see figure 4.2). Yet while geometric ideals formed a foundation for the Renaissance definition of an ideal character, they were not obeyed too strictly. Feliciano describes the R as a second-class character because it could not be defined in a purely geometric way. He advises that because the tail of the R "cannot be perfectly described with the compass[,] let yourself be guided by your eye."[6] Optical harmony was as much an ingredient in these attempts to define perfect lettering as any mathematical principles were. The square and its divisions, for instance, might strictly determine how far the arm of an E would extend, but adhering too firmly to the square would have produced H's that appeared too wide in proportion to other characters.

The study of ideal characterforms during this period seems to be intended for practical use. Robin Rider notes that the first Renaissance building in Verona completed after Feliciano's treatise bears an inscription that follows his definition of lettering exactly.[7] And Damiano Moille's definition of proper characterforms was printed as a single sheet rather than as a book—apparently intended for use by craftspeople rather than by scholars.[8] Motivated by practical use, rather than by metaphysical perfection, the notion of a singular ideal also waned as the history of Renaissance characterform studies progressed. Later accounts, like that by Albrecht Dürer, abandoned the notion that there is a single ideal. Instead, a number of possible ideals were offered, and while one proportion might be favored over the others, all were said to produce beautiful characters.[9]

In this early period of attempts to define the essence of linguistic characters, we should note a few details. To begin with, although these studies were completed after the development of movable type printing, they were not intended explicitly for the perfect design of typographic characters. The men completing these studies were often artists or calligraphers, not punchcutters. Second, because these studies took as their model the perceived perfection of ancient Roman inscriptions, they tended to describe only uppercase characters. These characters have more uniform appearance in both their height and widths (with the exception of I, J, and often S) than the lowercase. It was, therefore, easy to imagine the kinds of definitions being produced—uniting all characters in the alphabet by a single proportion, and setting each character within uniform squares. Were these thinkers dealing with the diversity of the lowercase, their definitions might have been more complicated.[10] Finally, while these studies attempted to locate in our alphabetic characters the perfect order of nature, they did not maintain a strict adherence to that perfection. Many of those who produced these treatises stated the ideals, but presented characters that were more optically pleasing than geometrically perfect. When French bureaucracy got involved in the definition of characters at the end of the seventeenth century, the call to perfection became more adamant.

The committee involved in the design of the typeface known today as Romain du Roi saw their work as scientific, and their description of a perfect alphabet was formed from mathematical ideals and set out on detailed grids of 2,304 units. The typeface was designed within King Louis XIV's Academy of Sciences as part of a broader project to define all the practical arts, and the resulting typeface would eventually be used exclusively by the King's Imprimerie Royale. The committee was made up of scholars rather than craftsmen—the bibliophile Gilles Filleau Des Billettes; the mathematician and designer of educational games, Jacques Jaugeon; and the priest and admirer of measurement and tabulation, Father Jean Truchet. In 1699, six years after the committee began its work, they described their progress as follows: "We have begun with the art that preserves all others—namely printing. Monsieur Jaugeon, who took it upon himself to describe one aspect, has first of all gathered together alphabets of every language, both dead and living, with a supplement to each one, showing characters peculiar to certain sciences such as astronomy, chemistry, algebra, and music. Next, no longer restricted to simple description, he showed the Academy a new French alphabet that had been chosen to please the eye as far as was possible."[11] These men studied the history of typography and previous treatises on perfect characters, and in response to these studies they defined their alphabet in perfect, rather than practical, terms. The committee's ideal design was then manifested in two ways, and by two craftsmen. Louis Simonneau produced engravings for each of the gridded upper- and lowercase character designs; and Philippe Grandjean began cutting punches for Romain du Roi in 1695, though this would take him and others two decades to complete.

The resulting typeface is seen as an early typographic triumph of the engineer, of rationality, of mathematical principles, and an early example of the Enlightenment's striving toward encyclopedic knowledge. Yet while this is certainly a typeface that emerges from a belief in one's ability to perfectly define the most pleasing (and perhaps pure) typographic characters, Grandjean altered the designs of the committee in his production of the punches. The grids that laid out these ideal characters are significant as ideas, but Grandjean seems to have used his experience as a punchcutter to alter the designs for practical use. As in the earlier treatises on perfect characterforms, we can once again see the tension inherent in these projects between definitions with numerical and geometric perfection on the one hand, and the preferences of the reading eye, or of the materials of production, on the other. Up to this point in typographic history, it seems the human exceeds the reach of the mathematical definition.

Even in the original designs for Romain du Roi we can see the human (and perhaps the royal ego) sneaking in. As much as the committee's process seems to be one of aggregating the best and most essential from previous examples of type and other lettering, there is a thorn that appears in the side of this collected essence. The lowercase l features an excessive detail, a mark with no mathematical relevance, no scientific purpose—about halfway down its left-hand side is a small spur (see figure 4.1). Daniel Berkeley Updike argues that this spur was a mark of royalty; it was intended to identify this (and later faces from the Imprimerie Royale) as one of the king's typefaces.[12] It can also be seen as a historical link,

Figure 4.1
A spur appears on the
l in both Romain du
Roi (ca. 1695) and
Gutenberg's Textura
typeface (ca. 1450).
Source: author.

reaching back to Gutenberg's original typeface, where a similar spur appears on the l. But whether the scientific ideals of the Academy's committee break down at the point of production, or at the point of royal property, Romain du Roi remains an important typeface for opening the way to ever-more modern and geometric faces.

These attempts to define typographic shapes through scientific and mathematical principles influenced future typographic design, but were unlikely to arrive at an irreducible skeleton for the medium as a whole. They are useful as cumulative studies, looking for similarities across designs—common forms and ratios. However, the set of shapes they compare is limited largely to Roman inscriptions and book typefaces. Furthermore, while they identify certain skeletal qualities like stroke ratios, they have not removed enough detail to arrive at a formal essence of the typographic shape. The modernist typographers working in continental Europe in the early twentieth century were more explicitly invested in defining something essential. After a Victorian explosion of typographic novelty, they sought to return the medium to its purest forms.[13]

Modernist Purification and the Sans Serif

Frequently in modernist artistic movements, the philosophy was one of reduction—the elimination of excess, of ornamentation, or of illusion. At times, this reductive move was seen as a sort of purification, a distillation of an art to its essence. In typography, continental European modernist designers set about removing both the excesses of Victorian commercial design, and the idealization of Old Style typefaces and handcraft taking root in England and America. Clarity of communication was generally the motivation, and the tactics were largely geometric. Three movements in particular affected the modernist views of typographic essences: constructivism, De Stijl, and the Bauhaus.

The constructivists in Russia rejected the spiritual in art and sought to serve Bolshevik aims with design that created clear messages through the combined force of foundational elements—monochrome, geometric shapes, and the objective record of the photograph. They were using their design to reflect (or even bring about) a new sociopolitical order, while in the Netherlands the minimalist designs produced by members of De Stijl were motivated by a larger cosmic order. Their palette was restricted to black, white, and the three primary pigments; and their forms reflected a belief that the entire universe is ordered by the opposing forces of the vertical and the horizontal.[14] Influenced by both of these movements, but also ultimately more influential itself, the Bauhaus in Germany sought the unification of art and technology. These designers embraced industrialization by experimenting with new materials and technologies, and also by adopting certain ideals from the mechanical realm, such as efficiency, precision, and geometry.

Collectively, the typographic production of these three movements has been referred to as New Typography. The adoption of the particular philosophies behind this kind of typographic design may not have been widespread, but the styles, and in particular sans serifs, were. Jan Tschichold maintained that "Among all the types that are available, the so-called 'Grotesque' (sans-serif) or 'block letter' ('skeleton letters' would be a better name) is the only one in spiritual accordance with our time."[15] By the time New Typography became codified in the late 1920s, countless typefaces were already available, but for these designers only an efficient, streamlined typeface would speak to the contemporary reader. Sans serifs (or "skeleton letters" as Tschichold advocates we call them) eliminated the trappings of convention, and instead sought to communicate through the simplest possible geometric forms.

To an extent, all sans serifs are an exercise in constructing a simplified geometric definition of characters, and some modernist faces kept one foot in the Renaissance definitions discussed above. Edward Johnston's Railway Sans (1916), for instance, uses ancient Roman capitals as a model, and shares its stroke width-height proportion of 1:7 with that prescribed by the tenth-century Arabic calligrapher Ibn Muqlah.[16] But Railway Sans also adopts the ideal of perfect geometric forms and the belief that sans serifs would communicate more clearly to those attempting to navigate the then newly redesigned London Underground.[17] Rudolf Koch, like Johnston, was a skilled calligrapher, and he too designed a modernist sans-serif—Kabel (ca. 1928). Named in honor of industrial technologies, Kabel also mixes the Roman capitals discussed above with the purified geometry of modernism. This face features both perfectly circular O's and equilateral A's, as well as a Venetian e (slanted crossbar), and a two-story a, uncommon in sans-serifs. In Kabel's unique reimagining of the geometry of the g (see figure 4.3), one can see the new terrain of possibilities that are opened up through the attempt to strip down typographic shapes to a geometric core. Perhaps the best example of this project is Paul Renner's typeface Futura (1927).

Futura was an exercise in defining typographic forms using only perfect geometric shapes—circles, triangles, and straight lines. "In contrast to the then fashionable Constructivists," Renner wrote, "I did not want to glorify the compass as a tool, instead I wanted to lead form out of the wilderness and back to its origins."[18] One can see in early versions of this face that some familiar characterforms become distorted when one attempts to describe them in such strict terms. Under the strain of strict geometric ideals, the a can become a circle sheltered under a right angle (see figure 5.1), and the g can become an odd stack of shapes resembling a logo rather than a character (see figure 4.3). When the typeface went to market, unfamiliar variations like these were ultimately offered as optional characters in an otherwise tamed set of geometric sans-serif forms. The final harmony that Renner achieved, while maintaining the flavor of pure geometry, has ensured Futura's continued popularity, and his exercise reveals some of the challenges in this modernist version of typographic skeletal definition.

In the mapping of Roman capitals by Renaissance scholars, the contours of characters were defined by geometry—circles, for instance, centered the character, or defined the curve of the serif's brackets. But the characterforms themselves were not constructed strictly out of these geometric shapes (see figure 4.2). As noted above, even these external definitions of characters ran into challenges that led scholars and craftspeople to stray from the original geometric ideals—for instance, by making an H narrower than a square would prescribe. The modernist application of geometry to typographic forms was even more ambitious, and likewise ran into challenges. As Tschichold's description of the sans serif suggests, in the modernist era simplified geometric forms were seen as the skeleton of typographic shapes, that is, as their core rather than simply a tool for drafting. But the lowercase g's from faces like Futura, Kabel, or

Figure 4.2
Renaissance scholars used geometry to map out the ideal proportions of characters (left), while modernist designers attempted to construct characters themselves out of perfect geometric forms. *Source*: author.

Herbert Bayer's universal (1925) (see figure 4.3) suggest that attempts to uncover the geometric skeleton of such a complex character resulted less in a revelation than in experimentation.

Of course, the geometric sans serif is only one style of sans serif, so perhaps the skeletal quality that Tschichold refers to comes not from the reduction to perfect geometric forms but rather from the simple removal of the serifs themselves. The serif was seen as an inefficient ornament in the modernist age, a form without a function. Though the first sans serifs were designed in the nineteenth century, the proliferation of these faces in the twentieth century is a testament to the desire to reduce typography

Figure 4.3
The g's from Futura (Paul Renner, 1927), Kabel (Rudolf Koch, 1928), and universal (Herbert Bayer, 1925). *Source*: author.

to an essence in which the serif is seen as unnecessary. It is tradition, it is habit, but it is not essential.[19]

In the 1930s, Edward Catich, a priest, paleographer, and professor of lettering arts, conducted a study of Roman capitals, and from this study established a new theory of the origin of serifs (published in 1968).[20] It had been assumed that the serif was a finishing mark—that Roman stone carvers had produced serifs as a way of marking the end of a chiseled line. They were seen as practical embellishments that were then carried over into typographic design thanks to the Renaissance admiration for ancient Rome. The basic theory, expressed by people like Warren Chappell and Raymond Ballinger, was that the serif was carried from stone carving to calligraphy and then typography thanks to its utility as a guide or finishing mark.[21] While the account of the continuation of the serif into typographic design is more or less accurate, Catich revealed that the serif was a remnant not of the stone carver's chisel, but rather of the letter-painter's brush.

Catich lists a number of questions that the chisel explanation leaves unanswered: Why are some serifs bowed rather than straight? Why are some bilateral serifs shorter on one end than the other? If the stone carving tool is the explanation, then why do serifs appear in ancient Roman stone carving, but not in ancient Greek? And perhaps most basically, why would the carver go to the effort to bracket the serifs, rather than leaving them as unbracketed horizontal lines? Then, through a close analysis of the shapes that appear in these inscriptions, and through intimate knowledge of the arts of lettering and stone carving, Catich argues that serifs emerge from characters that are sketched onto the stone surface before being cut. Given the rough surfaces and large scale of these inscriptions, Catich concludes that these initial sketches were produced by a brush rather than a reed pen, and it is from the handling of the brush that serifs naturally emerge. He argues that Roman letterers used a square-edged brush, and each character produced with such a tool begins and ends with an edging stroke (edging-in or edging-out); these strokes are the origin of the serif.

Apart from being an impressive piece of visual analysis and visual thinking, Catich's argument reveals the serif to be a naturally occurring mark of one technology that has been repeatedly translated into new technologies for no practical reason. It is a mark that emerges from the typical use of the square-edged brush, which is then copied by the chisel, and then in the early Renaissance and beyond, copied again by the calligrapher's pen, and by the typographer's punch, film, and pixels. It belonged to the brush, but it remained throughout these other technologies out of habit.

As a remnant of antiquated tools, the typographic serif is superfluous—it is not an inherent part of the typographic shape. This allowed modernists to define the sans-serif as the skeletal core of typography. Yet even a historian like Henry Lewis Bullen, who would adamantly disagree with the notion of the serif as extraneous, viewed the skeleton of every typeface as the sans serif. As the librarian for the American Type Founders, Bullen was not only familiar with the diversity of typefaces populating this medium, he was also a contemporary of many of the modernists who advocated for the sans serif. In his theory of typeface classification, he proposed that the serif is the defining feature of each group of variations. As the title of one of his articles proclaimed, he envisioned an "Evolution of Type Faces by Change of Serifs."[22]

According to Bullen's theory, the sans serif, or gothic, is "the model or basic form, which remains unchanged in all examples."[23] When serifs of different sorts are then attached to this basic form a new category of typographic shapes is created, and the basic form responds to the influence of the serif. Adding square serifs to the skeleton creates the group known as antiques, adding beveled serifs creates the Latin group, and so on. Rather than seeing a bit of ornament held over from a previous age, Bullen views the serif as a force, transforming the basic form of typographic characters when the two come into contact. Although this theory presents an interesting view of the serif, as a system for defining the population of typographic characters, it reveals one of the central problems with the modernist definition of the stripped-down sans serif as the skeleton of type. Given that the sans-serif group has its own diversity of forms, we would have to ask what the skeleton of the sans serif is. Bullen produced a system that could describe a number of different kinds of typefaces, but couldn't describe the sans serifs themselves.

In the modernist era, the reduction of typography to a geometric essence invited, in some cases, unfamiliar forms that seemed to describe *unique* typographic shapes, rather than defining the purest g, for instance. And the reduction of typographic diversity to a sans-serif essence ignored the diversity that exists among sans serifs themselves. At the very least, the failings of these attempts to define typography suggest that neither pure (Euclidean) geometry nor sans serifs dig deep enough into the typographic medium to locate an essence. Later in the twentieth century, the uphill battle of teaching computers to recognize and produce our alphanumerical characters introduced a new angle from which to consider their essential definition.

Computer Programs

The way of thinking involved in computer programming is unique.[24] In daily life, when asked to define or describe something to another human, we can easily rely on the other person's use of context, experience, and common sense, to overcome hurdles like vagueness, anaphora, or metaphor.

The computer, on the other hand, does not make assumptions, and does not yet possess the flexibility of the human brain. To define a typographic character for a computer, then, requires more rigor than was needed (or perhaps even imagined) in either the Renaissance or the modernist period. Most attempts to create a definition for computers tended to involve first a dissection of some sort, followed by a set of rules for the manipulation and recombination of those dissected parts. The computer age, furthermore, had more practical need for such definitions—namely, to facilitate both the production of digital type and also the computerized "reading" of optical character recognition (OCR) machines (which we'll explore more in the next chapter). A number of innovators in digital typography from the 1960s and '70s attempted to achieve such a definition by dividing characters into constituent parts that could be controlled by a designer manipulating parameters (like serif length, ascender height, relative x-height, etc.).

In 1968, for instance, Harry Mergler and Paul Vargo proposed a system called ITSYLF (Interactive Synthesizer of Letterforms).[25] The goal of this program was to help the designer create a consistent set of typographic shapes by automating the basic quantitative details that make one form in a typeface harmonious with the others.[26] The program, that is, would not only assure characters of appropriate height, weight, and proportional widths, but would also make sure that the leg on the R bears resemblance to the leg on the k, or that the bowl of the b mirrors that of the p. This, Mergler and Vargo argued, would free the designer up to make more detailed design decisions. In the process of defining the routines to produce typographic forms, Mergler and Vargo divided the characters into five classes:

1. Straight horizontal and vertical only: E, F, H, I, L, T
2. Straight, not necessarily horizontal and vertical:
   A, K, M, N, V, W, X, Y, Z
3. Straight and/or curvilinear: B, D, O, P, R, U
4. More complex curvilinear: C, G, S
5. J and Q, which were not produced by the program, given
   that they were essentially simply I and O with tails.[27]

These five categories base the definition of each character type in its "significant geometric properties," so Mergler and Vargo could ground each definition in an understanding of what kind of character they're trying

to define.[28] The program would produce twenty-four uppercase characterforms based solely on the mathematical descriptions the program
contained and the parameters the user entered. While users could enter
parameters for each character individually, it was not necessary to do so.
They could merely enter information about the E, information about serifs, and from there the computer would generate the rest of the characters
in the typeface—one version with serifs, one version sans.

The designs that emerged from this program were not at all typographically pleasing, and Mergler and Vargo themselves recognized that
there remained many imperfections in their program, and many problems to be solved in the programming of text generation more generally.[29] But significantly, ITSYLF introduces the idea of a programmable
typographic skeleton on two levels. On the one hand is the assumption
(found throughout early digital typographic programming) that one can
mathematically define each *character* (one definition for A, another for b,
and so on), and these definitions can then be programmed in such a way
that designers can achieve unique designs merely by changing parameters in that one definition. In Mergler and Vargo's system the designer
set the initial parameters of the E, but then could also tweak the parameters of other individual characters if they did not like what the program
generated.

On the other hand, ITSYLF assumes that each *typeface* has a skeleton—
an aesthetic quality that unites every shape in the typeface and that can
be programmed as various kinds of proportions. However, one of the
critical flaws in ITSYLF, from a design perspective, is that Mergler and
Vargo identified the E as the basis for the typeface's skeleton. The parameters set for the E would unify all other characters in the typeface, and
their reasoning for this starting point was linguistic—"E" is the most
commonly used letter in the English language (and several other Latin-
based languages).[30] The goal of a skeletal program like ITSYLF, however,
is to design shapes, not a language; and the E does not contain enough
information about the shapes around it to be an effective starting point.

Matthew Carter, one of the most respected type designers of the contemporary era, begins the design of his typefaces with the h, follows this
with the o, and then the p.[31] This order is not about frequency of use, but
rather about opening up, with each step, more information about the
other letters in the typeface. The h contains information about straight
lines, curves (and what will happen to stroke-width around these curves),
and about ascenders. From the information in this character you can

form the n, m, and u (see figure 4.4). The o provides information about round characters, and the p that follows is both straight and round, and contains information about descenders. Similar to the h, from the p one is able to form q, b, and d. To be fair to Mergler and Vargo, their program was only producing uppercase characters. But even here, the designers Jonathan Hoefler and Tobias Frere-Jones have noted that they begin (for similar information-density reasons as Carter) with the H, followed by the O.[32] Even if these characters are not used as frequently as the E, they are richer in terms of the information they contain about the other shapes around them.

The fact that certain more densely informative characters are a better starting point for design than others is evidence of the redundancy that appears in writing systems. As we'll see in chapter 7, this redundancy is certainly not unique to the Latin alphabet. In designing a Hebrew typeface, for instance, one would be wise to begin (as Martin Mendelsberg does) by designing the Yud (ʼ), since this form appears within every other character in the script.[33] It is not unreasonable to think that there is a skeletal definition of a typeface, in addition to the skeletal definitions of each character, but that skeleton has to be defined visually, rather than verbally.

Mergler and Vargo's method was to divide characters into different groups (recognizing that different kinds of character skeletons exist), and then write their definition from there. This same basic process characterizes the work of Philippe Coueignoux from the early 1980s, though he based his system on a deeper dissection of the alphabetic characters. Rather than identifying shape-groups, he identified common shapes that

Figure 4.4
When one is designing a typeface, much of the information for forming the n, m, and u can be derived from the design of the h. *Source*: author.

appear across such groups. The stem in Coueignoux's system appears in Mergler and Vargo's groups 1–3 (and technically 5).[34] The bow or arc appears in groups 3 and 4, and so on. All told, Coueignoux identifies twelve "primitives" that can be combined to describe all Latin characters (with the exception of diacritical marks and italic variants; see figure 4.5).

To this list of primitives Coueignoux adds a grammar for how the basic units can and cannot be combined; he identifies two sets of rules: rules of proportion and rules of construction. Rules of proportion work to ensure harmony across a typeface (similar to Mergler and Vargo's aims), they relate "the values of parameters of the same nature involved in different primitives within a given font."[35] Rules of construction, on the other hand, limit the number of possible shapes that can be made by limiting how the primitives can be combined with one another. For example, Coueignoux notes that "the rule of construction states that a character must have at least one and at most three fundamental primitives, the latter term referring to complete stems and to bows."[36] This general rule suggests that in addition to creating a list of primitives, Coueignoux has also created a hierarchy of use. The most specific and rarely used primitives are the three tails (of the Q, R, and g), and the belly of the a. While the broadest, and most used is the stem.

The stem, as a category of basic units, highlights an interesting challenge for this kind of skeletal definition. The stem is a broad category, including the vertical strokes of I or l, as well as the diagonal strokes of V or k. Coueignoux notes that such a broad category could be seen as defying one of the laws he set out for the construction of primitives themselves (as opposed to the rules governing their connection). The laws governing primitives are as follows:

(0) characters are formed of primitives,
(1) the form of a primitive is stable across the characters in which it appears.
(2) the variability of this form is the result of a small number of parameters whose values depend largely on the font that it characterizes, and for a very few letters, embellishes.
(3) a description of a character from primitives depends entirely on the letter it represents, and not on the font to which it belongs.
(4) a primitive usually appears in the description of more than one letter.[37]

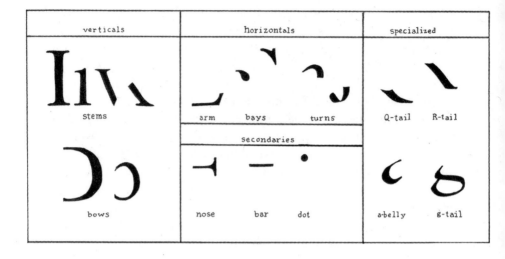

verticals	horizontals			specialized	
stems	arm	bays	turns	Q-tail	R-tail
	secondaries				
bows	nose	bar	dot	a-belly	g-tail

Figure 4.5
Philippe Coueignoux, ca. 1975, identified twelve "primitives"—shapes that can be used to create characters in the Latin alphabet. The verticals were the most commonly used shapes, the horizontals and secondaries second-most commonly used, and the specialized shapes were rare. *Source*: author.

Rule (2) states that what variability does exist in primitives (which according to (1) are stable across characters) is minor. That variability is attributable to those details that set one typeface apart from another, rather than to differences in the characters themselves. It would seem, then, that the somewhat drastic variability among stems would violate this law. The diagonal versus vertical slope of a stem seems to be a difference emerging from the characteristic lines of the character, not from a specific typeface design. Coueignoux admits there is great variability in this category, writing, "we see that the slope, the thickness, and its serifs are far from constant."[38] In response to this, he identifies the stem as a somewhat exceptional category that draws together similar rather than identical shapes. Some of the variability he sees as mere embellishment, while other variability is necessary. The slope of a stem, he argues, is a necessary variable—allowing for the difference between A and H, for instance. The thickness of a stem and the serifs, on the other hand, are mere embellishments.[39]

Coueignoux elaborates on this distinction between necessity and embellishment further with a number of colleagues, Charles Cox, Barry Blesser, and Murray Eden. In their attempt to define digital typographic characters skeletally, they recognize the following puzzle: if you begin with a roman font, and remove all the embellishments, what you end up with is *not* a general definition of characters, but rather a description specific to the original font; on the other hand, if you begin from a general definition, this will be insufficient for producing a well-formed font. Defining the character as a visual manifestation and the letter as an abstract concept, Cox and his colleagues note that "letters and characters . . . are mutually disjoint."[40] To facilitate the transition between letter and characterform, they propose the development of skeletons. Partly abstract, partly physical, the skeleton is a "description in terms of vertices, spatial orderings and vertex/edge relations" that describes how a particular abstract letter can become a concrete characterform.[41]

Drawing primarily on the work of Blesser and R. Shillman, this skeletal program first establishes a notational system to describe different constituent parts, and their means of combining. The parts include a vertex (*), an explicit edge (—), and an implicit edge (- - -). These edges have four possible orientations (horizontal, vertical, and two diagonals), and the connections that can be made are: meeting, joining, linking, and crossing. With these basic ingredients in place, Cox and the other authors construct skeletons for the fifty-two upper- and lowercase Latin characters (see figure 4.6). They then set out a series of rules of transformation based on eight of Coueignoux's primitives (excluding the tails and belly from the original twelve). With these rules one can create characters from the skeletons (see figure 4.7). One of the advantages of beginning with such a skeletal notational system, rather than with Coueignoux's already-formed basic units, is that this notational system could conceivably be used to map out non-Latin shapes as well, even if arriving at the final non-Latin typographic shapes may require different rules of transformation. It seeks to capture topology, rather than the contours themselves.

Cox and his colleagues present the most explicit version of a skeleton that we've seen thus far, and its potential to capture a wide variety of shapes is impressive. However, there is still a problem worth noting in

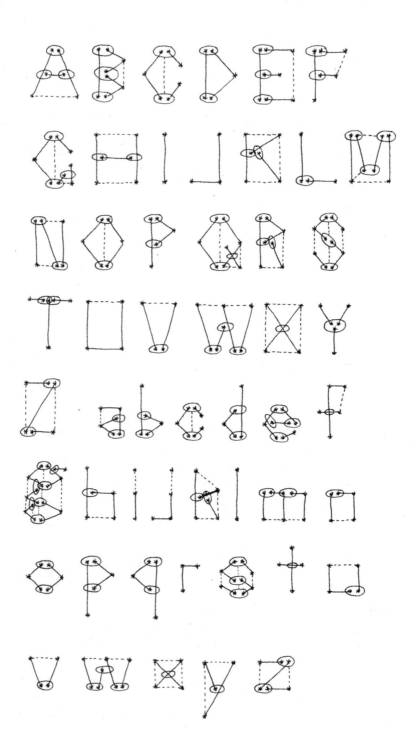

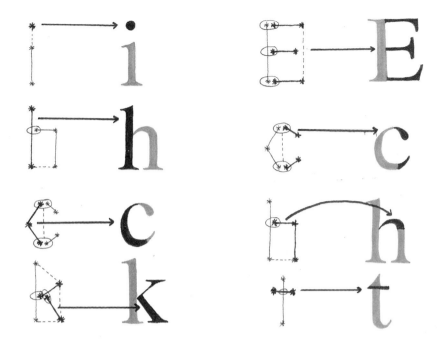

Chapter 4

Figure 4.6
Charles Cox et al. (1982) developed a notational system for the construction of typographic skeletons, to mediate the transformation of alphanumerical concepts into computer-generated typographic forms. This notational system included three parts: vertex (*), edge (—) and implicit edge (- - -), which could be combined in four ways meeting (e.g., left side of the C), joining (e.g., top of the A), linking (e.g., crossbar of the A), and crossing (e.g., tail of the Q). *Source*: author.

Figure 4.7
Charles Cox et al. (1982) established rules of combination for how their skeletal notation is transformed into Coueignoux's primitives. First column: isolated vertices become dots; an edge that covers the height of the skeleton becomes a stem; two edges that meet at one vertex and have an implicit edge between their other vertices become a bow; a nonhorizontal edge with one free vertex becomes a truncated stem and maintains its orientation. Second column: a horizontal edge that joins with a stem and has a second unattached vertex becomes an arm; an edge that shares a join with a bow becomes a bay; a horizontal edge with one vertex that meets the stem becomes a turn; all other horizontal edges become bars. *Source*: author.

their notion of the skeleton. Consider the following summary: on the one hand is the character, which they define as a visual manifestation; on the other hand is the letter, an abstract concept; and these two are mutually exclusive. One cannot begin with a character, remove the embellishments, and end up with the abstract concept of a letter. Nor can one begin with the abstract concept of a letter and use that general description to produce a well-formed (typographic) character. The skeleton, then, is to be the intermediate stage between these two. It is partly physical, and partly abstract; it is derived from the abstract letter, and through a set of rules can be transformed into a concrete character. The problem arises, however, from their idea of the "letter." What they have been calling a "letter," I have referred to as a "character," and what they call a "character," I have called a "typographic shape."

Notice that the skeleton that Cox and his colleagues present for the lowercase a, for instance, is a two-story a. This suggests that the "letter" on which this is based is *not* an abstract concept of "A," but rather an abstract *visual* concept of a particular kind of "A." It is a skeleton based on the mental image of a two-story a, rather than a single-story ɑ, or any other shape that could function as an a. When, in the next chapter, we explore the outer limits of the set of typographic shapes (rather than the inner limit of the skeleton), we will see that there is a wide variety of shapes that can function as an "A," even if they do not resemble the a's (or A's, or ɑ's) we are used to. Because the "letter a" that Cox and the other authors are dealing with is a mental image of a particular kind of "a," the skeleton with which they define "a" will never produce the full diversity of shapes that could function as an "a."

In a sense, the approach that Cox and his colleagues take is the opposite of the modernist approach. Whereas modernist typography was concerned with reducing, or distilling, already concrete characters down to their skeletons, Cox et al. were interested in beginning with the concept of a character, and defining the skeleton from there. Still, they end up with the same problem—failing to reach a satisfying core of a given character-group (such as all ɑ's, or all a's). While the notion of the sans serif as skeleton ignored the fact that the sans serif itself has particular qualities that exceed a skeletal level, this digital skeleton ignores the fact that it describes a *particular* mental image of a character—not the pure concept itself. The allure of being able to define such a purely general concept, or to create a program that could create every conceivable G was one of the motivations behind Donald Knuth's work on digital typography.

Beginning in the late 1970s, Knuth developed METAFONT, a digital program for the design of typographic forms, and along with it, the concept of a meta-font.[42]

As with Mergler and Vargo's system, METAFONT was based on the idea of mathematical descriptions of characters that could be altered by adjusting a variety of parameters. Rather than creating lines to fit the outside edge of a shape as others were doing, Knuth constructed META-FONT's forms with a metaphorical pen—first following the center of this elliptical pen, then finishing off the edges of the form.[43] By 1982 there were forty-five parameters, including pen width, x-height, ascender and descender length, and serif length. Much of the improvement of the program over time involved increased numbers of parameters, thereby better reflecting the incredible amount of detail involved in typographic design. By focusing on parameters, this program was intended to encourage the design of type families rather than individual typographic forms or faces. Even the sans serif is viewed in this model not as an individual typeface, distinct from an equivalent serifed face (nor was it a base to which details are added). Rather, the sans in METAFONT is a stylistic variant—a typeface with a serif length of zero. So, in one illustration of METAFONT's flexibility, Knuth set a single text to show a gradual transition from an Old Style serifed typeface to a modernist sans serif. These are not conceived of as two separate type families, but as a gradient of varieties of the same type family.[44]

The conceptual content of the METAFONT project is as important as the practical achievement of a functioning program. Knuth identified his project as a possibility unique to the computer age and vital to the future. He even saw it as a responsibility, a contribution he owed to print as it moved further into the digital realm.[45] At the same time, he saw his mathematical study of type in the same tradition as the Renaissance studies of Pacioli and Feliciano.[46] While he recognized the failings of these attempts to use Euclidean geometry to describe typographic characterforms, he nonetheless believed that the expanded forms of geometry at his disposal could lead to a meta-font. This was to be meta "in the sense that it deals with fonts from outside, at a higher level."[47] The meta-font strives for the substance of an idea rather than the mimicry of a particular form. Knuth argued that more of a character's intelligence is captured by a set of instructions than by a single drawing of that character—the patterns and the shared information among varieties of a character are made more explicit. He wanted to formulate a description that was rigorous and general, one that was detailed enough in its available parameters that it could be the basis for all possible A's, H's, f's, etc.

According to Knuth, "a 'meta-font' is *a schematic description of how to draw a family of fonts*, not simply the drawings themselves."[48] Some of the typographers who responded to Knuth's concept of a meta-font in a 1982 special issue of the journal *Visible Language* found this to be an unprovocative proposal. Charles Bigelow and Gerard Unger (both innovators in digital typeface design themselves) argued that Knuth's project was merely a continuation of a long history of establishing the type family as the standard unit, rather than the typeface.[49] However, while METAFONT was intended to encourage the design of type families as opposed to individual faces, a meta-font is not equivalent to a type family. A meta-font is a set of instructions; it is not the end result. Knuth was motivated by a love of books and beautiful typography, but he was also a computer programmer, interested in ensuring a rasterized stability for these typographic shapes. He conceived of METAFONT as a way to ensure that even as the resolution of computer displays improved, as they inevitably would, the typographic shapes he was constructing around the raster would be able to "stay the same forever."[50] The mathematical skeleton that Knuth developed was conceived to provide stability and infinitude to digital typography.

Knuth's idea and demonstration of METAFONT raised objections from a number of typographers who insisted that type design cannot be done by purely rational means.[51] Some argued that a computer was only a useful tool if it was used by an expert in calligraphy or type design; a mathematician like Knuth was out of his depth in the world of typographic design. Although they overlook the fact that Knuth did work with experts like Matthew Carter and Hermann Zapf, the core idea that these protests seem to be raising is that typography is not a mathematical art; rather, it is an intuitive art, mastered through years of experience shaping a particular set of characters. This viewpoint seems to be Knuth's starting point as well—that is, until he began to notice that if a lowercase i had a width w, then the lowercase n would be 2w, and the lowercase m would be 3w. There were patterns that Knuth noticed as he studied well-formed typography more closely, and these are what made it possible for him to translate these typographic shapes into o's and 1's. Further rebutting his critics, Knuth points out that "it is most inconceivable that more than 2000 years of accumulated knowledge about geometry and curves will prove to be irrelevant to alphabet design."[52] While some type designers may have protested the unsatisfying results of METAFONT, the underlying idea of a mathematical skeleton able to generate an infinite number of typographic forms is compelling. The two-pronged question that remains is: is it possible to develop a skeleton that will be general enough to capture all possible G's, yet specific enough to generate only G's? Perhaps the strongest critique of Knuth's concept of the meta-font comes from the polymath Douglas Hofstadter. His critique focuses on METAFONT's logical implications, and is based around this two-pronged requirement of completeness and consistency.

Hofstadter focuses on what he notes may seem like a throwaway sentence in Knuth's article in this special issue of *Visible Language*, but which in fact is conceptually significant. Knuth, playing devil's advocate for his own idea, asks, "The ability to manipulate lots of parameters may be interesting and fun, but does anybody really need a 6 1/7-point font that is one fourth of the way between Baskerville and Helvetica?"[53] In raising the idea of a typeface that is "one fourth of the way between" two typefaces as different as Baskerville and Helvetica, Knuth is suggesting that one could parameterize these two typefaces with a single knob—turning the knob to a point where the face becomes 25 percent Baskerville and 75 percent Helvetica. Through the logical rule of transitivity, Hofstadter points out, the further implication is that *all* typefaces could be parameterized with a single knob. If *any* two typefaces can be parameterized together, then *all* typefaces could; if *any* two G's can be parameterized together, then *all* G's could be.

There are significant challenges to parameterizing even a single character—determining, for instance, which parameters are worth including and which are not.[54] To achieve the joint parameterization that Knuth imagines, one cannot simply parameterize each character individually—Baskerville and Helvetica would never meet if each is defined on its own. Instead, one would have to determine the parameters for every possible A, B, C, and so on. One would have to determine the essential features of a Q, and in particular what sets it apart from an O or a G. This is a common theme in the skeletal view of typography, but no matter what definition of Q one decides on, Hofstadter points out that there will always be some variants that don't share the common features you've settled on, or that have more than one (e.g., no discernible tail, or more than one). And still other variations are not even the result of altering parameters.[55]

In considering how to define the possibilities open to a Q, Hofstadter warns against what Carl Sagan refers to as "chauvinism"—our tendency to restrict our sense of the possible to what we're used to. In imagining life on other planets, for instance, we imagine it will be of the same sort as life on our own—carbon-based, reliant on water, or a particular range of temperatures, and so on. We assume Q's will be round shapes with a particular range of thickness, range of slopes, and a tail, but there is nothing to say they must be. The risk of character parameterization is that we assume that all Q's will be what they have always been.

While Hofstadter is not convinced by Knuth's means, he doesn't dismiss the ends. That is, even if parametrizing isn't the way to go, he supports the idea of capturing the intelligence of a character—the intention or the substance. Hofstadter argues that there is an essence to an A, a Platonic ideal, even. "The shape of a letterform," he writes, "is a surface manifestation of deep mental abstraction."[56] In his theory, the spirit of an A is made up of certain "conceptual roles," which, he notes, bear a resemblance to Blesser's notion of "functional attributes"—that is, attributes that disambiguate letters from one another (e.g., an A from an H). Roles include "crossbar," "post," "bowl," and in this way appear to be similar to Coueignoux's primitives. They do not define particular characters, but rather indicate the probability of particular characters. A post and a bowl in a particular orientation does not guarantee a d, but rather indicates that it is probable that a d is present.

What is perhaps most interesting about Hofstadter's idea of conceptual roles (and perhaps of Coueignoux's primitives) is that they are not confined to individual characters—the crossbar, for instance, is shared by A, H, e, and others. His attempt to define the spirit of a character, then, is relational. He argues that "letters mutually define each others' essences, and that is why an isolated structure supposedly representing a single letter in all its glory is doomed to failure."[57] What is explicit in his argument is implicit in the other skeletons considered throughout this chapter. The strength of these skeletal ideas—whether Renaissance ideal forms,

Figure 4.8
Even this form can be a skeleton for a lowercase a. *Source*: author.

modernist sans serifs, or digital recipes—is not the successful definition of an essence of typographic shape, but rather the studied comparison of those shapes that goes into developing the skeleton.

Ultimately, no skeleton can define all typographic shapes. A collection of primitive parts can always be divided again into a more detailed collection, or expanded by new designs. A line will always have dimension that can be divided one more time into something more basic. And topological definitions will never capture all the possible forms that might function in the typographic medium. As the expansionist method of defining typographic shape will show in the next chapter, the flexibility of the category will always exceed any skeleton we can imagine. Even if we agree on a skeletal shape for the lowercase a as a vertical line with a circle, or bowl, to the left of it, we will find a's with a skeleton like that in figure 4.8.

5 Type's Outer Limit

Design is about creating something new each time we approach a problem,
even if it's the same problem.
—Zuzana Licko[1]

We saw a search for the skeletal essence of typographic shapes in the attempt to define them through pure geometric forms. In the hands of a designer like Paul Renner, we also saw it as a test of how far these shapes could
be pushed toward a concept and still remain viable. In his typeface Futura,
Renner was motivated by heavily practical aims—distancing the lowercase
from the calligrapher's pen, thereby better integrating the two cases.[2] And
he was dedicated to the concept of perfect circles, triangles, and squares
as a means of accomplishing this. Yet Renner found ultimately that "the
artistic value of a typeface has to prove itself before the human eye; that
is, in the sphere of appearances and not the sphere of mathematical concepts."[3] While his final version of Futura settled on simple forms like
the single-story a and the double-story g, the early stages of experimentation with the forms of a, e, g, n, m, and r reveal some of the flexibility
of the category of typographic shapes (see figure 5.1). In the n and m, we
see Renner avoid curves (and thereby also divorce these two characters
from their relatives h and u). The r is simplified dramatically into a stem
and unattached dot. And the e becomes an unusual hybrid between the
upper- and lowercase e's we are used to—the three bars found in an uppercase E curve in on one another to approximate, but not reproduce, the
traditional eye and aperture of the lowercase e. Through this and other
experiments performed throughout the twentieth and early twenty-first
centuries, the class of typographic shapes proved to be remarkably flexible. The question in light of these experiments is, Can an outer limit be
located and then used to define this class of shapes?

Figure 5.1
A collection of unconventional shapes in Futura (Paul Renner, 1927). *Source*: author.

Not all of the designers discussed in the following chapter were actively seeking the outer limit of typography. Some were motivated by a desire to reform the alphabet; others were addressing the limitations set out by early digital technologies; and still others were interested in unmasking the (authoritarian) conventions of print. But whatever their explicit motivations were, they all needed to accept to some extent the idea that the typographic shapes we would consider normal are not the limit of what a typographic shape can be.

Alphabetic Reforms

In the first half of the twentieth century, a number of typographers were interested in using design to reform what was seen as a flawed alphabet. Sometimes focusing on pronunciation, other times on simplifying the fifty-two-character Latin set of the upper- and lowercases, their experiments were ultimately about using form to affect function. Herbert Spencer captured a number of the motivations guiding these modernist experiments when he critiqued the Latin alphabet as both "extravagant and inadequate"—it is both complexly constructed and yet not useful enough.[4]

The idea that typographic design could affect pronunciation did not originate in the twentieth century. In the sixteenth century, for instance, Geofroy Tory published a book that protested the inconsistent pronunciation of the French language, and maintained that the design of Latin characters could correct this problem. Each character, he argued, was to reveal its proper pronunciation—the two legs of the A meet at an angle to resemble the voice emerging from an open mouth, and the crossbar represents the point at which the voice must be cut off to make this particular sound; the two lobes of the B are meant to resemble the two parted lips through which the sound for that character is made; and so on.[5] But in the twentieth century, this equation between the shapes of characters and phonetics took on new seriousness.

Eric Gill, the British typographer and artist, poked fun at the assertion that the Latin alphabet is a phonetic one. Pointing out the lack of phonetic logic of the combination "ough," he writes, "'Though the tough cough and hiccough plough me through, my thought remains clear' and it is this: that it is stupid to make pretence any longer that our letters are a reasonable means for rendering our speech in writing or printing."[6] Like his contemporary, George Bernard Shaw, Gill supported the use of a phonographic writing system—what we refer to today as shorthand. Though most proponents of shorthand viewed it as a useful alternative for handwriting, Gill's discussion of it in his *Essay on Typography* suggests that he supported phonetic typography as well. It was his position that the characters we use are irredeemable thanks to their lack of phonetic logic. Unlike Tory, he did not believe they could be usefully redesigned; they would need to be replaced.

At the same time that Gill was declaring the futility of the Latin alphabet, a number of German modernists were developing phonetic typefaces in concert with their broader desire for a universal typeface (discussed briefly in chapter 3). In 1929, Jan Tschichold's "universal" alphabet bore the basic appearance of other universal typefaces—a geometric sans serif made up of uniform thickness, and using only a single case. And yet, Tschichold also defied his own belief in a universal typeface that would cross linguistic and national borders, by paying particular attention to sounds common to the German language. In the phonetic version of this typeface, he developed a number of new shapes, both for characters and for diacritical marks, in particular creating new shapes for common German sounds represented by "sch," and "ch" (see figure 5.2).

In this way, Tschichold's system reduced the number of characters involved in representing particular sounds, and he reduced redundancy in other ways as well. For instance, repeated letters were eliminated, so that a word like *dass* would become *das*. Other characters were replaced

Figure 5.2
Jan Tschichold's universal
(1929) introduced new
shapes for common
letter combinations "sch"
(top) and "ch" (bottom).
Source: author.

with more accurate representations of their pronunciation, so the z came to be represented as "ts," and the "eu" in a word like *neu* became "oi." Other characters draw a distinction between two different sounds that had previously been represented by a single character. So, while he keeps the n in a word like *neu* unchanged, when that n is voiced as an "ng," it appears as in figure 5.3. Similarly, Tschichold's system has two e's, one of which is used for less voiced instances of the e—so a word like *jedem* appears as in figure 5.4. Tschichold's phonetic alphabet diverged only moderately from what would have been familiar to readers. But through its small innovations, this typeface did raise the prospect that typography's outer limit would need to be far out enough on the horizon to allow for the introduction of entirely new characters.

A fellow advocate for universal type, Herbert Bayer also developed a phonetic typeface, though long after Tschichold. Bayer designed Fonetik Alfabet (1959) with the English language in mind, when he was living in America. Its geometric forms are more minimalistic than Tschichold's, and its revisions of how one represents sounds is even more extreme. Some of this typeface's forms seem to be motivated merely by a desire to simplify shapes—the A has no crossbar, and the n is simply an arch (the u likewise is a mirror image of this simplified n). As the spelling of its name suggests, other forms are meant to provide clearer phonetic alternatives to certain letters and letter combinations. The "ph" is replaced by an f, and k takes the place of any hard c's. Bayer also created a few new forms—the common combinations of "ion" and "ing" are replaced (see figure 5.5). Bayer adds an ash (æ) for the long a sound, and an open-topped o for the vowel sound in words such as "of." And like Tschichold, he eliminates redundant letters—for instance, rewriting "common" using

TSɑiTpuʞT

Figure 5.3
Jan Tschichold's universal
(1929) introduced a
new shape for an n
that is voiced as "ng."
Source: author.

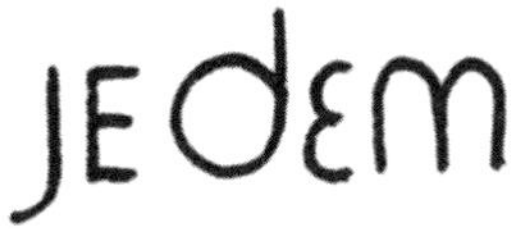

JEɒɛm

Figure 5.4
Jan Tschichold's universal
(1929) has two e's; the
second is a less-voiced
e. *Source*: author.

Figure 5.5
Fonetik Alfabet (Herbert
Bayer, 1959). To simplify
the alphabet, Bayer
created new characters
to stand in for commonly
used letter combinations
"ing" (left) and "ion"
(right). *Source*: author.

a single m with a line underneath it. Bayer's alphabet also features attempts at disambiguation. The b and d, for example, are not mirror images of one another; instead the b has a normal, curved bowl, while the d's bowl is flat on the top (see figure 5.6).

A contemporary of both Tschichold and Bayer, though not well known as a type designer, Kurt Schwitters developed his own phonetic alphabet, or *Systemschrift*, in 1927. His motivation was not one of universalization, but rather of systematization—he viewed the existing alphabet as unsystematic, not because there was no system at play, but because there was more than one.[7] In an explanation of his Systemschrift, he points out how illogical it is that E and F should have such great visual similarity, given that they have little phonetic similarity; and conversely, E and O, which have phonetic similarity, have little in common visually. In his system, then, the vowels are made to be heavy and round, while the consonants are lighter and narrow. To achieve this, certain characters have to be contorted—the E adopted into the system is a lowercase e, and the I is an uncommon shape, closer to a J (see figure 5.7). Schwitters developed a few versions of this writing system, most of which used primarily recognizable shapes. His priority in these versions seems to be distinguishing

Figure 5.6
Fonetik Alfabet (Herbert Bayer, 1959) breaks with the usual symmetry of characters like b and d.
Source: *author.*

Figure 5.7
Vowels from Systemschrift (Kurt Schwitters, 1927). To create a more systematic alphabet, Schwitters believed characters that sound similar should reflect that similarity in their appearance.
Source: author.

between vowels and consonants and simplifying some of the commonly used letter combinations found in German (such as "sch" and "ch").

In addition to these more moderate versions of his Systemschrift, Schwitters also developed a set of marks that he described as purely systematic, based on an analysis of where various sounds are made in the mouth and throat. In this system none of the consonantal sounds, besides those represented by T and F, look familiar. All are constructed out of a vertical stem with varying combinations of notches at the top, middle, and/or bottom of the stem (see figure 5.8). The vowels are of the same form as in the more moderate versions, but also have new variations in this system depending on whether the vowel sound is long or short.

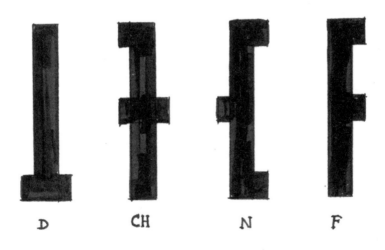

D   CH   N   F

Figure 5.8
Consonants from Systemschrift (Kurt Schwitters, 1927). All consonants in Schwitters's most systemic version of this typeface involved a vertical rectangle with varying combination of notches. *Source*: author.

Without Schwitters's explanation (and perhaps even with his explanation), this system would be extremely difficult to read with any fluidity. This is not merely because of the lack of familiarity of these shapes, but also because of the lack of diversity among the shapes. In this experiment, Schwitters maintains that an entirely new set of symbols can be successfully introduced to replace our existing script. But his purely systematic alphabet raises the question of whether a set of shapes must be able to be easily read in order to be considered typographic shapes. Readability did not appear to be a concern for Schwitters, whereas Tschichold and Bayer both kept their reform typefaces closer to expectations, taking advantage of reading by context, rather than introducing an entirely new system.

It may seem counterintuitive that modernists such as Schwitters, Tschichold, and Bayer attempted to reform the alphabet through typography. As we saw, the dominant modernist edict was that form should follow function, but these experiments present form as means of altering function. They assume both a linguistic function for typographic shapes, and a correlation between characterforms and speech. And they wagered that entirely new forms not only could be incorporated into the existing class of typographic shapes, but could influence linguistic evolution. Of course, linguistic evolution does not occur by shape alone—such evolution is successful only through repeated use by a linguistic community. And while none of these modernist attempts to reform the alphabet were adopted by such a community, they do provide openings for future, more practical redesigns.

Running through all three of these systems is a desire to simplify the alphabet, or to eliminate what nonsense it contains. It's notable, for instance, that all three are single-case typefaces—even if they borrow shapes from both the upper and lower cases, they eliminate the use of two separate sets of shapes.[8] This was the primary innovation in Bradbury Thompson's Alphabet 26 (1950) as well. Thompson's redesign is not a revolutionary shift; instead, it presents the argument that the single case is not merely a reduction of redundancy, but in fact makes reading easier for more people. Alphabet 26 merely combines certain characters from the upper and lower cases of Baskerville, rather than designing an entirely new typeface; but it is significant for its attempt to improve literacy. Inspired by his son's difficulty in dealing with the ambiguities and redundancies in the existing fifty-two-character Latin script, Thompson wanted to see if a twenty-six-character script could improve ease of reading and reduce confusion for early readers.[9] The set he collected is made up of seven characters for which the upper and lowercase forms are basically the same: C, O, S, V, W, X, and Z; he uses the lowercase for a, e, m, and n; and the uppercase for B, D, F, G, H, I, J, K, L, P, Q, R, T, U, and Y. All the characters are then made the same height.

In this typeface one no longer has to learn that A and a are equivalent, nor when you're supposed to use one or the other. Additionally, ambiguities between characters are dramatically reduced. Some of these ambiguities, such as that between the I and the l, are consistent throughout a reader's life, while others are specific to early readers and those with dyslexia. The mirrored shapes, like b and d, p and q, u and n, often cause problems for those whose reading brains have remained mirror symmetrical. Today, the underlying goal and certain lessons from Thompson's Alphabet 26 can be seen in typefaces designed specifically to help readers with dyslexia. Christian Boer's Dyslexie (2011), for instance, uses strategically placed weight, variable bowls, and unusual stem angles to decrease the ambiguity among characters in the alphabet (see figure 5.9).[10]

Whereas these reforms seek to improve literacy, S. B. Telingater proposed a reform in 1968 that would facilitate international commerce and telecommunications. He proposed a new set of streamlined and reorganized graphemes for all the languages that have developed from the Latin

Figure 5.9
Dyslexie (Christian Boer, 2011). *Source*: author.

and Greek alphabets (see figure 5.10). With practical concerns in mind, he suggests that this reform would require a number of steps, including removing all unpronounced characters from our written language.[11]

These reform alphabets show that there is a distance between the letterforms we are used to and the outer limit of typographic shapes. In their own ways, they maintain that we do not have to continue reproducing the same shapes—we can use the standardizing power of the typographic medium's mass production to push the forms and functions of these shapes past tradition, and perhaps toward greater efficacy. Yet even if these reform typefaces reveal the existence of a more distant outer limit, they are unlikely to locate it, because they are tethered to phonetics

Figure 5.10
Standardized global graphemes (S. B. Telingater, 1968). *Source*: author.

and literacy. Not only is there a conservatism in these goals that sells the potential of the typographic shape short, but many other goals or motivations are possible and if followed will exert their own influence on shape. For instance, typographic shapes can be pushed toward an outer limit by following specific formal constraints.

As a founding member of De Stijl, Theo van Doesburg developed a set of typographic forms in 1919 that were informed by the movement's belief in the cosmological tensions between the forces of the horizontal and the vertical. Restricting the available shapes to those produced with vertical and horizontal lines resulted in typographic characters being pushed in new directions. Consider the contortion that occurs in previously diagonal shapes like the K and X (see figure 5.11). These shapes emerge not only from strict horizontality and verticality, but also from the need to be distinguished from H. Some of the peculiar shapes in this typeface come from the fact that it is uppercase only, that the strokes are of uniform thickness, and, with the exception of the I, that the face is fixed width. But most of the face's peculiarities emerge from the constraints of designing a purely rectangular typeface. Comparable formal distortions can be seen in a 1900 typeface by Adalb Carl Fischl, which emerges from the art nouveau movement and accordingly (and again with the exception of the I) is produced primarily out of curves rather than straight lines.[12] A typeface motivated by triangles would similarly introduce a new variety of unfamiliar shapes into the class of typographic shapes.

Similar to van Doesburg's type, in the late 1960s Wim Crouwel (1967) and Timothy Epps and Christopher Evans (1969) designed purely vertical and horizontal faces. But these fixed-width rectangular typographic forms had yet another motivation for pushing toward the outer limit—a technological one.

Figure 5.11
Characters from
Theo van Doesburg's
De Stijl typeface (1919).
Source: author.

Digital Raster and Digital Readers

As discussed in the previous chapter, the binary logic and raster-based displays of computers introduced new challenges for the type designer. But this technology also brought with it programmability, which allowed for computer-designed typefaces, digital printing, and computer reading. A number of designers, like Wim Crouwel, Hermann Zapf, and Adrian Frutiger, quickly accepted the digital as the future. Even if these new technologies called for unfamiliar shapes, they believed the designer should work with the technology rather than against it.[13] As a result, the 1960s and '70s saw the development of a number of faces that pushed the bounds of typographic shapes further, not so much to accommodate the human reader or particular geometric beliefs, but rather to accommodate the machine. To meet the computer where it was, these shapes were designed with unique geometric restrictions, and with the goal of eliminating ambiguity. The letters designed had to be either an A or an H, with no in between.

Wim Crouwel designed New Alphabet (1967) as a response to the scaling problems he saw exhibited in the early digital printing produced by the Hell Digiset machine. Given the raster-based system, a typeface that might look perfectly fine at 10 point would become distorted when scaled up or down in size, so Crouwel designed a typeface with characters that would speak the formal language of the machine, and therefore would be able to scale without mutations. "Because circular and diagonal lines are least suitable for this technique of [cathode-ray tube] screen reproduction," he wrote, "the proposed basic alphabet consists entirely of vertical and horizontal lines."[14] Given the prevalence of curves and diagonal lines in traditional typographic shapes, this produced a number of unfamiliar forms, just as van Doesburg's typeface did.

Crouwel's project was even more ambitious than other straight-line experiments, however, because it sought to produce a lowercase set of characters under these strict requirements. In the resulting single-case typeface (in which capitalization would be indicated by a line above the character), not only the k, but also characters like a and g, had to be reformed into strict raster-based grids. Some of the resulting shapes are easily recognizable—for instance the p, e, and b in figure 5.12. Other shapes, however, barely resemble the way these letters are usually represented; figure 5.13 shows the g, a, s, and k. These distortions arise partly from the emphasis on the horizontal and vertical, but also on Crouwel's broader belief that typefaces for the computer age should be designed around the computer's own structure of individual, uniform cells.[15] The shapes in New Alphabet, then, are constructed of equilateral units—designed not merely on a grid, but out of a grid.

What is perhaps most remarkable about New Alphabet is not the design of twenty-six characters and ten numerals out of equilateral vertical

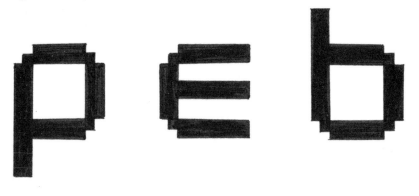

Figure 5.12
A collection of recognizable forms from Wim Crouwel's New Alphabet (1967).
Source: author.

Figure 5.13
Unconventional forms from Wim Crouwel's New Alphabet (1967). Here: g, a, s, k.
Source: author.

and horizontal lines, but rather, the fact that even with its unfamiliar forms, New Alphabet is legible. The first shape in figure 5.14 is able to function successfully as an a not because it is recognizable as such, but because the characters around it are recognizable. By way of context, we can read this shape as an a (see figure 5.14).[16]

Crouwel himself claims he never intended New Alphabet to actually be used for setting text; this was more of a thought experiment, an "initial step," as he put it.[17] And his alphabet does have shortcomings—for instance, the more unfamiliar shapes that appear in a single word, the harder it is to read. Likewise, Crouwel's means of capitalizing creates further ambiguity; the capitalized T, for instance, looks like an F (not a New Alphabet F, but the F we are used to; see figure 5.15). Still, the New

Figure 5.14
New Alphabet (Wim Crouwel, 1967) relies on contextual reading in order to maintain its legibility: here the unconventional a is able to function as an a thanks to the context of the more recognizable forms around it. *Source:* author.

Figure 5.15
Wim Crouwel designed New Alphabet (1967) as a lowercase typeface that indicates capitalization by adding a line to the top of characters. This creates some challenges as here the capitalized T takes on the appearance of a conventional F (not a New Alphabet F). *Source:* author.

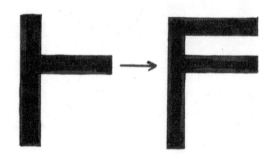

Alphabet is significant for how far this thought experiment was able to push forms, while remaining legible.

Two years after New Alphabet, Timothy Epps and Christopher Evans designed a similar typeface, likewise intended to fit cathode-ray tube displays. The Epps Evans Alphabet features the same requirement of no curves or diagonals. But rather than being prompted by poor printer output, this alphabet is inspired by the "infancy of the mechanical brain."[18] Epps identifies three paths for the development of a reading, mechanical brain. One path is laid out by those who believe machines should be built to handle any human-produced text that is fed to them. On an opposing path are those who believe an entirely new set of shapes should be designed to fit the computer, and humans would then need to learn to use these shapes. And between these two is the path that maintains machines and humans should work with one and the same set of symbols that are legible to humans, but also appropriate for machine handling. This is the middle ground that the Epps Evans Alphabet seeks to establish.

Each typographic shape in this alphabet is designed on a 5 × 5 grid, and Epps and Evans attempted to eliminate as much redundancy in the forms as possible. For instance, the required information for telling an E apart from an F is a single line—the bottom-most arm of the E. To design these two shapes as distinct, then, requires only three horizontal lines for the E, and two for the F. This would be enough information for the computer to identify which character is which. However, in the interest of the human reader, Epps and Evans added back some redundancies. In an early design the E appears as three horizontal lines, but in the final version the vertical stem is restored. The characters in the Epps Evans Alphabet are generally more familiar than in Crouwel's New Alphabet, but overall the typeface is less harmonious. Though they wanted their characters to be recognizable to the human reader, the requirements that contort shapes such as K and Q are intended to accommodate the computer reader (see figure 5.16).

Although straight vertical and horizontal lines are easier for computers to deal with than curves and diagonals, it turns out that faces designed specifically for computers did not need to be so formally strict. The most important thing for such typefaces was in fact disambiguation, which itself is a motivation that invites new varieties of shapes. Prior to the development of omnifont optical character recognition (OCR) scanners, the late 1950s and '60s saw the design of a handful of typefaces specifically for use in machine reading. Machines have been useful readers

Figure 5.16
Characters (K and Q)
from the Epps Evans
Alphabet (Timothy Epps
and Christopher Evans,
1969). *Source*: author.

for bureaucracies that sort considerable amounts of paper, such as postal services and banks. For magnetic ink character recognition (MICR) machines (used primarily in banks), there were two main faces: E13B used in the United States and Canada, and CMC7 in Europe. For OCR machines, major faces were OCR-A, OCR-B, and Farrington's 12L/12F Selfchek.[19] By and large, these were purely functional faces intended for error-free recognition by machines, and to varying degrees, ease of use for humans. Though some of these avoid curves and diagonals, the peculiarities in these alphabets are primarily to set ambiguous shapes apart from one another. The numeral 1 is often among the most unusual characters in these faces, to help set it apart from the lowercase l, the upper- and lowercase i's, and the ! (see figure 5.17).

Perhaps the most peculiar of these faces is CMC7 (1960s), in which each characterform is constructed by seven vertical strokes of uniform width. This technique introduces new disambiguating requirements, different from those found in the other typefaces. Now, not only does one have the potential ambiguities of thin vertical characters like I, T, 1, and 7, but the 4 oddly comes into potential conflict with characters like C, F, and G (see figure 5.18). One of the advantages of an MICR face like CMC7 is that the identification of each character is written directly into the ink itself. But as Adrian Frutiger notes, this required high-quality printing accuracy, and produced shapes less pleasing to the human eye.[20] Beginning in 1963, he designed a typeface for standardized OCR readers that would also have an aesthetic as close to traditional typographic shapes as possible. Interestingly, his design process for this typeface incorporated both a

Chapter 5

skeletal theory and also an eye toward the outer limit. Each characterform was designed around a centerline, to ensure the OCR scanner's ability to identify a character regardless of the weight in which it was set. But at the same time, technical requirements forced Frutiger to sometimes adopt what he saw as imperfect, unfamiliar shapes.

His typeface OCR-B is first of all a fixed-width face, like New Alphabet and the Epps Evans Alphabet. At least in early versions of the face, each character is the same width, in part because this face was developed for

Figure 5.17
The numeral 1 from: E13B (1958), CMC7 (1960s), OCR-A (ATF, 1965), OCR-B (Adrian Frutiger, 1968), Farrington 12L/12F Selfchek (Farrington Manufacturing Co., ca. 1966). *Source*: author.

Figure 5.18
CMC7 (1960s) is an MICR typeface in which each character is constructed out of seven stripes, introducing unusual sites of ambiguity among the 4, C, F, and G. *Source*: author.

typewriting, and in part because it is easier for an OCR scanner to determine where one character ends and the next begins if they all have the same width. The rest of the typeface's features are intended to set individual characters apart from one another. This, for instance, is why the face is sans serif. Frutiger argued that the "repeated presence of horizontal strokes [i.e., serifs] would have considerably increased the letter likeness, uselessly creating minor shapes common to all letters."[21] It was necessary in this face that no one character could appear in its entirety within another character, that each had to have a distinguishing feature that was unique to it and only it.[22] The l could not appear in the T, the n could not appear in the h, and so on. More specifically, the minimum difference between any two characters had to be at least 7 percent, regardless of the weight of each character.[23]

This 7 percent requirement led to design details, such as a cap height shorter than both the numerals and the ascenders of the lowercase characters, a B that was uniformly wider than the 8, and an & with a smaller bottom counter than top (see figure 5.19).[24] Although Frutiger constructed this face around the principle of a centerline, it is important to note that this skeleton did not define the *identity* of a character. Instead, it was excessive features, like the serifs that remain on the i and j, that

Figure 5.19
A successful OCR typeface, like Adrian Frutiger's OCR-B (1968), needs to clearly disambiguate similar characters, like the B, 8, and &. *Source*: author.

Chapter 5

distinguished the uniqueness of each character. One might think that the way to design an unmistakable W would be with four straight-edged diagonal lines. However, the W in OCR-B has curved outer strokes in order to distinguish it from characters like U, V, and even H.

Though MICR and OCR typefaces do not stretch the set of typographic shapes nearly as far as New Alphabet or even the Epps Evans Alphabet do, they introduce more explicitly the formal interests of another (nonhuman) reader. This is a reader that has no interest in phonetics, semantics, or tradition. Were the human reader not an issue, typographic shapes could stretch far beyond even Schwitters's purely systematic alphabet. As is, digital readers emphasized the piecemeal information of pixels and the binary logic of being either one character or another. Frutiger and his fellow MICR and OCR designers revealed that what sets apart each member of the set of typographic shapes is not a unified skeleton but an individualistic collection of details. Omnifont OCR machines, increasing pixel density, and techniques like anti-aliasing and vectorial rendering allowed designers in the 1970s and beyond to produce digital typefaces that were more familiar to the human eye. But when the computer became an attainable tool for individual designers in the mid-1980s, a new wave of digital experimentation emerged. The pixel, binary code, and programmability formed new constraints within which type designers pushed the typographic shape, playing with identifying details, and reimagining their craft and legibility itself.

Testing Legibility

In an interview from 1990, type designer Zuzana Licko identified two goals behind her work. The first was to explore the design possibilities that are unique to the computer. Second was "to see how much the basic letter shapes can be changed and still be functional."[25] One of the earliest designers to adopt the Macintosh 128K, Licko viewed the computer's poor resolution and general display logic as a productive constraint. The rasterized and binary nature of this tool created a delimited space in which Licko was then free to create new shapes. This led to unapologetically bitmapped faces like Oakland (1984) and Emperor (1985). The latter of these even embraced the scaling issues that Crouwel's New Alphabet was protesting. Emperor was a typeface built as a system that purposefully allows the forms of characters to be altered as the face scales. At 8 point, each character in this face has a stroke width-to-cap height ratio of 1 pixel to 8. At 10 point, that ratio is 1:10, at 15 point it would be 1:15. That is, the width of the strokes never changes, even as the height stretches or shrinks. The only core ratio that is maintained in this face is the 1:2 ratio of stroke width to counter width. The overall shape of these characters, then, changes freely as the size of type changes, challenging the conventions of what makes a unified typeface (see figure 5.20).

Licko's second goal (not unrelated to the first) is an explicit expression of the desire to locate the outer limit of the typographic shape. With the new possibilities opened up by the personal computer, she did not want to take for granted the rules that had been set out over previous centuries for the legibility of typographic shapes. In Variex (1988), for

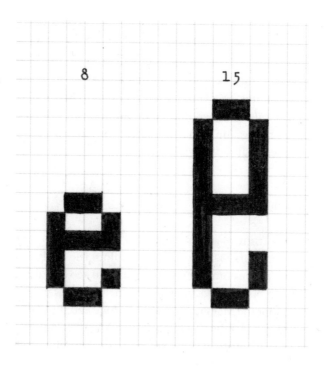

Figure 5.20
Emperor (Zuzana Licko, 1985) embraces the pixel and the ways scaling on low-resolution digital displays distorts character designs. As Emperor's characters scale up and down in size they maintain a stroke-width to counter-width ratio of 1:2. *Source*: author.

instance, Licko and her partner Rudy VanderLans created a type family that tests the durability of character shapes as their weights change from light to regular to bold. In Variex Light, each character is formed by a thin stroke of uniform thickness, which serves as the centerline for the two other weights. The weight of the characters is increased by adding lines of equal width on either side of this centerline.[26] Using this systematic means of increasing weight, Licko and VanderLans created a typeface with a variable x-height, and characterforms that slowly lose their distinct identifying qualities. What begins as a clearly decipherable e, g, or 9 soon becomes an unfamiliar or ambiguous shape—still functional, as Licko says, but certainly inching toward the outer limit of a recognizable e, g, or 9 (see figure 5.21).

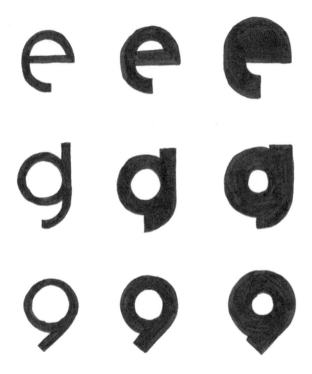

Figure 5.21
The increasing ambiguity in e, g, and 9 in Variex (Zuzana Licko and Rudy VanderLans, 1988) as weight increases. *Source*: author.

For Licko, to "still be functional" meant to be legible, but her definition of legibility, and that which dominated the late 1980s and 1990s in type design, was more flexible than it had been earlier in the century. Licko is often quoted as saying, "You read best what you read most."[27] Among early twentieth-century advocates for legible type design, like Beatrice Warde and Stanley Morison, this sentiment might be interpreted as advising that one design type according to existing expectations.[28] If we read Times New Roman most, then we should have text set in this and similar faces in order to ensure the best reading. But Licko and her contemporaries saw the relationship between legibility and typefaces as conventional, arbitrary, and therefore open to change. If we come to read best that which we read most often, then legibility is not a naturally occurring phenomenon, and we can, therefore, train ourselves to read unfamiliar forms simply by reading them more often.

In the 1980s, Licko and VanderLans founded *Emigre*—a magazine and digital type foundry in California, both focusing on new faces that challenged typographic traditions. In England, *Fuse* magazine—founded by Neville Brody and Jon Wozencroft—served a similar function. These publications and the design culture that arose around them are indications that Licko's two goals were not unique to her; they were a common pairing seen in the late 1980s and 1990s. The rise of the personal computer in design was accompanied by a new wave of experimentation pushing at the limits and legibility of typographic shapes.

This period of exploring typography's outer limits can be seen as inspired by earlier iconoclasts, like Wolfgang Weingart, who began in the 1960s and '70s to break with the clean, orderly designs of Swiss Modernism.[29] But it has also been attributed to a number of other factors that are technological, social, and philosophical. First, the computer made experimentation quicker and less costly, so designers may have been more willing to push into unfamiliar formal territories. We also see in Licko's work the idea that the computer creates productive constraints, forcing new forms of creativity by necessity. Second, design writers Chuck Byrne and Martha Witte have argued that the computer introduced a new social climate to which these exploratory designers were responding. They describe this as "a world agitated by more and more complexity."[30] Many of the unusual typefaces being designed during this period, like Keedy Sans (Jeffrey Keedy, 1989), Template Gothic (Barry Deck, 1990), and Beowolf, reflected this sense of complexity, instability, and imperfection. Just as the sans serif was seen by modernists like Tschichold as the typographic shape best suited for his age, late twentieth-century designers like Barry Deck believed that the imperfection of humanity, of language, and of society should be matched by imperfection and sometimes even chaos in design. These designers were willing to sacrifice legibility, because, as Phil Baines argued, "legibility represents information as facts rather than as experience."[31]

The third factor often named as an influence on this period of experimental type is the philosophical impact of semiotics and deconstruction. Through the writings of people like Roland Barthes, Michel Foucault, and Jacques Derrida, some designers were inspired to challenge the typographic values that had become naturalized over the course of centuries.[32] Once designers had identified the constructs of typographic characters, the uses of punctuation, or the commonly occurring layouts as convention, these typographic domains were subject to being broken up, disorganized, and put back together in nonnormative ways. Type historian Rick Poynor has noted that this period saw several hybrid typefaces, which quite literally dissected traditional typographic forms and recombined the parts—creating forms reminiscent of Frankenstein's monster—in protest of the stability that modernism had created.[33] In Dead History (1990), P. Scott Makela freely combined serifed and sans-serif forms within single characters, while Jonathan Barnbrook's Prototype (1990) even spliced together upper- and lowercase features into single characters. Poynor notes that the variability of these hybrids reveal "that A—like any other letter of the alphabet—has the potential for limitless conceptual reinterpretation and remodeling."[34] Alongside these Frankenstein varieties were a host of dissected characters, which were never sewn back together.

While some designers were testing how distorted, elaborated, embellished a typographic form could be while still remaining legible, others were exploring how typographic shapes could be broken down into isolated and identifying forms. This wasn't a new form of minimalism in type design, but one that was heavily motivated by the fractured nature of the rising computer age. A few examples of these minimalist faces appear in the modernist period—A. M. Cassandre's Bifur (1929) features bold strokes that identify the essential minimum of each character, and which are then adorned with thin hash marks to finish out the character. Even more extreme is Bruno Munari's Essential (1935), in which all nonessential marks are omitted from a basic uppercase, sans-serif face (see figure 5.22).

The partial faces from the early 1990s do not appear to be about finding the essential part of each character (as the name of Munari's typeface suggests). Instead, the goal in a typeface like Gerard Unger's Decoder (1992) is about physically deconstructing the conventions of typographic tradition and handing the resulting parts to users to recombine at will. It's unclear whether one could actually say that Decoder has characters; instead, Unger hoped that readers of *Fuse* magazine (for which the face was designed) would take the bits he gave them and create their own characters (see figure 6.3).[35] Barbara Butterweck's Typeface F, Dear John (1992) similarly deconstructed typographic shapes; bearing a strong resemblance to Munari's Essential, it isolates even more minute identifying features of individual characters. Though individual characterforms in this face may not be identifiable in isolation, within the context of the concept behind the face and in concert with the other characters, Butterweck manages to produce a deconstructed but still legible set of shapes (see figure 5.23). This requirement that Licko set out of still being functional is perhaps most explicitly articulated in Phil Baines's typeface You Can Read Me (1991). Unlike Munari and Butterweck, Baines produced a *serifed* face in which significant portions of the typographic forms appear to have been erased. What remains are typographic shapes that—though partial by traditional standards—provide the reader with the minimum shapes required to still be read.

It is important to note here that what Licko and her contemporaries were exploring in their experiments was *not* readability but rather legibility. Legibility is necessary for readability (the greater the legibility is,

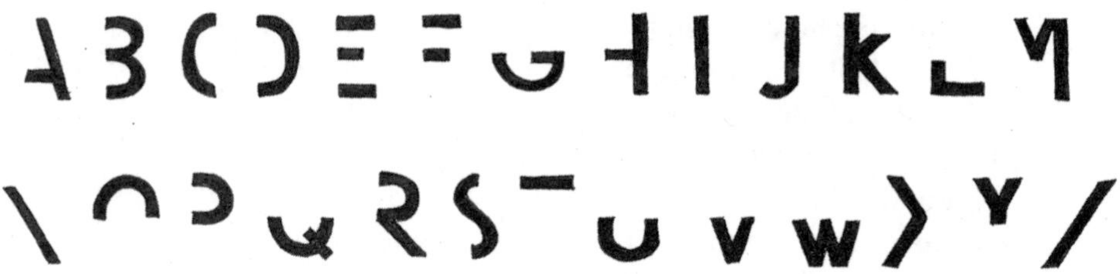

Figure 5.22
Essential (Bruno Munari, 1935). *Source*: author.

Figure 5.23
Typeface F, Dear John (Barbara Butterweck, 1992). *Source*: author.

the greater the readability is as well), but while they are related, they are distinct measures. Legibility is a matter of recognizing that a particular shape is presenting a particular concept or performing a certain function. Our knowledge of what those concepts or functions are need not be extensive. When we look at these shapes:

a lion

we are aware that the shape a is standing for a particular letter, indicating a particular sound, or is performing the role of an indefinite article. Likewise, if we see the shapes:

κινησις

while we might not know what the shape η represents, we are still aware that it is distinct from κ or σ, and so can assume it is indicating a concept different from those shapes. The legibility—our understanding—will be lower in this case, but there is legibility nonetheless.

Continuing this example to explore readability, we can assume that "a lion" is readable for most of us, while "κινησις" is not. This is of course a matter of one's knowledge of different languages, but only in part. This failure of readability is also a matter of shape—the Greek alphabet uses shapes that are unfamiliar to most who use the Latin alphabet. We learn to read through repetition, and we read by recognizing shapes that we've seen before. So, the more readily we recognize a shape and the purpose it serves, the easier that shape is to read. If we simply translate "κινησις" to "kinesis" it immediately becomes more readable.

Here I adopt the distinction that Walter Tracy sets out in his book *Letters of Credit*, where readability is about the comfort one experiences in reading large amounts of text, while legibility is more broadly about being decipherable and recognizable. "Legibility," he writes, "refers to perception, and the measure of it is the speed at which a character can be recognized. . . . Readability refers to comprehension, and the measure of that is the length of time that a reader can give to a stretch of text without strain."[36] It is unlikely that anyone would identify New Alphabet, Emperor, Prototype, or You Can Read Me as comfortable faces to read. They take extra effort from the reader to decipher. But there is no question that these remain legible shapes—not as quickly recognized as the ones you're reading now, but our reading brains are able to make use of them all the same.

We will discuss this impressive flexibility of legible shapes further in chapter 7. For now, notice that for many outer limit designers, legibility seems to be the measure of the typographic tipping point. Faces with names like Essential and You Can Read Me suggest that they are as far as the typographic shape can go before functionality is lost. Of course, one can point to typographic shapes that defy even this equation of the limit of legibility with the outer limit of typography. Typefaces such as Zapf Dingbats (ca. 1977), or Ji Lee's Univers Revolved (ca. 2004), provide radical challenges to what constitutes a typographic shape. Lee's typeface is derived directly from traditional typographic shapes: as the name suggests, the forms in Adrian Frutiger's typeface Univers (1957) have been revolved around an axis, creating the appearance of three-dimensional solids. Similar to the manipulations performed in Licko's Hypnopaedia, Univers Revolved highlights the fact that all typographic characters are abstract shapes first and foremost. Lee did intend for his typeface to be read, and this can be achieved, though in certain instances it requires more attentiveness to detail.[37] As solids, shapes like U and H look remarkably similar (see figure 5.24); quickly distinguishing one from the other is a challenge.[38] Setting aside what this face shows us about legibility, in the majority of Lee's book *Univers Revolved*, his new typographic forms are used to construct landscapes, robots, chessboards—pictures that have no interest in being read in any traditional sense of the term.[39]

A more traditional example of a typeface that challenges the equation of the limits of legibility with that of typographic form, Zapf Dingbats has

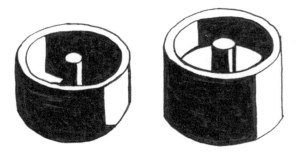

Figure 5.24
The U and H from Univers Revolved (Ji Lee, ca. 2004) look similar (unless viewed from below), challenging the ease of reading. *Source*: author.

precedents in the ornaments and symbols traditionally included in metal fonts. These symbols have long been part of the typographic toolbox and have been used in the production of traditional typographic texts, but they make no claim to legibility.[40] In the late twentieth century, the art director David Carson used Dingbats to challenge the supremacy of legibility directly, setting an article in *Raygun* magazine in the typeface—the article (which he deemed too boring to be read) was set and published word for word in Dingbats, but no one could read it.[41]

From the relatively moderate reforms of phonetic typefaces to the more extreme shapes of hybrid and partial faces, these experiments all recognize an outer limit of typographic shapes that is further away from tradition than we are likely to expect. They test the limits of what is possible within the set of shapes while still remaining legible—keeping in mind the influence of convention and context on our ability to read any given shape. The success of typographic experimentation should not be measured by whether or not these new shapes become our defaults; they do not need to usurp the place of more traditional shapes to be of value. Rather, typefaces that push at the outer limits of the category of typographic shapes are successful if they reveal something overlooked about the other shapes that populate this category. If they reveal the false equation of alphabetic shapes and phonetics, the difference between legibility and readability, or the flexibility of the human brain, then they can be considered useful designs. And they can certainly be considered constituent within the set of typographic shapes.

Ultimately, the shortcoming of the outer limit approach to defining the set of typographic shapes is the same as for Knuth's METAFONT—there will always be another variant another shape that can be added, particularly in light of typography's relational nature. The skeleton revealed a great deal of repetition and similarity among typographic shapes. This is what allows one to imagine that we can define an essence that unites all these variations. The idea of a typographic outer limit, on the other hand, reveals the great amount of flexibility that characterizes this set of shapes. People have been shaping and reshaping Latin typographic forms for nearly six hundred years, and certain other typographic forms for even longer. To expect there to be an outer limit to these variations is ambitious but, ultimately, foolish. The repetition revealed by skeletons and the variability revealed by the outer limit suggest that the best means of defining the set of typographic shapes will be relational rather than definitive.

chpN

ascender
bowl
brackets
aperture

aAqe

crossbar
eye
counter
descender

AfiB

cap-height
serifs
ligature

Ea

stem
thick & thin strokes

Source: author.

6 Relational Shapes

I guess I'm never sure that print is truly linear.
—Muriel Cooper[1]

The a in Wim Crouwel's New Alphabet looks nearly nothing like the low-ercase a's we're used to. If one adds a few details, we might be able to guess where it comes from (see figure 6.1). But on its own, the shape looks more like a J or a backward L than an a. Still, as discussed in the previous chapter, Crouwel's a can function as such not because it resembles an a, but because of its relation to the other shapes in the typeface. The rela-tional value of characterforms is explicitly visible in New Alphabet, but it isn't unique to peculiar faces like this. Ferdinand de Saussure's revelation of the arbitrariness of the signifier–signified relationship in linguistics suggests that none of our characters actually *resemble* the concepts they signify. This:

G

is able to stand unproblematically for a particular linguistic concept thanks to the construction of an arbitrary relationship. Of this linguistic arbitrariness, Saussure writes, "There is no internal connexion . . . be-tween the idea of 'sister' and the French sequence of sounds *s-ö-r* which acts as its signal. The same idea might as well be represented by any other sequence of sounds. This is demonstrated by differences between languages, and even by the existence of different languages."[2] In some respects, the differences between typefaces are comparable to those be-tween different languages. Both G and G are able to stand for a single con-cept; and just like "sister" and "soeur," both forms share certain common qualities. However, this is not to say that all the signs for a single concept

Figure 6.1
Source: author.

need share common qualities; because the relationship is arbitrary, the signifier connected to a signified could be nearly anything.

The challenge with arbitrary systems like this is twofold: they often conceal their arbitrariness, giving off a false air of inevitability (leading to the kind of chauvinism Carl Sagan warns against, or the hegemony that Stuart Hall critiques); and if left unchecked, they open up an unmanageable and unproductive amount of possibility. If there is no natural link between a signifier and a signified, then one could assume that absolutely anything can serve as a signifier for a particular signified. In Saussure's theory, we protect against this sort of extreme randomness by relying on linguistic communities. It is only by common use within a linguistic community that "sister" is able to refer successfully to its designated signified. However, when considering the arbitrary nature of character design, Saussure's theory is less useful.[3] It is not a linguistic community that allows New Alphabet's a to avoid mere randomness and to signify successfully; rather, it is a community of other shapes. This latter community is so flexible it allows the New Alphabet a to function despite the fact that it looks nothing like the a's we're used to, and in fact looks like characters other than a lowercase a.

Consider an example from neuroscientist Stanislas Dehaene's work; though used to illustrate the differences between the abilities of the reading human brain and the reading computer, it also illustrates the difference between a linguistic community and a community of shapes:

Chapter 6

Honey bees savour sweet nectar.[4]

Using experience and context, we are able to read this sentence as "Honey bees savour sweet nectar" rather than "Honey bccs sovovr sweet ncctar," as it is actually written. We can easily decipher this not because a linguistic community has assigned the shapes *savour* to the idea "savour"; it has in fact assigned a different signifier to that signified. Instead, we recognize (correctly or not) a combination of shapes. The *v* works in this sentence as a u, and the *c* as an e, because of the aesthetic context in which we find them, and the linguistic connections our brains make, based on that context. Although we may technically be misreading the sentence before us, our brains are able to make sense of its deviations from the edicts of the linguistic community thanks to the flexibility of the community of characterforms.

It may not seem likely that a shape as seemingly obvious as this:

E

would require relational definition in order to signify successfully. The commonsense explanation for that shape's ability to signify is that we recognize it as a particular combination of strokes that our linguistic community has decided will stand for the concept "E." But our ability to differentiate one characterform from another is always in question; that question is just more pressing in some cases than in others. As seen in the Epps Evans alphabet, a relational understanding of E is necessary to distinguish it from F. In faces designed for computer reading, we have seen the i, j, l, I, and 1 require such relational differentiation in order to refer successfully. Indeed, in every instance of Latin type design (that is, type design intended to be read), the h has to be designed in a certain relation to the n and the b, so that they will each remain distinct from one another. The arbitrary relationship of a signifier to a signified opens up vast amounts of formal possibility, but the typographic shape's ability to function linguistically merely requires the maintenance of certain relations to other shapes. As Douglas Hofstadter noted in his critique of Knuth's METAFONT, "Letters mutually define each others' essences."[5] It follows from this key point that the most effective means of defining the set of typographic shapes will be relational rather than individual or essentialist.

Using Family Similarities

In an often-cited section of Ludwig Wittgenstein's *Philosophical Investigations*, he proposes a means of defining a concept using relations rather than one common feature, or one clear outer boundary. It is worth noting that this section appears in his late philosophy—that is, after he had shifted from a strictly logical project to a use-theory of language.[6] In fact, Wittgenstein introduces the idea of family similarities in the midst of defending his philosophy from a hypothetical critic of this shift. Having just spent sixty-four sections developing a complex language game (as a means of getting at a clearer understanding of language itself), he introduces an imagined detractor who criticizes him for failing to define his key term—namely, *language*. Wittgenstein admits that he has not done this, but notes that it would be impossible to identify one necessary common feature present in all language, and thereby to define this concept in traditional ways. Instead of one common definition, he proposes a more rhizomatic form.[7]

Considering the process of defining something like *language*, Wittgenstein advocates we "don't think, but look."[8] That is, if you only think about how a definition should work, you may assume that there is some identifiable feature common to everything we house within a single concept—the concept of *language* or of a *game* (in Wittgenstein's other example). He argues that if we actually look at the specific items housed within a concept like *game*, we will see that they do share features, but not one single feature that could form the basis of a logical definition. Instead, "we see a complicated network of similarities overlapping and criss-crossing: sometimes overall similarities, sometimes similarities of detail."[9] These criss-crossing similarities are, collectively, the relational definition of what *game* means. The same is true of typography—we may think there must be a common core for all typographic shapes, but if we actually look at the medium, we see that it comprises only a network of similarities. Wittgenstein likens this kind of similarity to family traits that are passed on between generations—not every member of a family receives the same traits, and some traits skip generations, but the traits are the features that bind a family together genetically.

Wittgenstein notes that the similarities in a relational definition are sometimes overall and sometimes detailed—or in the original German, "Ähnlichkeiten im Großen und Kleinen," large and small.[10] In the definition of typographic shapes, the large (*Großen*) might be the sorts of common features that Coueignoux identified in his system (discussed in chapter 4)—particularly the verticals, horizontals, and secondaries (see figure 4.5). One might also think of the features common to typeface classification systems as another example of the *Großen*—slanted axis, ratios of thick and thin strokes, type or bracketing of serifs, and so on (see figure 3.2). The small (*Kleinen*) might be like the more specialized shapes in Coueignoux's system, specific details of the dimensions of these forms, more unusual typographic forms, etc. The *Großen* would be overall both in the sense of providing a more general description of typographic shapes, and also in being the more commonly appearing similarities in the system. The *Kleinen* would be detailed both in the sense of providing more specific descriptions of shapes, and in being less abundant—collecting a smaller number of similar shapes. Typographic forms in such a relational definition should be parsed at both levels.

Though Coueignoux's parts may be useful for describing the sorts of resemblance that exist in the typographic system, it is important to note that the relational definition proposed here seeks to embrace the complexity of typographic shapes that both Coueignoux's system and classification systems try to reduce. Making things manageable is not the goal here; it is instead to acknowledge the vast formal scope of the typographic medium, as well as the flexibility of legibility. As a thin slice of what a relational definition might look like, take something like figure 6.2. Though limited to a single character here, there are plenty of shapes that relate these g's to other characters: o's, 9's, commas, and so on.

Such a map—not only of single characters, but across characters—would not be simple, but there are technologies that might help us take on such a gargantuan task. In 2017, software engineer Kevin Ho developed a Font Map that performed a similar, though more sophisticated mapping of shapes according to formal relations. Using an object-recognizing algorithm, he produced a navigable map of A's from over 750 typefaces.[11] The computer sorted these typefaces according to a number of major distinctions—like serif versus sans serif, and roman versus blackletter—but also more subtle differences—like variably spaced versus monospaced faces. Interested in developing a tool that designers would find useful (e.g., for locating typefaces that work harmoniously with one another), Ho produced a map that does the same work a designer would do in sorting typefaces in her own font library, only more efficiently.[12] Useful as this technology could be to a relational definition, it's important to ensure that the program's goals are geared toward

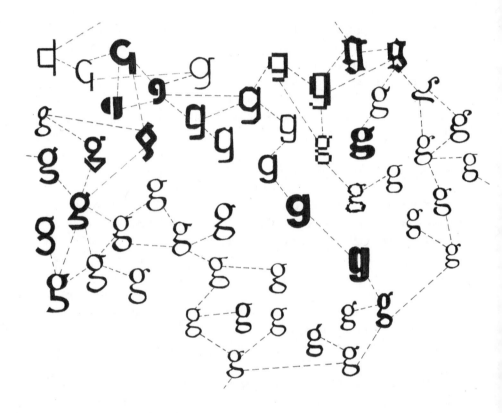

figure 6.2
Source: author.

typography's details and diversity. Impressed by his program's handling of unusual typefaces, Ho noted, "[A designer would] probably throw all these random fonts into a random bucket. The algorithm did the exact same thing."[13] While it is a common practice to have a "grab bag" category in classification systems (variously known as Fantasies, Graphics, and Decorative),[14] carrying this habit into such a sophisticated visual recognition program risks ignoring the features that even these outer limit typefaces share with more mundane faces. A relational definition of typographic shapes (which is admittedly distinct from what Font Map sets out to do) may very well have use for the processing power developed by computer learning, but the resulting system should be concerned less with the designer's use, and more with the nature of the shapes populating the typographic medium.

As a means of defining terms, it may appear that we've descended into chaos rather than the clarity we expect from dictionaries. But as Wittgenstein notes of his undefined term *language*, just because we cannot logically or neatly define a term does not mean this term cannot be useful.[15] And, though he was less admiring of this kind of use than Wittgenstein was, Friedrich Nietzsche would argue that the very reason we collect such a messy diversity within a single concept (like the concept *typographic shape*) is for our own convenience—that is, to enable use.[16] As long as we don't pretend that this messy diversity isn't there, as long as we don't limit the shapes to *our* utility, use can be understood as a force that holds this apparently chaotic collection of shapes together. A typographic shape does not need to meet a minimum or maximum requirement of definition to be included; rather, it merely needs to be useful within the set of typographic shapes. Perhaps that use is testing out an aesthetic limit, perhaps it is exploring a technological constraint, perhaps it is enacting a philosophy, perhaps it is even beyond human consideration; what's key to understand is that usefulness is not identical to legibility. For a time in the 1960s, manufacturers of duck decoys marketed their work as laboratory tested, informed by the latest scientific research to be life-like. They claimed that a decoy needed to fit as closely the features of actual ducks (that is, as close to the definition of a duck) as possible. But Mr. T. W. Sandoz—experienced hunter, and collector of duck decoys—argued in favor of simple, folk designs. "The ducks will sit down to something like that," he noted, "They're crude but they'll do the job."[17] Metaphorically speaking, as long as a duck will sit down to a shape, we can count it as typographic.

Use not only helps bind the set of typographic shapes together, it also informs the new shapes that seek admittance to the set. Recall that in the biological morphology of D'Arcy Thompson, a femur is not shaped the way it is in order to bear weight; rather, it is shaped in that way from having borne weight. In New Alphabet, the a functions as an a not because it is formed to do so, but because within the context or environment of the other shapes, it *does* so. If we consider less experimental typographic shapes, it is still possible to see that they are not formed to function in their assigned ways, but rather are able to function in those ways because they maintain certain relationships. Just as a femur is shaped by bearing weight, a conventional E is not formed to signify "E," but is formed by bearing the relationship, to other typographic shapes, of signifying "E." Beyond this morphological metaphor, there are a number of ways in which biological evolution can be a useful model for understanding the relational nature of the set of typographic shapes.

An Evolutionary Model

In the early 1990s, Ellen Lupton and J. Abbott Miller proposed an evolutionary view of typographic history.[18] Drawing on evolutionary ideas, they argue that we should reconceptualize "the alphabet as a system of infinitely changeable relationships between elements."[19] And they describe typography as "a flexible genetic code capable of breeding an infinity of new species."[20] This view captures the infinite variability made possible by basic elements, and the relational nature of typography as a medium. However, their natural history falters when they start to sketch out the history of those changes. They rightly suggest that the history of this medium is "a string of responses to random catastrophes in the philosophy and technology of design," rather than "a logical evolution toward perfect forms."[21] But the history they tell is a teleological one—designers progress from the idealization of the alphabet to the acceptance that signs are arbitrary forms that can be the subject of experimentation. In this narrative, the medium itself is not evolving; rather, designers are evolving it. Though they capture nicely the immense variability and responsiveness of the typographic medium, their natural history of typography does not take full advantage of the evolutionary model.

If evolutionary biology is taken as a model for thinking about the relational nature of typographic shape, there are at least three key features to borrow from it. First, the view of evolution by natural selection that Darwin proposed undermined teleology. Though there is clearly a development over time characterizing evolution, a movement from one form of being *toward* another, that movement is not toward a particular goal, or a particular idea of perfection. This we've already seen in Thompson's work and in typography—forms do not develop toward a particular functional goal; instead, they develop by functioning. If a particular feature proves to be advantageous it will be reproduced again; if a particular form of G proves to be advantageous it will inspire further G's. And similarly, if a particular typographic shape does not catch on, then its features will likely fall out of future shapes (e.g., the spur on an l, or the long s). As noted in chapter 3, this selective process is also influenced by technologies and which shapes they support. This technological selection is notable not only stylistically (e.g., a hairline typeface falling out of use in the early digital period), but perhaps most significantly in instances where a given character set needs to be reduced to fit the operations of a technology (e.g., in the development of Chinese typesetting and typewriters).[22]

Second, Darwin argues that adaptations don't occur in isolation, but rather that biological evolution is characterized by co-adaptation, or adaptation within environments. A particular species of bird evolves not in isolation but in environments in which members of that species develop various forms of "mutual relationships" with other beings (food sources, predators, and others).[23] An individual typographic shape develops not only in relation to all other shapes of its character-type (e.g., all other G's or all other &'s), but also within the context of its type family and the contexts of its production and use. For instance, in chapter 3 we saw that the technologies used to produce type have historically influenced how the shapes develop. In the early years of metal typesetting it was dangerous for a serif to be too thin, as it wouldn't survive frequent pressure from the press. The serifs that were most prolific during this period were stubby. Later, the flexibility of phototypesetting and dry transfer allowed for typefaces to develop in more elaborate and sometimes outlandish ways. Freer in relation to technology, the success of this gamble in development relied more on a symbiotic relationship with graphic designers. If graphic designers were brave enough to sometimes leave Helvetica behind, Neil Bold (Wayne Stettler, 1966) had a chance of survival.

Finally, the fact that evolution is nonteleological, and driven by the complex ecosystems in which it occurs, suggests it has no director—there is no designer deciding how the evolution will take place. Evolution is an emergent system, achieving fitness not through conscious or individual decision but through collective actions and collective intelligence. This may be the most difficult evolutionary idea to accept as a descriptor of typography, given that we know typefaces have designers who usually put considerable time and effort into the design and production of those faces. And after this there are graphic designers who make use of typefaces in particular contexts, which tends to influence not only the characteristic of or associations with that typeface, but also what sorts of faces will be designed in the future. However, typography is emergent in the same way a city is. While there may be identifiable designers of specific parts of it, there is no designer of the city itself. When left to their own devices, cities develop through use, and according to what the people living there need. As Jane Jacobs argued at the height of postwar city planning and suburbanization, a city suffers when an order is imposed on its already existing "underlying order."[24] In an emergent system, there is no hierarchical source of organization, from either inside or outside. Within the typographic medium this means no shape or group of shapes sets standards for all the others (no skeleton or essential definition calls the shots).[25] But neither is the set of shapes held together by some external force of language (there is no outer limit defined by the limits of signification).

As a system, then, the typographic set of shapes wanders aimlessly from variation to variation, informed (but not directed) by internal and external forces. Though the variations are often minor in scope, they are frequent, creating a massive and dynamic system, one that is best captured by relational ways of thinking.

A Relational Definition of Typographic Shape

The typographic set of shapes is *a set of shapes regularly identified as typographic, for the reason that each member bears notable formal relations to other members in the set, and contributes some utility to the set of shapes as a whole.* Note that this is different from a nominalist definition (that typographic shapes are shapes we refer to as typographic). The relational definition maintains that we are able to refer to these shapes as typographic in a meaningful way *only because* of the relationships they maintain among themselves. The relational definition comes from the shapes more than from us. One might think the typographic shape is defined by its ability to be used to set readable texts. However, we have seen typefaces like Zapf Dingbats and Univers Revolved that complicate this assumption. Alternatively, one might assume that a typographic shape is defined by its maker. Similar to the logic behind Marcel Duchamp's readymades, one might think a typographic shape is that which a typographic designer declares as such.[26] However, what makes a typeface like Tobias Frere-Jones's Fibonacci an example of typographic shape is not *his* impressive career and authority as a type designer but rather the fact that this set of shapes reveals something useful about the nature of the typographic medium. These shapes, as unconventional as they are, are useful for the set of typographic shapes.

We have already seen in the previous two chapters examples of typefaces that, to some degree, address this relational quality. The outer limit shapes discussed in chapter 5 rely on the relational to keep themselves within the fold, and to make unconventional shapes functional. In Tschichold's phonetic alphabet, for instance, the two e's are able to produce two different sounds thanks to their relationship to one another. Similar to the queen's relationship to the king or pawn in chess, the short e can be recognized as such only in relation to the longer, or standard e (see figure 5.4). In the OCR and MICR typefaces, peculiar characters like the ꓲ in OCR-A signify successfully because of their *differential* relationship with other characters like the 1. More broadly, any typeface that seeks to introduce unconventional shapes will function as typically expected only if those shapes continue to maintain some formal relationship to other typographic characters.

In the skeletal experiments we explored in chapter 4 there was less a sense of reliance on relation and more of an implicit acknowledgement that there is something relational among the typographic shapes that exist. In the modernist attempt to define the essence of typography there was an assumption that these shapes all share a common geometric language. While designers like Paul Renner may have defined that language in limited terms (as perfect geometric forms), this assumption nonetheless acknowledges that there are shared formal features. The same is true in piecemeal computer definitions like Coueignoux's and Cox's. By identifying a number of basic ingredients that can be combined to form any typeface, these systems suggest that there are basic features that appear repeatedly within a wide variety of typographic shapes. In a far more whimsical and less practical version of this, Woody Leslie's idea of molecular typography similarly breaks up typographic forms into component parts (atoms of various sorts), which have rules of combination (that involve positive and negative charges). Each character has its own chemical formula, and the fact that some characters have the same formula is said to reveal their relation to one another (e.g., 6 and Q).[27] Though clever at times, this fictional case of the relational quality of typography draws its relations too close. It lacks a clear understanding of how the *differential* relationships are produced in addition to (or out of) these relationships of similarity. The more successful (and actual) form of this repeated-features-view of type is the modular typeface.

As we saw in Gerard Unger's Decoder, modular typefaces are deconstructed typefaces, though they also predate the period of deconstructivist design. These typefaces consist of a number of parts that, when combined by the user, form typographic characters (see figure 6.3). Fregio Mecano (attributed to Giulio da Milano, 1933), perhaps the most famous modular typeface, has twenty parts; Patrona Grotesk (V. Kánsky, 1931), an earlier Czech modular, has thirty-eight parts; and Aleph (Philippe Apeloig, 1994), a partially modular typeface, has only two or three parts.[28] (I refer to Aleph as partially modular because it creates its characterforms out of a limited number of basic parts, but it does not make those parts themselves available to users.) These typefaces can be seen as placing a part of the creative process in the hands of users; for instance, Unger notes that what he "wanted to do was get Fuse-lovers [fans of the magazine in which the typeface was published] to make their own series of shapes."[29] They can also be seen as part of the modernists' purifying project, particularly given that both Patrona Grotesk and Fregio Mecano were designed in the 1930s, and the Bauhaus's Josef Albers also has a partially modular typeface, Kombinationsschrift (1931), from this time period. Whatever the underlying philosophical motivation, modular typefaces necessarily recognize that typographic shapes are related to one another through the presence of repeated forms.[30] This is particularly true of individual typefaces, but the same basic principle applies to the set of typographic shapes as a whole. This principle is what Coueignoux's work hinges on, but both his set of shapes and these modulars are too narrow to accommodate the entire network of relations in the typographic medium. As seen in the challenges to Knuth's METAFONT, no one modular set will be able to produce every typographic shape imaginable.

The repetition (or even approximate repetition) of formal features is only one of the ways in which the typographic medium can be understood

Figure 6.3
Modular typefaces. Clockwise from the top left: Decoder (Gerard Unger, 1992),
Patrona Grotesk (V. Kánsky, 1931), Aleph (Philippe Apeloig, 1994), Kombinationsschrift
(Josef Albers, 1931), Fregio Mecano (Giulio da Milano, 1933). *Source*: author.

as relational. The differential relation obvious in OCR and MICR faces (but present in all typefaces) is another kind of relation, which we've already discussed. Beyond these, one of the most important relations in the typographic medium is that of figure and ground. Gerrit Noordzij argues that characters are two shapes—one black, the other white (or dark and light)—and when you change the form of one, this changes the form of the other. In his view, it is using the black forms to shape the "white in the word" that unites all forms of writing and type, no matter how their scripts may differ.[31] As with any other central typographic feature, designers have experimented with this figure/ground relationship as well (see figure 6.4). Herbert Bayer's Shadow typeface (1925) draws attention to the relation of figure and ground by designing the ground to reveal the figure, rather than the other way around. He allows the unfamiliar shapes of the ground to reveal familiar shapes in their gaps. Optica Normal (Manolo Guerrero, 2010), on the other hand, uses the ground to obscure the figure, nearly obliterating this differential relationship. In this design, Manolo Guerrero uses varying orthogonal lines across the figure and ground to create a typeface in which the letterforms barely appear. Somewhere between these two, the brand consultants Superunion recently designed a typeface, apparently inspired by blockchain, for a cybersecurity company.[32] It too uses obscuring stripes, but is more of a shadow face—the characters emerging from the design of the ground, rather than the figure itself. Finally, Neville Brody's Antimatter (2003) plays with the idea of particles and antiparticles.[33] As though located on the event horizon of a black hole, each character stretches from a central point, both up and down in space, existing in the end not at a single point, but along a continuum that spans the figure and the ground.

Typographic shapes relate to one another in countless ways, and we have formalized some of these relationships into taxonomies such as typefaces, type families, and typeface classification systems. But unless we can allow these categories to stretch beyond what we're used to, or what we expect, we haven't yet glimpsed the full scope of the typographic medium (see figures 6.5a and 6.5b).

The set of typographic shapes already allows for this diversity of shape—typographic shapes exhibit "infinite creativity," which Hofstadter notes cannot be captured in a single meta-font.[34] We now need to adjust our own understanding of typography to foreground this diversity as well, confident in the idea that the medium's own operational logic is what holds this diversity together.

Figure 6.4
Typefaces that play with the relation of figure and ground. Clockwise from top left: Bayer Shadow Type (Herbert Bayer, 1925), Optica Normal (Manolo Guerrero, 2010), Antimatter (Neville Brody, 2003), Blockchain type (Superunion, 2018). *Source*: author.

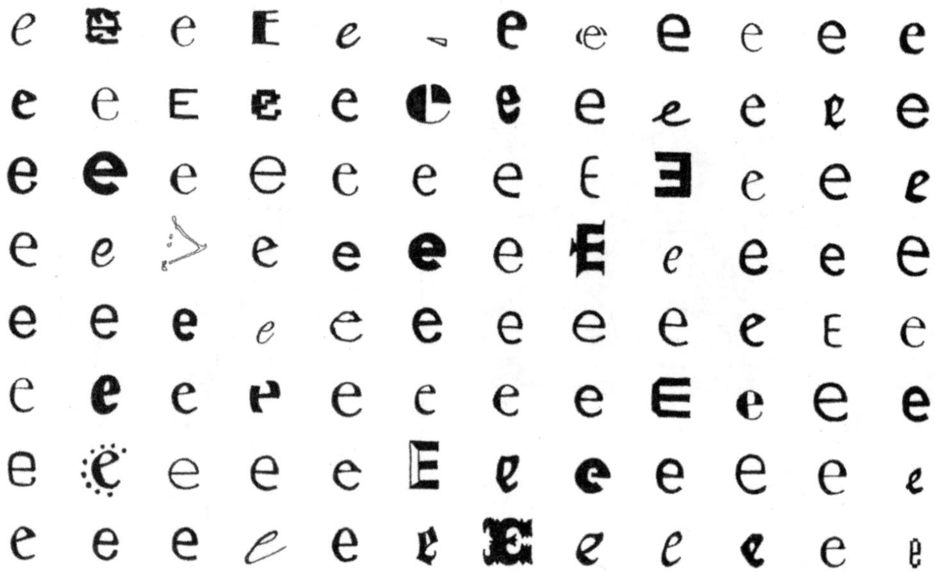

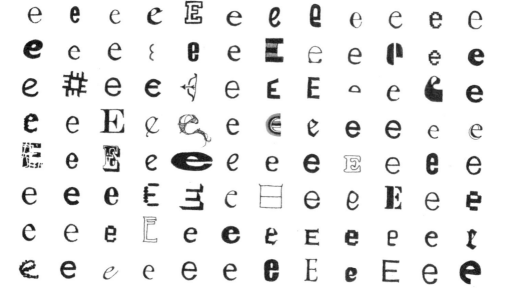

Figures 6.5a and 6.5b
Source: author.

The Diversity of the Typographic Shape

A given typographic character is a shape, both useful and aesthetic. It is a shape influenced by millennia of human writing and reading, and by centuries of typographic technologies. It is also influenced by cultural tastes and cultural colonialism (as evidenced by the dominance of Latin forms), and by the interests and ideas of individual designers and clients. However, while it is influenced by these substantial forces, the typographic shape is not determined by any of these factors in a strict sense. Instead, the set of typographic shapes is a vast and growing network of formal relations—an ongoing conversation among numerous variables, balancing external and internal forces.

As we've seen, perhaps the most insistent variable is language, an external force. Typographic shapes are easily mistaken for letters, and the purpose they serve is easily reduced to linguistic communication. But we've also seen that these errors are the result of typography's linguistic function obscuring their formal essence. Typographic shapes are distinct from the alphabet—their forms are separable from even their linguistic function, as Hypnopaedia makes clear. Rather than emerging naturally or obviously from the rules of linguistic signification, these shapes are usually the result of considerable work and artistry—even a typeface as ubiquitous and seemingly innocuous as Times New Roman. They can be described geometrically (and computationally), but are not, as a set, fully parameterizable, given the possibilities for radical creativity. And even among the majority population of typographic shapes distinguishable from one another by only minor differences, there is near-infinite possibility in the forms these linguistically identical characters can take.

Not only are typographic shapes separable from the alphabet, it may be possible to reform language (or even thought) through the reform of these shapes. Typographic experimentation has seen the outlandish ideas behind Geofroy Tory's graphic instructions for proper pronunciation. But it has also seen more practical, if still utopian, ideas in the phonetic type of Kurt Schwitters, Jan Tschichold, and Herbert Bayer; in the literacy and comprehension interests of Bradbury Thompson and Christian Boer; and the global communication interests of S. B. Telingater and Google. Typographic shapes are able to do more than convey an author's ideas—they can express power and politics, conquering the world for better and worse. However, the only reason these shapes have the potential to exert such power is through their technologies of mass production.

Technology is a second external force acting as a variable in the relational network of typographic shapes. While external (typography is not defined by one technology or another), it is a more integral force on this set of shapes than language is. Typographic shapes are informed by individual technologies in numerous ways, responding to (among other things) the constraints of punchcutting, the metal rectangle, the pressure of the press, the binary logic of the pixel, and tendency of ink and light to spread. But they're also influenced by pretypographic technologies. The calligrapher's pen or stone carver's brush are rarities today, but still their curves and serifs populate our world. Though evidence of typography's conservatism, this is also a reminder of the typographic medium's longevity.

Typographic shapes are informed by technological constraints, but the typographic medium has also managed to survive several technological deaths and upheavals. Across this long history, there are formal patterns that span technologies even as they are influenced by them—most notably the discreteness and modularity of the typographic shape. Though deeply dependent on context and function, these shapes are discrete and combinable units. This is the case even when characters are collected into ligatures (whether Latin, Arabic, etc.), when individual characters are linked in script faces, or in recent handwriting-based typefaces like Julia Sysmäläinen's Mister K (2008) and Harald Geisler's numerous typefaces based on famous hands.[35] The revolutionary power of the typographic medium has always emerged from overcoming the multiple individual strokes that make up characters in handwriting, and introducing fully formed, individual shapes that can be combined, separated, and combined again.

The countless individual typographic shapes are themselves a third significant variable influencing the set of typographic forms. Obviously an internal force, typographic shapes are informed by other typographic shapes. This set of shapes is emergent, driving itself nonteleologically through formal relations. Today it is an incredibly dynamic system. Not only does it contain between about 580 and 1,000 years of existing shapes, but new shapes are being designed each day. Though dynamic, it is also subject to habit and conservatism. As Jon Wozencroft noted when introducing his experimental typography magazine *Fuse*, even some typefaces we consider well-established classics today were resisted when they were first released. "Typography," he writes, "continues to be an innately conservative medium, resisting anything that challenges the familiarity of its 'classical' past."[36] Additionally, styles that are centuries old are often revived or cannibalized, even after the technology that influenced those forms is long gone.[37]

This influence of the traditions or conventions of typographic shapes is significant, but it should not be mistaken as a limit on the potential for experimentation. Existing shapes have inspired not only mimicry but also resistance, divergence, and challenge. And the most successful experimental typefaces tend to be those that combine the familiar with the unfamiliar—the conservative shapes among them helping us to make use of the radical ones. Though typographic shapes are influenced by the force of existing typefaces, there are no essential features shared among all these shapes. As long as a shape is of use to the set of typographic shapes it will be included within that set.

Use links together the three major variables discussed so far, and is itself a fourth (and internal) force acting on the nature of the typographic shape. Whatever the technology producing these shapes, they are formed through functioning—informed by standards linked to that functioning. Typographic shapes can vary widely as long as they are still able to indicate their functions and to remain within the network of formal relations with other typographic shapes. Given language's tendency to obscure these diverse forms, it should be remembered that the function of the typographic medium is also variable—functioning is a force distinct from that of language (and will be discussed more in the following chapter).

These forces interact, creating a vast expanse of formal diversity, but this diversity belongs not to any one of these forces but rather to the medium as a whole—it is the heart of typography's mode of presentation. Language contains formal diversity in the existence of different scripts. But beyond this, and in most cases, the diversity of typographic shape does not belong to language. One possible exception is the existence of pseudo-fonts, by which I mean typefaces that disguise their script. Historically, these are Latin typefaces that are designed to look like other scripts (pseudo-Chinese fonts, pseudo-Hebrew fonts, etc.).[38] The diversity of forms in these instances does come from language's own formal diversity—with one script mimicking another. However, at their heart, even these instances are linguistically identical with any other Latin typeface. Linguistic communication can be helped or hindered depending on the shapes, but on the whole the linguistic identity of any variant of L, w, and so on suggests that formal typographic diversity is not attributable to the influence of language.

Some amount of the diversity of shape, on the other hand, *does* belong to technology. We have seen that typographic technologies put formal restrictions on shape, or even suggest new areas of formal diversity to explore. The pixel, for instance, invited a new way of thinking about the grid, typographic forms, and how they behave in the hands of "users." However, we have also seen technology's ability to mimic forms that bear the marks of other technologies. That is, we've seen that some diversity of shape not only is *not* determined by technology, but openly transgresses its boundaries. The typographic shape is independent of technology in a way that typographic technologies are not independent of shape, given the way they've been built up to accommodate typography's modularity.

The source of formal diversity in typography seems most closely related, then, to the two major internal forces acting on this medium—most obviously, the influence of the set of typographic shapes on itself. Diversity is what makes the conversation among typographic shapes possible—otherwise typography would be an endless echo of itself. It is worth remembering that this conversation inspires both conservatism and radicalism in design, but in both instances, formal diversity is present. And finally, given its centrality to what makes up the broad mechanics of the typographic medium, and its distance from language and particular technologies, at this point it's safe to wager that diversity of shape has something to do with the functioning of the medium as a whole.

Enabling reading may have been the functional spark that first set off this swarm of shapes. But as an emergent system the typographic medium appears to be working something out through variation of its own forms. This is true of a number of different kinds of shapes—architectural forms, chess pieces, duck decoys, belt buckles, and so on. No doubt some changes in form do make these better able to serve the functions to which *we* set them. But in all of these cases, there is far more variation than improved utility alone can explain, particularly if that utility is defined simplistically (as signification, in type's case). The argument that this diversity serves changing cultural tastes is also not strong enough to explain the full diversity of these forms. If changing taste were the explanation, one might expect a typeface over a century old, such as Goudy Old Style (Frederic Goudy, 1915), to have fallen out of use. Further, one might expect more people to be more aware of the detailed differences in typographic shapes if their designs truly are serving the public's tastes.

One answer for why there are so many typographic shapes is because this set is negotiating these four expansive forces—hundreds of languages (each of which is itself vague and variable), technological constraints and possibilities, centuries of already existing shapes, and a variety of functions. Within these four there are subforces that add to this complexity as well (e.g., a designer's intent, or a client's interests). The possible ways for a typographic shape to respond to the numerous ways these forces can be combined is seemingly limitless. Given that the force of function is a common factor in the other three forces as well, let's return to the question of function, now equipped with a richer understanding of the scope of these forms.

N brackets f fi serifs B

ligature

ear bowl g g g g link loop

O O

sloped axis

Source: author.

7 Why Am I a Triangle?

Our sensibility—that is our visual perception and our aesthetic
sense—is superior to geometric construction, and it is to this sensibility
that we must appeal.
—Emil Ruder[1]

Typographic characters are functional shapes; they are formed by performing a function, and they indicate their functions through their forms.
However, there is incredible flexibility not only in those forms, as we've
seen, but also in the medium's functions. In a typeface like New Alphabet, we see a designer who never intended for his typeface to be used to
set text—its function was to be a thought experiment, a possible solu-
tion to a particular design problem, and perhaps an invitation to others
to respond.[2] In Hypnopaedia, Licko intended to illustrate a point about
the nature of typographic shapes as shapes. These patterns were meant
not to contain and communicate someone else's argument but to be an
argument themselves. In 2003, Erik van Blokland and Just van Rossum
designed Twin, a typeface for the city of Minneapolis that was intended
not only to provide the city with a graphic identity but also to communicate weather information. The typeface has multiple variations for most
of its characters and is linked to weather data. When the weather is cold
the typeface appears harsher and more formal (with slab serifs); as the
weather warms, the characters become rounder and more playful (and
sans serif).[3] While van Blokland and van Rossum's face adds a layer of
information to its design, FE-Schrift (1980) was intended to safeguard
information. Designed by Karlgeorg Hoefer in Germany, FE-Schrift was
intended to undermine the forging of German license plates—a common
practice of the radical Baader-Meinhof Gang in the 1970s. It is a typeface
widely criticized for its design peculiarities, but it is designed specifically
to prevent similar characters being transformed into one another. The O
is shaped like an egg, preventing it from becoming a Q with its straight

edges, and uneven base. The bowl on the P is rounded and a small serif extends to the upper left of the stem, preventing it from being turned into the R, which has a clean stem and a squared bowl (see figure 7.1).

One of the most challenging typefaces—both formally and functionally—is Jonathan Barnbrook's Rattera (2012). Designed for *Fuse* magazine, it is said to have been inspired by the notes of an outsider artist and schizophrenic, Alfred Rattera.[4] According to Barnbrook, Rattera conceived of a new "philosophical alphabet" that would gradually be released to the public. Once learned, this alphabet would provide a new way of communicating, thinking about, and therefore of organizing the world. The over 18,000 (proposed) characters were meant to simultaneously create a new worldview, while also illuminating the problems Rattera saw afflicting his contemporary (late 1990s) society.[5] Rattera's new philosophical alphabet is largely ridiculous, basing characters on static

Figure 7.1
FE-Schrift (Karlgeorg Hoefer, 1980) was designed to forestall the counterfeiting of license plates, by making it impossible for characters to be transformed into similar characters (the O cannot become a Q, the P cannot be transformed into an R, etc.). *Source*: author.

coming through televisions, for instance, or on the trajectory of a space shuttle mapped out by the slope of Michael Jackson's nose (see figure 7.2).[6] However, the idea is enticing—a typeface that is meant to entirely re-organize the way in which we capture and therefore conceive of the world.

All of these typefaces illustrate possible non-obvious functions of the typographic medium. The obvious function of the medium is to aid reading, though being obvious doesn't mean this is simple. In OCR and MICR technology, we can see that the ability to read is more or less flexible depending on who, or what, is doing the reading. It also has different outcomes—the most immediate end of human reading is the decoding of a message, while for the computer the end is encoding (translating printed forms into digital code).[7] Even if we limit the reader being discussed to a human reader, it should be remembered that typography is not merely a vessel, the clothing worn by words, branding for an idea. Its

Figure 7.2
The A, F, and H (that is, characters linked to these keys on a computer keyboard) from Rattera (Jonathan Barnbrook, 2012). *Source*: author.

function is not simply *to be read*; rather, typography participates in the reading process. It should also be noted that here I am not looking at reading primarily as a linguistic (or conceptual) activity, nor is it seen as a literary activity—readers and authors working together to produce the meaning of a text. Instead, what follows considers reading as a physiological (and cognitive) activity, involving the materiality of the characterforms, the eyes, and the brain, plus thousands of years of written language and hundreds of years of typographic technologies.[8] As the designer Jost Hochuli defines it, reading is "the conversion in the brain of the perceived succession of letters."[9] Of course, I would not use the word *letters*, since typographic characters are not primarily letters but shapes. Consider, then, the relationship between these shapes and this physiological process.

Optical Comfort

Hochuli's book, *Detail in Typography*, concerns itself with micro-typography: all the minor but vital decisions one makes in designing quality typographic work—not simply typefaces themselves, but type on the page. The topics Hochuli discusses are intended to serve not the tastes of any particular society or time period but rather the reading eye. For instance, certain character combinations should be kerned (i.e., spaced) more closely together than others. We noted in chapter 3 that the combination VA should ideally be nested in order to be most aesthetically pleasing (a task that was difficult in the age of rigid metal type). The formation of ligatures, at least in the Latin alphabet, is another minor aesthetic decision based on creating a more harmonious appearance. Not only is this decision not about serving taste, in Latin it also serves no linguistic purpose:

fi and fi

are linguistically identical. A number of the other decisions Hochuli highlights are less intuitive, and are rejections of geometric harmony for optical harmony, similar to the decisions Grandjean made when cutting the punches for Romain du Roi, deviating from the designing committee's ideals. Our eyes play tricks on us, and typographic designers respond.

In designing optically comfortable characterforms, circular, triangular, and rectangular characters need to be treated differently. Our eyes perceive circles and triangles as smaller than squares or rectangles of equal height. This means that triangular and circular characters need to be designed to be slightly larger in order to appear to be the same size (see figure 7.3).

Similar optical illusions affect stroke width and the bisection of characters. While one might assume that all comparable strokes in a typographic character (all thick strokes, all thin strokes) would be of the same width, the actual width of a stroke needs to take into consideration whether it is vertical or horizontal. We perceive a horizontal stroke as being thicker (or heavier) than a vertical stroke of equal width, hence the horizontal needs to be made slightly thinner in order to appear to be the

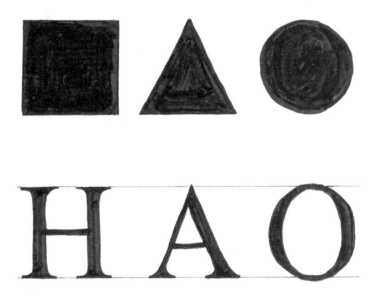

Figure 7.3
In order to appear to be the same height, triangular and circular characters have to be made slightly taller than rectangular characters. Drawn after Hochuli's *Detail in Typography*. *Source*: author.

same width. Following a similar pattern, in characters with two lobes (e.g., E, B, 8, x), while it may make geometric sense to split these shapes in the center, optically this makes the top half appear heavier than the bottom. And so, the crossbars, or intersections of strokes in these shapes are generally positioned slightly higher than the midway point (figure 7.4).

These are all static considerations in the design of typographic forms, but an understanding of the moving, reading eye also informs micro-typography. When we read, our eyes do not move the way we type—sequentially down the line of text, character by character.[10] Instead, the eyes make jumps, or saccades, along the line of text, fixating on certain points, taking in others only in the periphery, and sometimes retracing its steps. The reason for these jumps is that we read with a specific part of the eye, the fovea (see figure 7.5). This is a spot on the retina (located on the rear wall of the eyeball) that provides the most focused vision. While we can perceive familiar and large text in our peripheral vision (e.g., recognizing an EXIT sign), reading smaller and more novel text requires that it remains within a limited range of our visual field. The saccades keep the text in view of the fovea, and are approximately 7 to 9

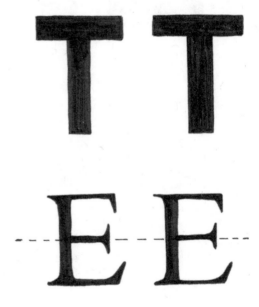

Figure 7.4
In order to avoid appearing top-heavy, horizontal strokes need to be made slightly thinner than vertical; and the crossbars for double-lobed characters need to be positioned slightly above the midway point. Drawn after Hochuli's *Detail in Typography.*
Source: author.

characters long. Our brains even adjust to the size of text in determining how far the eye will jump next, keeping the number of characters it takes in within that range. These saccades vary a bit in reading different scripts—Chinese characters, for instance, have greater information density than Latin, so the saccades for reading Chinese are shorter, taking in fewer characters at one time.[11] In 1975, researchers found that when reading Latin, we perceive information about letterforms only as far as ten or eleven characters from the fixation point. A similar range exists for perceiving information about word shapes.[12] The size of these saccades and the scope of our peripheral vision when reading indicate the extent to which a page of text is a blur, apart from the immediate surroundings of what we are reading. Decisions about line length and linespacing, are consequently intended to make the significant amount of eye movement involved in reading more manageable.

Hochuli notes that typographers variously recommend line lengths anywhere from fifty to seventy characters, and that anything too short or too long is tiring for the reader.[13] There are of course exceptions to this, such as the short line length in reference works, where the reader is only

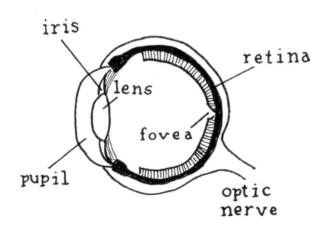

Figure 7.5
The basic anatomy of the eye. *Source*: author.

taking in small amounts of text to begin with. Robert Bringhurst, the author of what is widely viewed in the Latin world as the typographers' bible, notes that anything from forty-five to seventy-five characters is acceptable. He writes that justifying a line of text (that is, setting the text to be flush on both the left and right margins) with too few characters will lead to an uncomfortable amount of white space between words. And a line with too many characters, he claims, gets in the way of "continuous reading."[14] The space, or leading, between lines of texts also affects optical comfort—it should be large enough to avoid lines running into one another in the eye's perceptual field, but not so large that the eye gets lost as it moves from the end of one line to the start of the next. That being said, some kinds of typographic shapes (like the delicate forms designed by John Baskerville or Fermin Didot) require more white space around them, overall.[15] And writing systems (like Arabic) or type styles (like script faces) with more pronounced ascenders and descenders will likewise need more space.

Concerns such as these seem directed at creating as smooth a surface as possible for the reading eye to move along. The minor differences in character form and stroke width, the spacing and length of lines, are intended to avoid distractions for the eye as it moves rapidly and frequently through a text. The ideal for setting large amounts of text is an even, gray color for the page, where *color* refers to the overall lightness or darkness of a page of text. How closely individual typographic shapes are set to one another influences the color, as does the distribution of "ink" in the characterforms themselves.[16] For large amounts of text, typographers generally favor serifs over sans serifs, whereas for wayfinding signage they tend to favor sans serifs.[17] One of the main details typographers have traditionally viewed as increasing legibility is a large x-height and corresponding counter size.[18] While one can sketch out these standards for setting an effective or pleasing text, all this is about readability rather than legibility—about ease, comfort, and beauty rather than converting or processing shapes in the brain.

Neural Processing

As Stanislas Dehaene and others have pointed out, humans have not been reading long enough for us to have *evolved* a dedicated reading area of the brain.[19] And yet we do seem to have an area of the brain that is consistently *used* in reading—Dehaene has proposed that when we learn to read, we repurpose existing neurons for this task. Once information is taken in through the fovea, it is transmitted to the visual cortex, located at the back of the brain, in the occipital lobe. This is where all visual information starts out, before being transmitted to other areas for further processing. Text is sent from the visual cortex to the left occipitotemporal area, which Dehaene and his colleague Laurent Cohen refer to as the "visual word form area" (VWFA) (see figure 7.6).[20] The existence of a VWFA

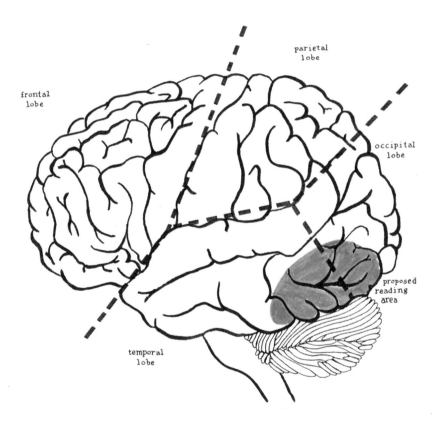

Figure 7.6
The basic anatomy of the brain, and location of proposed visual word form area.
Source: author.

is not, however, settled fact. Cathy Price and Joseph Devlin note that this area of the brain is also activated during other activities that have nothing to do with reading; so at the very least, reading is not the only task this area of the brain carries out. While they don't argue that this region of the brain is *not* involved in reading, they note that reading involves a number of different regions working in concert, a cooperation that the directness of the name "visual word form area" obscures.[21] Whether or not this area of the left occipitotemporal region is the key to understanding reading, this area that is active in reading, is located near other areas that are dedicated to recognizing other kinds of visual things: faces, objects, houses, landscapes. From here information is transmitted to areas of the brain that focus on language—associations or meaning, speech, and so on. Note that though this all happens in a very short amount of time, typographic characters (as well has handwritten characters) seem to be treated in the brain first as shapes, then as a certain kind of shape, and only then as a linguistic thing.

Although this reading process has been described in linear terms, the real-time process is more complicated than this. The brain's efficiency is thanks in large part to an architecture that uses parallel processing to save time. It appears that when reading, we take in multiple characters at once and are processing multiple clusters of characters in the brain, often transmitting information back and forth between numerous areas. As Dehaene describes it, "All the brain regions operate simultaneously and in tandem, and their messages constantly crisscross each other."[22] While reading is a network of simultaneous processes, and while reading familiar and unfamiliar words will involve slightly different processes, some studies of the reading brain have found that the same region of the left occipitotemporal area is involved in reading regardless of what script is being read, or even the direction in which that script is read.[23] Numerous languages make some use of this region of the brain.

The commonalities among pathways of reading suggests there may be some *aesthetic* universality across writing systems.[24] This idea of a common formal basis has been explored in tangential ways in both philosophy and typographic theory. The French aesthetician Jacques Rancière argues that there is a shared formal language between the works of the French poet Stephan Mallarmé and the German designer/architect/engineer Peter Behrens. Mallarmé was an innovator in the use of typographic layout to add meaning to poetry; Behrens was a pioneer in the idea of total design, unified aesthetics across fields of design (architectural, graphic, and industrial). According to Rancière, both the poet and the engineer participated in the streamlining of their subjects. In Mallarmé's layouts one finds the same kind of abstractions one finds in ballet—not a literal representation of a theme, but the adoption of metaphor in its place. For Behrens, the streamlining was a reduction of consumerist variety in favor of a unifying essentialist design. The result of these streamlining moves is the production of "types," which Rancière usefully defines as characterized by a correspondence between objects and their function. He argues that Mallarmé and Behrens reveal, through this shared use of "types," "an equivalence between the forms of art and the forms of objects of everyday living."[25] He argues that there is a common surface of design upon which artists and engineers work, a common store of recurring elements. Independently, Ellen Lupton argues that typographic design exists at "the frontier between language and objects, language and images."[26] Typography is fluent in both the language of things and pictures of things. This idea of a common store of shapes spanning typography and other objects in the world, though speculative in these theoretical works, is supported by research by the neuroscientists Mark Changizi, Shinsuke Shimojo, and others.

The shapes of different scripts may use the same region of the brain not because these shapes developed together (they might have done this only up to a point) but rather because they developed in more or the less the same way. It seems that because the brain has not evolved to read, what we read has adapted itself to the preferences of the brain. Studying commonalities across 115 writing systems from throughout recorded history, Changizi and Shimojo found that most characters are made up of about three strokes, and that individual characterforms contain a significant amount of redundancy (allowing characters to be recognized even if partially obscured).[27] They found that even when a writing system has a large number of characters (they looked at systems with up to two hundred), the average number of strokes used in each character did not increase; instead these systems create more characters by increasing the variety of strokes used in the system overall.[28] The uppercase Latin alphabet, for instance, creates twenty-six characters with a set of fifteen strokes, but still each character has about three (see figure 7.7). In another study, Changizi, Shimojo and two other colleagues propose two more similarities across writing systems: (1) they are optimized for reading rather than writing, and (2) their stroke combinations are based on forms regularly seen in natural surroundings.[29]

/ ı ⁄ _ _ . \ ⟍ C Ɔ J O ꟼ S U

A K M N V W X Y Z

E F H I L T

B D G P R

C J O Q S U

Figure 7.7
Fifteen strokes are combined to make up the twenty-six uppercase characters of the Latin alphabet. *Source*: author.

Rather than isolating strokes, in this second study Changizi and his colleagues focus on frequently occurring stroke combinations. Comparing these to common stroke configurations in shorthand and trademarks, they conclude that the most commonly occurring shapes in our writing systems are optimized for reading rather than writing. Shorthand, which is an optimized form of writing, shares few stroke combinations with the other writing systems studied, while trademarks, which are intended for visual recognizability, share many of the common configurations.[30] It would seem, then, that the characterforms humans have developed over time are best suited for recognition, rather than production. What makes them suitable for recognition is explained by what Changizi and his colleagues refer to as the "ecological hypothesis": our writing systems use configurations that are commonly found in natural settings. They compare "signature configurations" found in both our writing systems and images of natural scenes.[31] It's important to note that what they are comparing here is not the contours of shapes, but the topology—we wouldn't mistake the contours of a Y for a tree, but we can see in its general arrangement of strokes an echo of the ways in which branches are configured in relation to a trunk. Seeing in their analysis a strong correlation between the distribution of stroke configurations in both natural images and our writing systems, they conclude that the scripts we use have developed to best fit what our brains are already primed to perceive.

Dehaene explores similar evolutionary sources for our character-forms, noting that macaque monkeys have been found to have neurons prone to respond to what he calls "proto-letters." This includes two lines in the form of a T, two circles forming an 8, and three lines forming a Y. He proposes that these shapes gradually developed a privileged place in the primate brain because "they constituted a generic 'alphabet' of shapes that are essential to the parsing of the visual scene."[32] A number of these proto-letters appear where edges of objects meet, and the work of Irving Biederman has shown that these meeting points are more important for identifying objects than the contours of objects are.[33] In figure 7.8, we can see that if we gradually remove either segments of contours (left) or segments of edges meeting (right), the object becomes harder to recognize without those meeting points. As a result, topological shapes like F, T, or Y are important for the brain to be able to recognize objects quickly. This all suggests that our writing systems have evolved using a basic set of topological shapes that exist throughout the natural world and that our brains were already skilled at identifying. At this point it's worth acknowledging that the topological shapes discussed in this research are skeletal, compared to the diversity of detailed shapes found in the typographic medium. The one comment Changizi and his colleagues make concerning typography is to note that "typeface and computer fonts are two classes of script where there is no selective pressure for writing at all, and characters in these scripts are qualitatively quite similar to those of the typical writing system."[34] That is, typographic shapes, just like the other scripts they study, are optimized for visual recognition rather than writing.

This evolutionary explanation for why all languages perform some of the processing of characters in the same region of the brain, and share similar basic characteristics of topological form, suggests a limited foundation for the typographic shapes our brains will process best. But with

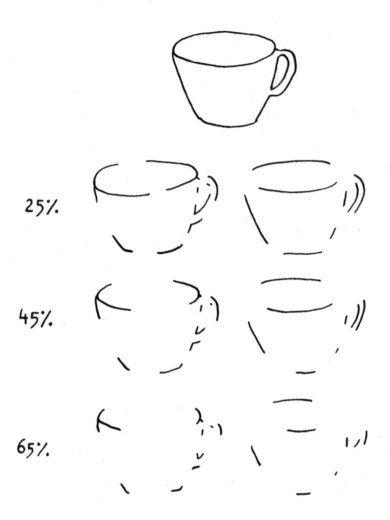

Figure 7.8
This illustration (drawn after Irving Biederman's "Recognition-by-Components," 1987) shows it is easier to recognize an object if the meeting points of contours—the vertices—remain visible. In the left column contours are progressively deleted, while vertices remain; and in the right the vertices are deleted, though the midsections of contours remain visible. *Source*: author.

that foundation in place, the brain is able to make sense of a *wide variety* of text, regardless of significant variables like size, position, and style. Within a reasonable range, the size of text has no effect on our ability to read it. One instance in which there is an effect on reading is at the smallest sizes, generally 6 point and smaller. In 2005, Thomas Huot-Marchand designed a typeface, Minuscule, that seeks to address the challenges of reading at these point sizes. The shapes at these sizes have to adjust in order to preserve our ability to distinguish characters. Based on the research of legibility pioneer Émile Javal, the shapes in Minuscule become increasingly less round and less open as the sizes scale down (see figure 7.9).[35] At 6 point, the somewhat square forms have a large x-height, relatively open counters, and unnecessarily closed shapes have been eliminated (like the bottom half of the g's loop). The goal at this point is to keep strokes from closing in on themselves. The serifs for sizes 6 to 3 point are bracketed slabs, which are bilateral on some strokes, and unilateral anywhere they would threaten to close an aperture (e.g., a bilateral serif on the right leg

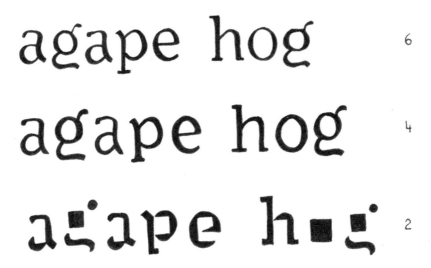

Figure 7.9
Minuscule (Thomas Huot-Marchand, 2005) is meant to be legible at sizes of 6 point and below. Here the characters are enlarged to show the ways shapes must change in order to remain legible at these small sizes. *Source*: author.

of the h threatens to close this characterform, making it appear to be a b). At 4 point, counters have been opened more widely, and more space is provided between the characters. By 2 point (the smallest size), this inter-character space is even greater, but the typographic shapes have also undergone extreme modifications. Some of the counters have been closed entirely—the p, g, and o are closed, and now entirely square. Other counters, like the belly of the a and the eye of the e, have been opened up—the strokes that once closed these shapes are now broken. Finally, the slab serifs are, at this size, entirely unilateral, only pointing outward from any counter or aperture.

Another area in which the size of text has been known to matter is in wayfinding—signs for which legibility is key, and the reader is also moving. The general rule that has been established for signs like those that guide us through airports is that there should be one inch of cap height (the height of an uppercase character) for every fifty feet of viewing distance; and highway signage has its own equation to factor in the speed limit.[36] Dehaene notes that the general size invariance is related to location invariance as well. Not only do saccades rarely land the fovea at the center of a word (without negatively affecting reading, and with the exception of reading Arabic), but we can read on the peripheries as long as character size makes up for the text's distance from the fovea.[37] We can, for instance, perceive the uppercase at a greater distance from the fixation point than lowercase characters.[38] Considering some of the basic variations common in typographic shapes, Dehaene also notes that differences in weight (**bold**, regular, etc.), and dIffERencES iN CasE, have little effect on our reading ability.[39] It has even been fuond taht we are able to raed small amoutns of text in whcih the letetrs hvae been miexd up, as long as the frist and last lettres remian in plcae.[40] According to Jonathan Grainger and Carol Whitney, the ease of reading jumbled text likely has something to do with the supporting context of the other words that are not mixed up. But they also see this phenomenon as evidence that the brain processes text using bigrams, or pairs of characters—a theory that we'll see depends not only on the forms of characters, but on their placement in space as well.[41]

Grainger and Whitney carried out a priming experiment in which subjects were shown a word to prime their reading of a second word, hypothetically speeding up the recognition of the second. They found in this experiment that being primed with "garden" or even "grdn" made reading "GARDEN" easier (illustrating case invariance). Characters could be removed from a word and the word could still be an effective primer, but they also found that "bagde" was an effective primer for the word "badge," while a cluster of characters like "barte" was not. One might think that "bagde" and "barte" would be equally effective as primers, since in both cases three out of the five characters are correct. However, Grainger and Whitney argue that we in fact make sense of words not as a collection of characters, but as a collection of bigrams—BADGE would contain the string BA, BD, BG, BE, AD, AG, AE, DG, DE, and GE. If the order of DG is switched, this means that only one of these ten bigrams has been changed, whereas "barte" alters seven of them.[42]

Dehaene likewise, and independently, has proposed a bigram theory of neural processing. However, he adds to his hypothesis two requirements having to do with position and spacing. He notes that irregular spacing slows down our reading, and that a bigram theory needs some way of explaining how we differentiate between words like ANNA and NANA, which share the same bigrams (AN, AA, NA, and NN). He proposes first that our bigram neurons would have a preference not just for a particular bigram, but for that bigram at the beginning or end of a word—a neuron for NA at the start of a word would be activated when we see NANA, but not ANNA. He and Laurent Cohen have also found that while we can recognize a bigram when there is a character between them, more than 1.5 character's worth of space between them will slow down reading.[43] Yet text read slowly is still legible text. We *can* st i ll r e a d t e x t wi t h u nu su a l let ter s p a c i n g.

Not only do we not read character by character, or entire words at once, we don't even need to read an entire character in order to recognize it (given the redundancy that Changizi and Shimojo noted). While radically sparse typefaces, like Butterweck's Typeface F, Dear John (see figure 5.23), or Baines's You Can Read Me, show us that we can recognize a character as long as enough unique information is offered (e.g., the eye of an e, or the loop of a g), as a general rule in the Latin alphabet we are able to read the top half of characters, without needing the bottom half (see figure 7.10), though this is more effective with serifs than without (see figure 7.11). This was illustrated in 1843 by a notary by the name of Leclair, who published an entire book *Impression Mi-Type* (*Mid-type Printing*), using only the top half of text (presumably as a cost-cutting proposal).[44] This phenomenon varies among scripts—Arabic, like Latin, is top-half-dominant, but Hebrew contains most of its information in the bottom half of characters. This allowed Liron Lavi Turkenich to design Aravrit

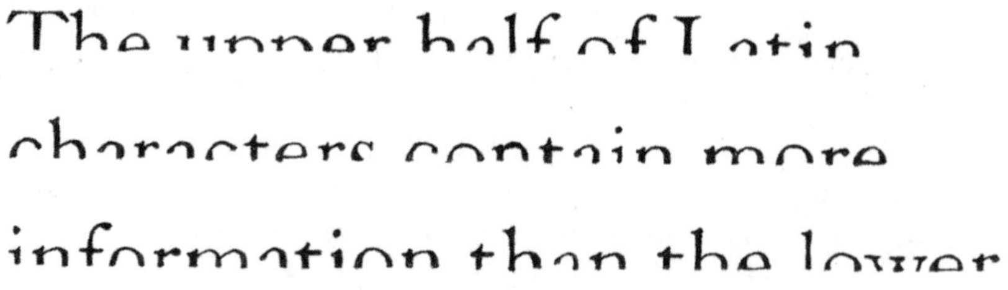

The upper half of Latin

characters contain more

information than the lower

Figure 7.10
In the Latin script, it is easier to read the upper half of characters than the lower.
Source: author.

(2017), a typeface that combines the bottom half of Hebrew and top half of Arabic characters in the hopes of creating a unified script for Palestine and Israel.[45]

What has been described so far has to do with reading alphabetic characters (primarily Latin at that), but typographic characters also include numerals, and the human brain handles these shapes differently. At the end of the nineteenth century, neurologist Joseph-Jules Déjerine began to study a patient who, following a stroke, lost the ability to read but was still able to write, a condition known as "pure alexia."[46] This patient, Mr. C, also remained able to recognize Arabic numerals and perform calculations. This is evidence that linguistic characters and numerals are processed by different pathways in the brain.[47] Because of these different pathways, Dehaene and Cohen have been able to observe people with brain injuries who regularly make errors in naming numbers but are nonetheless able to carry out accurate calculations with those same numbers. They describe, for instance, a patient who erroneously read the equation 8–6 aloud as 5–4, and yet also provided the correct answer of 2.[48] While, graphic information will still be processed through the fovea and the visual cortex, numerals appear to be processed next in the left

Figure 7.11
Upper-half legibility is limited by whether the typeface is serifed or sans serif.
Source: author.

and right parietal lobes, and names of numbers appear to be handled only in the left hemisphere.[49]

Another patient, known as VOL, had injuries to her left posterior cerebral artery; Dehaene and Cohen observed that she had more success naming the single-digit numerals she saw if she counted up to that number name. She essentially associated the numeral with a quantity in her mind's eye, and then counted that quantity to arrive at the correct name.[50] Within a manageable range, this is what we all do—associate a number with a quantity in our brains.[51] Humans share an innate "number sense" with several other species of animals (including other primates, various species of birds, insects, etc.). It is, as Tobias Dantzig characterizes it, a weak number sense. We share a sense of 1, a sense of 2, a sense of 3, and generally following this is "many."[52] What has allowed the human species to move beyond this weak number sense and to develop complex arithmetic is symbolic media—the numerals (particularly zero) that were developed not only to keep records but also eventually to calculate. This innate number sense and its limits are both reflected in the forms of the numerals we use. Across a variety of number systems, we find that 1, 2, 3, and sometimes 4 are expressed by a quantitatively accurate number of strokes, while the larger numbers are represented by abstract forms. The numeral 1 has one stroke, 2 has two, 3 has three, but then 4 has three; similarly, in Roman numerals: I, II, III, but then IV. The same pattern holds for Cuneiform, Mesopotamian and Syrian Aramaic, Etruscan, Mayan, Chinese, ancient Indian numerals, and so on.[53]

Numerals clearly bear a different relationship to the reality they represent than letters do; they maintain a link to quantities in the world, both mentally and, to a lesser extent, formally. One of the other key formal and operational differences between alphabetic characters and numerals is the consideration of order and the importance of space. Today we use a positional number system, thanks to the ancient development of the abacus, counting board, and most notably, the zero.[54] More efficient than earlier cardinal and ordinal number systems, a positional system allows fewer signs to represent more information.[55] In a positional number system a numeral means different things depending on where it appears in a string of numerals. So, 4 means something different in 304, 421, and 547. Unlike an alphabetic character, the position of a numeral is highly significant for our ability to decipher it. We are also not be able to read partial numbers in the same way we're able to read partial words—we have to read each digit in order to determine the quantity represented.[56] Additionally, whereas we're able to recognize words with unusual spacing between alphabetic characters, we cannot do the same with numerals: 54 3 9 01 will look to us like four separate numbers, even if the intended quantity was 543,901.

Both numerals and letterforms are broadly developed over time to fit our brains' biases; but our brains are also influenced by the forms we consume. Dehaene notes that while all languages do make use of the left occipitotemporal area, in brain scans this area is activated less in readers when they see characters they don't recognize (i.e., a script they cannot read).[57] He argues that this area of the brain is trained by the individual reader's cultural experience of reading, that is, by the habits our cultures have developed.

On Habits, Broken and Maintained

Given the flexibility of legibility, many typographic conventions are based not on necessity but on habit. We expect to see serif faces in books and newspapers. And while there has long been a debate over the relative legibility of serif and sans-serif typefaces, in most cases there is no significant difference in reading speeds between the two.[58] When a book, like Jan Tschichold's *New Typography*, is set in a sans-serif typeface, we may be surprised, and we may experience some discomfort in reading these shapes compared to others, but this discomfort can have advantages, as well.

In psychology, the cognitive ease one experiences when reading something that meets their expectations (either visually or in terms of grammatical construction) is known as fluency. And there are instances when fluency is most desirable. Tests of typefaces for wayfinding signage, particularly for road signs, are certainly looking to produce fluency. When driving at high speeds, indecision about the information a road sign communicates can have violent consequences. Similarly grave consequences are sometimes associated with the informed decisions made in hospitals. A 2014 study of fluency in delivering medical information to pregnant women found that the patients' perception of the desirability and complexity of a procedure depended on the fluency of the typeface used. Comparing Arial to Mistral (Roger Excoffon, 1953)—that is, a clean and familiar sans serif to a graphic, bold, and densely set script face—the study found that the women who read the more fluent typeface (Arial) understood the procedure described more easily, and viewed it as a less complex procedure.[59] It's important to note that they didn't find fluency had the same effects among the midwives they also tested, suggesting that their professional expertise made them less vulnerable to changes in the information's formal appearance. Still, this study supports earlier studies that found that fluency, which takes advantage of habit and expectations, makes information more likely to be accepted.[60] Other studies have found that *disfluency* can make a reader more open-minded, more willing to consider a message's information deeply.

Building on William James's theory that human reason involves two levels—one quick and intuitive, the other slow and analytical—Adam Alter and his colleagues found that creating disfluency with type can cause a reader to reach beyond their superficial, intuitive level of reasoning.[61] In one of their experiments, they used a test designed to require the nonintuitive level of reasoning, and had some subjects take the test in a fluent font (12 pt. Myriad Web) and others in a disfluent font (10 pt. Myriad Web Italic). Those who took the test printed in the disfluent font answered more of the test questions correctly, suggesting that the type pushed these subjects to think beyond their intuitive level.[62] Their findings in this (and three other experiments that build on this) suggest that some amount of difficulty in reading leads people to be more analytical, to think more deeply about the decisions they're making. While we can easily assume some of the advantages of using a deeper level of reasoning, researchers have actually measured some specific advantages in education. Connor Diemand-Yauman, Daniel Oppenheimer, and Erikka Vaughan, for instance, found that disfluency in school materials improved students' retention of information.[63] In one of their experiments the fluent font was 16 point Arial, and the disfluent fonts were either 12 point Comic Sans (Vincent Connare, 1994) at 60 percent grayscale, or 12 point Bodoni MT also at 60 percent. In a second study they explored differences among various disfluent faces: Haettenschweiler (Microsoft, ca. 1995), Monotype Corsiva (Patricia Saunders, 1995), and Comic Sans Italicized (they found no measurable differences between the performances of these faces).

From the perspective of the diverse set of typographic shapes we've been considering, note that disfluency in these experiments is produced by only slightly unfamiliar typefaces. Diemand-Yauman and his colleagues point out that the disfluent faces they chose were typefaces that appear elsewhere in the classroom, and so are not completely unfamiliar to the students.[64] Nor are effectively disfluent typefaces illegible typefaces—they are merely typefaces with a lower degree of readability. Some have argued that simply setting a statement in bold type will alter a reader's predisposition to that statement, perhaps making it more believable.[65] Looking specifically at how readers process negations (statements that have a negative structure, and are more difficult than positive structures for readers to follow), Sara Margolin found that bold type didn't positively impact our ability to deal with this kind of statement. The effect it did have, however, was to draw more attention to a statement—both positive and negative.[66] The specific effects of specific sorts of typographic disfluency are still being studied, but the apparent ability of typographic shape to push readers to deeper levels of thinking raises the important question of whether one function of these typographic shapes might be to affect our perception of truth.

In a series of three articles in 2012, the documentarian Errol Morris performed a stealth experiment on readers of the *New York Times*. The first article claimed a desire to test readers' optimism. It offered a scenario in which an asteroid was hurtling toward Earth, and then quoted the scientist David Deutsch claiming that we, living in the twenty-first century, are in a new age of security where this kind of threat is concerned. Today, he claims, we know how to defend ourselves against such a cosmic threat. The reader was then asked whether they agreed with Deutsch or not, and how firmly they agreed or disagreed.[67] What these questions were actually testing was how believable different typefaces are. Each reader saw the passage from Deutsch's text in one of six typefaces, and Morris wanted to know if there would be patterns in how readers responded to a single statement set in different type. He used three serifed faces (Baskerville, Computer Modern, and Georgia) and three sans-serif faces (Comic Sans, Helvetica, and Trebuchet). What he found (in an admittedly uncontrolled experiment) was that one typeface stood out as being both most believable and least unbelievable: Baskerville.[68]

Looking at the weighted measurements of agreement and disagreement (that is "strongly agree" is weighted more than "slightly agree"), Morris and one of his collaborators, David Dunning, found that the three typefaces that generated the most agreement were Baskerville, Computer Modern (Donald Knuth, 1978), and then Georgia (Matthew Carter, 1996)— that is, the three serifed typefaces. Oddly, the three typefaces that produced the *least disagreement* were Baskerville, Computer Modern, and then Comic Sans. Georgia, for some reason, was associated with the highest-weighted level of disagreement. However, all three of the sans serifs had markedly higher levels of disagreement than Baskerville and Computer Modern.[69] At the very minimum, what Morris's experiment suggests is that readers were more likely to believe a scientist's statement if it was set in a serifed typeface—the style of typeface in which we most often set authoritative texts.

Beyond this we can speculate about why different typefaces fared differently in this experiment. Comic Sans had the lowest level of agreement, and only a somewhat high level of disagreement, a combination that might be explained by the lack of seriousness with which this typeface is viewed, yet also the friendly, open appearance that makes it a favored typeface among teachers and those working with dyslexic learners.[70] Helvetica's low level of agreement and high level of disagreement may have something to do with its association with advertisers or corporate actors, rather than trustworthy scientists.[71] Baskerville's success, particularly over the other serifed typefaces, might have something to do with tradition, given its old age relative to the other two computer-aged serifs—or with "starchiness," as Morris implies.[72] But it may also have something to do with its relatively low x-height. Both Computer Modern and Georgia have higher x-heights, suggesting that they are more readable; so perhaps Baskerville has a level of disfluency about it, and perhaps this made readers more open-minded about Deutsch's claim. Finally, of the six typefaces tested, the two with *both* the highest agreement *and* with the lowest disagreement were Baskerville and Computer Modern—these are also the two likely to be the least familiar to the average reader of the *New York Times*. The other four typefaces selected are either ubiquitous because they are members of the eleven core web fonts, prominent in word-processing software and operating systems (Comic Sans, Georgia, and Trebuchet), or ubiquitous because it is Helvetica.[73] It would seem the typefaces that fared best in this experiment were those that push in some small way at the limits of the contemporary reader's habits.

The relationship between habit and typographic form has been addressed by two giants of typography—Zuzana Licko and Herbert Bayer. As we've already seen, Licko is often quoted as observing that we read best what we read most. This comes from an interview carried out by her partner Rudy VanderLans, and after noting this truism about reading and familiarity, she continues: "However, those preferences for typefaces such as Times Roman exist by habit, because those typefaces have been around longest. When those typefaces first came out, they were not what people were used to either."[74] Licko's view suggests that while form's relation to reading may be deeply habitual, that habit can be achieved by conservative and radical shapes alike. The equation of most and best on the one hand assumes conservatism—if type exists in the service of readability, and, given reading's preference for familiarity, should conform to habit. But on the other hand, it invites experimentation—simply because it is difficult to read a set of unfamiliar shapes now does not mean that we can't someday read those shapes best.

Bayer offers his own equation: "the more we read, the less we see."[75] In his view, the role of the typographer is to wake up the reader's eye, to use their formal skills to present a new experience of the alphanumerical characters that, as Judge Hale noted in *Goudy v. Hansen*, "have been known to the world for many generations of men."[76] Though he never referred to it as disfluency, Bayer understood that there is value in standing outside of habit, of venturing into the unfamiliar as a means of communicating more effectively. He proposed typographers play with column widths; with square clusters of text, rather than lines; or with varying colors of paper.[77] And he argued that the designs of characters should be informed by an understanding of vision, not linguistics; that these *visual* forms should instead be used, in collaboration with images, to attempt to bridge linguistic boundaries, and expand communication. In his equation, the familiar lulls us into stasis and chauvinism; it leads us away from imagination and invention, and also from effective communication.

In both Licko's and Bayer's views, as in the typographic medium itself, conservative and radical forms are of equal importance. Not only can time transform the radical into the conservative, but one can design radically with the conservative aim of exact communication in mind. Within the typographic medium as a dynamic set of shapes, the conservative and radical similarly play mutually beneficial roles. The formal experiments that have been discussed throughout this book may have shifted thinking in the typographic medium somewhat, but the majority of the type we read on a daily basis, the type you are reading now, is conservative. The most radical shift in type design is likely the introduction of sans serifs in the nineteenth century, and even today we are reluctant to use it to set a book. The minor differences between most typefaces are valuable iterations, expanding the medium's limits quietly but persistently. Unless they are allowed to become habit, they also establish a ground for other kinds of expansion.

During his career, Gerard Unger designed functional wayfinding typefaces (e.g., M.O.L., 1974; and Capitolium, 1998), innovative digital faces (e.g., Demos, 1975), and radically experimental typefaces (e.g., Decoder, 1992). Considering the flexibility of type design, he wonders whether "it is possible to invent so many unconventional designs precisely because convention is so strong."[78] We could ask similarly whether it is because the primate brain is primed to recognize a set of basic topological shapes that our brains can be so flexible when it comes to reading. Conservative developments are important insofar as they allow for ever-further experimentation. The major deviations, the wild or utopian experiments, extend the medium's limits more abruptly, and have the added advantage of making us uncomfortable at the same time. They push us to notice type, to question what it can be instead of simply what it has been. They allow us to see more even if, for the moment, we read less.

The British designer and writer Herbert Spencer was open to such experimentation. His book, *The Liberated Page*, compiled writing on typographic experiments from his magazine *Typographica*, and following its publication in 1987 was a key influence on the late twentieth-century digital experiments in design.[79] However, throughout the 1960s, Spencer also carried out a series of studies on the legibility of typography, as a means of giving (ultimately conservative) guidance to designers. In one of his books on legibility he argues that because typography is not an end in itself, designers should study legibility in order to "avoid fruitless innovation."[80] While Spencer was willing to embrace experimentation in *The Liberated Page*, his warning against fruitless innovation is surprisingly common in, and dangerous for, typography. Such a warning misunderstands the relationship between function and form, as well as conservative and radical forces in the typographic medium.

If there is great flexibility in both the typographic medium and the reading brain, then there is no reason to allow conservatism to become habit. There are advantages to changing typographic shapes (however radically we may choose to), and those advantages may be for us, or they may be for the typographic medium itself. The reason the warning against fruitless innovation is dangerous is because one never really knows ahead of time which innovations will be fruitless. As Abraham Flexner, the founding director of Princeton's Institute for Advanced Study, pointed out: it is difficult to know, in the moment of research, development, or creation, what will be fruitful in the future. Comparable to Sagan's warning against chauvinism, he warned against allowing the "useful" to be defined too narrowly. The free mind in Flexner's view is the site of true innovation, even when we can't see that innovation yet—he argued for a mind that follows its own curiosity, rather than premeditated interests.[81]

In Hannah Arendt's recipe for comprehension, one similarly needs an "unpremeditated, attentive facing up to," but also a "resisting of, reality."[82] In an exploration of totalitarianism, it is clear what that resistance would be against: totalitarianism itself, the unthinking following that maintains its power, but also the tendency to reduce totalitarianism to the abstraction "evil," as something outside of ourselves. What is the equivalent resistance in the case of typography? First, as we've seen, an unpremeditated facing up to the typographic medium reveals a vast system of shapes that are informed by, but not limited to, technology, linguistics, tradition, and use. The system is constantly churning, reviving old shapes and introducing new ones. Organized internally by small similarities and differences among the shapes themselves. Formally, it is held together by a set of topological shapes that our brains favor, and above that is convention; but rather than stopping there, it continues to expand, as far as imagination and use will take it. It is a collection of shapes that is full of questions, and few clear answers—to face it is to acknowledge how huge this system is, and how difficult it will be to fully understand it on its own terms.

What is to be resisted in this reality is the tendency to simplify, to rest in the comfort of the language of language. Habit is the reality worth resisting. Yes, we most often use these shapes as language. Yes, we read most easily shapes we are most used to seeing. But to unthinkingly assume that this is the only possible reality, or even just the most responsible approach to design, is stultifying. It is comforting for us but limiting for the medium. Daily we entrust the typographic medium with our collective knowledge. If in its own functions it isn't limited to characteristic lines, to a particular technology, or to meaning, why would we limit it, or understand it in such limited terms? The reality of the typographic medium's formal and technological complexity is what we've been resisting. But this we must face. The radical diversity of its conservative forms, and the utilitarian value of even its most radical forms, cannot be explained away with abstractions like aesthetic taste or designer intent. At the heart of the medium's mode of presentation is the typographic shape, in all its variation. This is the medium's own logic, its own driving force.

Toward the Operational Logic of the Typographic Medium

As unsettled as the sciences of reading may be, what comes through when looking at the role shape plays is (1) that there is great flexibility in the reading brain, and (2) that there is some value in following conventions—but given the brain's flexibility, there may be *more value* in breaking with convention. Our brains can handle the diversity and are apparently stretched into more analytic territories by moderate diversion from norms and expectations. More importantly, for the interests of this book, the typographic medium not only can handle diversity and experimentation but seems to thrive off it. The diversity of form acts as a check on the tendency to use the typographic medium to standardize, or to fix in place.

To be sure, convention plays an important role in the typographic medium. But within the medium itself, and unless we impose limits, the stasis of convention is unlikely, given typography's endless search for forms. We've seen that, in this medium, form is not there to serve function; function is instead the broad terrain on which typography explores forms. This exploration of form stands in contrast to the flexibility of the reading brain. That is, there is an asymmetry between how little the basic linguistic function requires of typographic forms, on the one hand, and the reality of their diversity, on the other. It is that asymmetry that suggests typography is doing something more than signifying in a medium other than its own ("print media," "digital media"). It is this asymmetry that suggests that which belongs not to our use, but to the medium itself—namely, diversity of form. However, it is not enough to merely say that the typographic medium is a set of diverse shapes—the nature of its diversity is particular.

The primary function of the typographic medium is the communication of information, and by its diversity alone it communicates the malleability of things. Through the mass-production and combinability of its diverse forms, the medium also communicates the modularity of things. Both malleability and modularity are integral to typographic diversity, and both contradict the idea that typographic forms are merely for the construction of something else—like bricks for a building. As we saw in the US debate over copyrighting typefaces, opponents have argued that type is like brick—building blocks for another work of art, not creative on its own. This comparison leads to the conclusion that since copyrighting or patenting bricks would impede the creation of buildings, copyrighting typefaces would similarly impede the creation of literature.[83] But while both type and bricks can be used in the creative production of other works of art, they aren't involved in creativity in the same ways. There is some variability in the style of bricks, and great artistry in bricklaying. But the brick's creativity is found in its modularity alone, in the combination of bricks. This justifies the protection of collections of bricks rather than the bricks themselves. Typographic shapes, on the other hand, are creative both in their modularity and in their individual forms, their malleability.

These are not merely two separate forms of dynamism—combination (modularity) influences individual forms (malleability). We can see this today in the increasing number of multiscript typefaces being designed. In the example of Qandus, discussed earlier, we saw that the combination of multiple scripts exerts an influence on the individual character forms designed for each script. Arabic forms are the starting point, and all three scripts exert some formal pressures on one another, in order to be able to harmonize aesthetically in the end. But this formal pressure of combination is not unique to multiscript faces; it is equally present in the design of a typeface in a single script. The design process generally involves testing out shapes within words, or word-like combinations, to allow for the likely combinations to influence the design of individual forms. And finally, in Pauthier and Legrand's attempt to design divisible

Chinese type, we can see what a failure to consider modularity's influence on malleability looks like. Because they didn't pay attention to the details of how combination works in the Chinese script, the design of their individual forms suffered.[84]

As I finish writing this book, variable fonts, now in their infancy, are beginning to play new games with the modularity and malleability of the typographic medium. Developed in a rare collaborative move by four major design tech companies (Adobe, Apple, Google, and Microsoft), variable fonts are, at their most basic level, a more efficient way of storing digital fonts. It allows for multiple styles of a single typeface to be stored in a single digital file—cutting down on both storage space and bandwidth. A variable font file allows users to slide between variations of a design, not unlike a knob that allows one to produce a typeface that is 25 percent Baskerville and 75 percent Helvetica.[85] The conservative uses of the technology, so far, allow one to slide between weights or styles of type. But some of the early experimentation with variable fonts, like that carried out by the Dutch/Finnish type firm Underware, reveals that one can slide between writing systems and characters themselves. Safari Braille (Underware, 2017) offers the ability to slide between Latin and Braille—potentially significant for increasing universal accessibility in design—while Safari from A-to-B (Underware, 2017) allows users to slide between any two uppercase Latin characters. In some respects, these are a shift away from modularity—a conceptual shift from the sense that the typographic character is a discrete, digital unit. Instead, variable fonts have the ability to highlight the extent to which typographic characters are in fact in close conversation with one another—across scripts, across contexts, speaking a common language of forms.

The other reason it is not enough to merely conclude that the typographic medium is diverse is that its diversity of form is intimately tied to function. Jacques Rancière is right when he defines a "type" as a correspondence between an object and its function. Although we may have assumed this correspondence meant typographic shapes are letters, this is now clearly a conclusion for our own convenience. The asymmetry between the requirements of linguistic function and the diversity of typographic form is not a sign that typography is an excessive medium; it is an indication that the functions of the typographic medium exceed linguistic use. Facing up to what looks like the excesses of typographic design reveals the complexity of the typographic medium, and can reveal the ways it stores and communicates information.

This communication is, first of all, full of redundancy—few scripts have only one typeface, or style of type, and even these rarities likely share qualities with other typographic shapes (for other scripts). As we've noted, the set of typographic shapes often settles into conventions, differentiating forms from one another in such minor detail that it becomes difficult, for instance, for judges to recognize the originality of design required for intellectual property protection. But these redundant, conservative forms are so numerous they cannot be accidental. As a transmission view of communication would suggest, they may be clarification of the signal—cutting down on the noise. But we shouldn't assume that the signal being clarified is necessarily for us. As an emergent system, these minor variations in shape may simply be the typographic medium working something out on its own, attempting to perfect its position, as a medium, between two things—a position that is never fixed.

In some respects, the minor details that set apart typefaces like Caslon and Baskerville bear a resemblance to the concept of *shanzhai*. In contemporary Chinese, it refers to what we in the West would call fakes (knock-off cellphones, for instance). Yet as the philosopher Byung-Chul Han discusses it, the concept is subtler than "fake" or "knock-off" allows, and it is embedded in a deeper aesthetic tradition of copying in Asian art and architecture. Mirroring the evolutionary creativity of nature, in *shanzhai* products gradually "depart from the original, until they mutate into originals themselves."[86] There is a playfulness in this sort of creative copying—devoid of any attempts to pass itself off as the original, a *shanzhai* product will even draw attention to the ways in which it diverges. And in its redundancy, its playful variation on a theme, it resists the (Western) cult of the original, a value that typography's legal history shows us is defined too narrowly.

Of course, redundancy is not enough for successful communication; Shannon's set of possible messages needs to be an ever-expanding set. As Hofstadter's critique of METAFONT notes, we need both consistency and completeness to capture all possible shapes. And to avoid chauvinism or hegemony, communication needs to be both polysemous and pluralistic, in Hall's terms.[87] It may be in those places where *shanzhai* products are explicit about their divergence that their mimicry becomes most anti-essentialist. *Shanzhai* resists authority and being fixed in place or time; in its variation, it undermines hegemony.[88] Similarly, New Alphabet's ability to be read, Emperor's embrace of the pixel at the expense of ideal proportions, Qandus's graphic insistence that Latin characters adopt Arabic forms—these are all ways in which the typographic medium can insist that it is not only polymorphic but *also* pluralistic. These more radical divergences help us to see that which is always in front of our noses.

There is real possibility in the typographic medium, not merely for design, efficient linguistic communication, or branding, but also for thought, which Arendt argues is a natural and usefully dangerous human capability that "undermines whatever there is of rigid rules, general opinions, and so forth."[89] There is clearly more work to do to understand what is happening at the subsemantic level in this medium, what effects the designs of typographic forms have on the information they carry, what they communicate in themselves rather than through themselves. But the starting point for such understanding is the typographic form—a modular and malleable intersection of language, technology, design, and function—since this is what belongs to the medium itself.

Glossary of Typefaces and Type Systems

As in the rest of the book, all illustrations in this glossary have been drawn by the author.

Albert Einstein. Harald Geisler, 2015. A typeface based on the handwriting of Albert Einstein. To capture more of the natural variation that occurs when humans write, Geisler designed numerous versions of each letter and numeral. As the user types, the program selects different versions, so in the end a page of text will show a variety of different e's, G's, etc.

Aleph. Philippe Apeloig, 1994. A reductive and partially modular typeface that constructs its characters largely out of two forms—a vertical rectangle and a curved form, both inspired by calligraphy. The strokes appear to have been made by a square nib pen, but also recall modernist abstraction. Apeloig works primarily as a graphic designer, rather than a typographic designer, and has little attachment to legibility as a primary goal.

Alphabet 26. Bradbury Thompson, 1950. This alphabet (which uses Baskerville, and so is not a typeface design of its own) is an attempt to simplify the Latin script, eliminating one case. However, rather than selecting either the upper or lowercase, as some modernists recommended, Thompson decided to select some characters from each. Thompson was inspired by his own son's challenges in learning to read, and believed a simplified alphabet would reduce confusion around differing cases.

Antimatter. Neville Brody, 2003. Designed for *Fuse*, the experimental type magazine Brody cofounded with Jon Wozencroft, Antimatter is a typeface that draws inspiration from atomic physics. Each character seems to emerge from and recede into space, as though they are particles and antiparticles on the event horizon of a blackhole. From a typographic perspective these characters play with the relationship of figure and ground—in some ways articulated more by the ground itself, and in other ways spreading its figure out along a broad area of ground.

Aravrit. Liron Lavi Turkenich, 2017. This is a bilingual typeface intended to allow for individual signs in Israel to be read by both Israeli and Palestinian readers. Having noticed that most of the information required to identify a letter in Arabic is located in the top half (as it is in the Latin alphabet as well), and most of the required information in Hebrew is in the bottom half, this typeface combines Hebrew and Arabic into a single set of characters.

Arial. Robin Nicholas and Patricia Saunders, 1982. Initially named Sonoran Sans, this typeface was designed for IBM's introduction of its laser printer. Designed at Monotype, the typeface was intended to share its proportions with Helvetica so that Arial could replace it without altering the layout of a document being printed or displayed (when Helvetica wasn't available). Given how close its design is to Helvetica's (not only in proportions but in many of its forms), Arial has sometimes been accused of being a pirate typeface. A close examination, however, does reveal numerous notable differences between the typefaces. Today Arial, like Helvetica, is one of the most ubiquitous typefaces, largely because of its inclusion in Microsoft software and as one of the core web fonts.

Arnhem. Fred Smeijers, 1998. A typeface for a redesign of the newspaper *Nederlandse Staatscourant.* The design began as a face for headlines, but was then adapted for body text as well. As a newspaper face, Arnhem is relatively narrow, but with a high x-height to enhance legibility. In the end the typeface was not used for the newspaper, but it has found some popularity in book publishing and other design, thanks to its championing by publisher Robin Kinross at Hyphen Press.

Avant-Garde Gothic. Herb Lubalin, 1968. Originally designed as the logotype for the magazine *Avant-Garde*, Lubalin then expanded the design into a full set of characters for the foundry he co-founded, International Typeface Corporation. A key innovator in the use of phototypesetting, Lubalin took full advantage throughout his design work of the new ways in which characters could be overlaid and embedded. He developed illustrative typography, and this typeface was full of unique ligatures and exceedingly close character-spacing. It is a geometric sans serif with an extremely high x-height, and with weights that similarly reach to the extremes.

Ayna. Tarek Atrissi, ca. 2006. Designed for the Arabic web portal, ayna.com, this typeface is based on square Kufic calligraphy. Square Kufic is a style that was developed in the thirteenth and fourteenth centuries, and was used widely in architectural inscriptions. Square Kufic type, like Ayna, is not only far more angular than other styles of Arabic typography and calligraphy, but often appears in square patterns—the characters interlinking both horizontally and vertically. In addition to its roots in Arabic lettering arts, Ayna can also be seen as bearing a relation to the modernist typographic experiments that came out of De Stijl, and out of early CRT type displays (Epps Evans, and New Alphabet).

Baskerville. John Baskerville, 1754. A perfectionist with a strange life and afterlife, John Baskerville based his roman on William Caslon's popular roman. But he introduced a new level of delicacy, which would inspire a shift from Old Style to Modern typefaces. Baskerville increased the delicacy of his thin strokes and serifs, and introduced more white space into his layouts. The increased contrast between the black and white of the page that resulted was not embraced by many in England or America, but would inspire even more drastic contrast between thick and thin strokes in the continental typefaces of people like Didot and Bodoni.

Bayer Shadow Type. Herbert Bayer, 1925. One of the experimental typefaces Bayer developed between 1925 and 1927. This face reveals its characters only through the presence of their shadows, essentially allowing the ground to reveal the figure.

Bell Centennial. Matthew Carter, 1976. Designed for use in AT&T's telephone books, this typeface had to meet unique design parameters. The phonebook printing would use cheap materials (ink and paper) on fast presses, meaning the ink was likely to spread significantly. And yet, the resulting typeface impression needed to be legible at small sizes, spaced closely together in tight columns. Carter therefore designed the typeface with notches dug out of any place where ink was likely to pool. In the finished product, these notches are not visible, and the finished shapes would not be made illegible by the pooling that did occur.

Bembo. Francesco Griffo, 1496. The primary source material for roman lowercase characters was the work of Southern European scribes; the primary source of inspiration for the uppercase were ancient Roman inscriptions. Given that these two sets of shapes came from two different sources, they did not always appear to form a unified alphabet in early roman typography. Francesco Griffo—punchcutter for the famous scholar-printer Aldus Manutius—designed Bembo with an interest in achieving a greater balance between these two cases. Most notably, he made the ascenders of lowercase characters taller than the height of his capital characters.

Beowolf. Erik van Blokland and Just van Rossum, 1989. A "random" typeface, Beowolf was an early experiment in the programmability of digital typography, and with imperfection. While the computer could be used to produce perfection in forms, van Blokland and van Rossum wanted to re-inject some humanity into digital type. Beowolf is a vectorial typeface, and the points defining its contours shift randomly when printed or typed. They designed three versions with varying degrees of randomness built into them. There's an interesting aesthetic parallel between Beowolf and Vojtech Preissig's Preissig Antikva (1923–1925).

Bifur. A.M. Cassandre, 1929. Designed for the French typefoundry Deberny & Peignot, this sans-serif typeface consists of thick characteristic lines, and thin hatched filling. The thick line in each character is selected to ensure recognizability, similar to the minimalist project of Bruno Munari's Essential. The N, for instance, is a thick diagonal line, with vertical shading forming triangles on either side of that diagonal. These shaded triangles take the place of the two vertical stems one would normally find on an N.

Bodoni. Giambattista Bodoni, 1788. A typeface inspired by the increased delicacy achieved by John Baskerville in his roman. Bodoni's Modern face has a perfectly vertical stress, strong contrast between thick and thin strokes, and extremely delicate, unbracketed serifs. In his *Manuale Typografico*, Bodoni illustrated his Modern type, and the large amount of white space that should be used in setting it.

Capitolium. Gerard Unger, 1998. Designed as a wayfinding typeface for the city of Rome, Capitolium is meant both to be highly legible and to capture some of the history of Roman inscription. A rare instance of serifs being used in wayfinding signage, the typeface draws inspiration from the work of Giovan Francesco Cresci, a sixteenth-century calligrapher.

Caslon. William Caslon, 1725. Inspired by the Dutch typefaces used by the Oxford University Press (known as The Fell Types), William Caslon's roman was designed to be a solid, legible, everyday typeface. With minimal contrast between thick and thin strokes; solid, short serifs—it was widely popular in England and the United States, where the typeface was used for John Dunlap's 1776 printing of the Declaration of Independence. Caslon's success was also attributable to the fact that William Caslon was one of the first to produce type in England, rather than importing type from the continent.

Caslon Bold. Keystone Type Foundry, 1905. An Old Style display typeface popularized by the Philadelphia-based Keystone Type Foundry. The typeface was involved in an unfair competition case, brought against Portland Publishing Co. for copying and selling Caslon Bold under the same name.

Century. Linn Boyd Benton, 1890. Designed for Theodore Lowe DeVinne's magazine *Century*. DeVinne argued his readers wanted something that was Modern, having tired of Caslon's angularity. The magazine's redesign required a bold face that would be legible in narrow columns. Benton achieved the appearance of bold modernity by using relatively high contrast between thick and thin strokes, but avoided purely hairline thin strokes, since this was seen as uncomfortable for reading lengthy texts. His design addressed the use of narrow columns not by making the typeface narrower, but rather by making its characters taller.

CMC7. 1960s. A Magnetic Ink Character Recognition (MICR) typeface, used primarily in European banking. Each character is made up of a combination of seven vertical stripes of equal width.

Comic Sans. Vincent Connare, 1994. Designed for Microsoft's program, Microsoft Bob. The program featured a cartoon dog with speech bubbles that were meant to guide users through Microsoft's new operating system, Windows. Comic Sans was designed for this dog's speech, and while it never made it into the program before release, the typeface was bundled into Microsoft products and later was identified as one of the eleven core web fonts. It is a friendly, open typeface, making it highly legible—particularly for the low-resolution screens and small sizes for which it was designed. Teachers and dyslexic readers have found use for it, but it is also subject to very vocal critiques; some have even called for it to be banned.

Computer Modern. Donald Knuth, 1978. A typeface designed by Donald Knuth using his METAFONT program, to be used in his digital typesetting program, T$_E$X. It is a Modern typeface, meaning that it is characterized by high contrast between thick and thin strokes, a perfectly vertical stress in bowled characters, and thin, largely unbracketed serifs.

Coueignoux's primitives. Philippe Coueignoux, ca. 1975. In the interest of developing computer-generated typography, Philippe Coueignoux began by dissecting existing typographic characters into a set of "primitives." These could then be combined using a set of rules of proportion and rules of construction to create fully formed characters. His work was later incorporated into the work of Barry Blesser and others in a refined program for defining and constructing digital type.

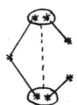

Cox et al.'s skeletons. Charles Cox, Barry Blesser, Murray Eden, and Philippe Coueignoux, 1982. A system for computer-generated typefaces, this proposal was developed by a group of computer scientists. They established a lexicon and grammar of strokes along with ways for those strokes to interact as a means of defining the construction of each character in the Latin alphabet. With this grammar, they formed skeletons and rules of transformation by which these recipes would result in typographic forms.

Data 70. Robert Newman, 1970. Designed for Lettraset, a dry-transfer type company, Data 70 mimics the aesthetic of MICR typefaces used in the banking industry. The characters are sans serif with rounded strokes of largely uniform width, apart from large tabs added along various sides or corners. The resulting aesthetic is a uniquely 1970s pulp science-fiction aesthetic.

De Stijl. Theo van Doesburg, 1919. A founder of the De Stijl movement, van Doesburg believed in the reduction of art to horizontal and vertical lines (though in some work he relaxed this, and controversially included diagonal lines as well). This typeface is a result of those beliefs—rendering familiar alphanumerical characters without diagonals or curves, and resulting in an unconventional set of typographic shapes. The elimination of curves and diagonals introduces new challenges in differentiating characters—for instance, the X and H now need to be distinguished from one another in a new way.

Dead History. P. Scott Makela, 1990. A hybrid typeface designed during a period often referred to as grunge design. Dead History draws attention to and challenges the traditional conventions of type—creating a typeface by cannibalizing elements from other typefaces (Linotype's Centennial and VAG Rounded), suturing them into a Frankenstein's monster of a face. Makela saw Dead History as an illustration of the computer's ability to serve as a tool for assemblage.

Decoder. Gerard Unger, 1992. A typeface introduced in the experimental type magazine *Fuse*, Decoder is a collection of typographic parts that the user can combine to produce their own characters. This modular typeface is far less extensive than earlier modulars—consisting only of seventeen parts. Unger's design seems less concerned, than earlier modulars, that typical characters can be formed out of the parts provided.

Demos. Gerard Unger, 1976. One of the first fully digital typefaces, for use with the Hell Digiset machine—a digital phototypesetting machine. As with Unger's typeface M.O.L., Demos has some rounded terminals and corners to anticipate light's tendency to round corners when it spreads. Its design also guards against the appearance of distortion at small sizes by minimizing the contrast between thick and thin strokes.

Didot. Firmin Didot, 1799. Member of a prominent printing family that served the French King, Firmin Didot developed type that reached new heights of refinement and rationality. Inspired by the stark contrast between thick and thin strokes found in Baskerville (and also by the work of Pierre-Simon Fournier), Didot is a Modern typeface with even greater contrast between its strokes. In addition, its serifs are so delicate and unbracketed that they at times seem to disappear into the significant amount of white space surrounding these characters.

DIN 1451. Linotype Co., ca. 1931. Designed for the Deutsches Institut für Normung, this typeface was meant to standardize the display of text on street signage, technical drawings, and vehicle identification. A clean, simplified sans serif with a relatively high x-height, it helped to set standards for wayfinding typefaces designed after it. In its narrow and mid-width version, the bowled characters have flattened sides, contributing to the typeface's efficient appearance. Since its introduction it has become emblematic of the aesthetic of German infrastructure.

Dyslexie. Christian Boer, 2011. Designed by Christian Boer, who himself has dyslexia, this typeface is intended to address some of the symptoms of dyslexia. It weighs down the base of characters to avoid the appearance of floating. It opens counters, and eliminates easily confused features of characters. It is a sans-serif face, and varies the height of peaks and valleys in characters like n, m, or v, w, y. It also introduces explicit distinctions between mirror letters—b and d, p and q. Results on Dyslexie's efficacy are inconclusive.

E13B. 1958. A Magnetic Ink Character Recognition (MICR) typeface, primarily used in American banking, this typeface had to balance the creation of completely unique characters for the MICR scanner to read with recognizable forms for humans to read.

Emperor. Zuzana Licko, 1985. When Apple released the Macintosh 128k, Licko was among the first to use the computer for typographic design work. Her earliest typefaces designed for the computer's 72 dpi resolution were bitmap typefaces that made no attempt to hide the aesthetic of the pixel. Emperor is a typeface that explores how typographic shapes change as they scale up and down in size. The point size of each character describes how tall the character is (e.g., uppercase in Emperor 8 is eight pixels tall), but the proportions of the stroke width and counter size do not change with the height of the character. Instead, each character in Emperor maintains a stroke width of one pixel and a counter width of two pixels.

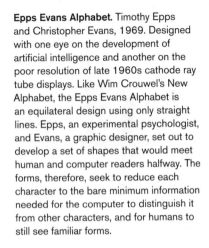

Epps Evans Alphabet. Timothy Epps and Christopher Evans, 1969. Designed with one eye on the development of artificial intelligence and another on the poor resolution of late 1960s cathode ray tube displays. Like Wim Crouwel's New Alphabet, the Epps Evans Alphabet is an equilateral design using only straight lines. Epps, an experimental psychologist, and Evans, a graphic designer, set out to develop a set of shapes that would meet human and computer readers halfway. The forms, therefore, seek to reduce each character to the bare minimum information needed for the computer to distinguish it from other characters, and for humans to still see familiar forms.

Essential. Bruno Munari, 1935. A modernist reduction of typographic forms to their bare necessity, Munari's set of characters is an attempt to limit these forms to the lowest amount of graphic information required to identify each character as distinct from others. It is an early attempt at what would be explored later in Barbara Butterweck's Typeface F, Dear John; and in Phil Baines's serifed version, You Can Read Me.

Farrington 12L/12F Selfchek. Farrington Manufacturing Company, ca. 1966. Developed for optical character recognition scanning technology, this typeface is a typewriter font, uppercase only, and was made to be read by the Farrington 3030 machine. In its design it seems to sit somewhere between the unconventional forms of OCR-A and more readable, but potentially ambiguous, forms of OCR-B.

FE-Schrift. Karlgeorg Hoefer, 1980. Commissioned by the German Ministry of Transportation for use on license plates, this typeface was designed not only to be read easily from a distance (and on a moving vehicle), but to prevent the counterfeiting of plates (FE stands for *Fälschungserschwerende*, "anti-counterfeiting" in German). To achieve this, similar characters (like O and Q, P and R, E and F) were designed so that one can't be transformed into another. This creates a typeface with unusual and often unpleasant forms, but the typeface has effectively been used for license plates in the European Union since the 1990s.

Fibonacci. Tobias Frere-Jones, 1994. Published in *Fuse* 10, an issue of Neville Brody and Jon Wozencroft's experimental design magazine, Fibonacci imagines what would be left of a typeface if one removed the alphabet. The resulting forms are orthogonal lines (in the uppercase), diagonal lines (in the lowercase), and curved lines (in place of numerals 0–9). The directions and proportions for these lines are apparently drawn from Fibonacci's Golden Section.

Fonetik Alfabet. Herbert Bayer, 1959. Designed by Bayer after he had moved to the United States, Fonetik Alfabet is a modernist sans-serif typeface that seeks to establish a more accurate phonetic representation of (primarily) the English language. This involved not only altering the way words are spelled to more accurately illustrate their pronunciation, but also simplifying characters to more essentialist forms, and creating new characters that would stand in for commonly occurring letter combinations like "ion" or "ing."

Fregio Mecano. Giulio da Milano, 1933. Designed for the prominent Italian type foundry Nebiolo, Fregio Mecano is a modular typeface. It contains twenty parts that can be combined to form typographic characters. The parts are covered in grid lines, so that when they are combined the joints between individual pieces seem to disappear.

Futura. Paul Renner, 1927. A geometric sans serif designed in the age of New Typography—a set of design principles that favored geometry, engineering, asymmetry, the sans serif, and forms shaped by their intended function—Futura is based on simple geometric forms of circles, triangles, and rectangles. Renner did not see this as a glorification of math, but rather as an attempt to lead typographic forms back to their origins. Renner designed a lowercase r that consisted only of a vertical rectangle with a small circle to its right; and a lowercase g that consisted of three shapes stacked on top of one another—a triangle at the base, a circle in the center, and a small square at the top. The typeface was released with these unconventional characters as alternates—the base font was more reined in, and has experienced a long and prolific life in graphic design and space travel.

Georgia. Matthew Carter, 1996. Inspired by a nineteenth-century style of serifed type known as Scotch roman, Georgia was designed specifically to work at small sizes on low-resolution computer screens. To meet the legibility requirements of suboptimal resolution, Carter designed Georgia to have a high x-height and thicker thin strokes than a traditional Scotch roman would have. The typeface has become a ubiquitous typeface in the digital age, given its inclusion in Microsoft software and its designation as one of the eleven core web fonts.

Goudy Old Style. Frederic W. Goudy, 1915.
An Old Style text typeface designed by one
of America's most prolific and enthusiastic
type designers, this typeface was initiated
by the American Type Founders (ATF),
and Goudy did have to compromise on
some character forms—such as shortened
descenders on characters like p and y. It
is a generous typeface in keeping with
the style favored in the private press
movement of the day, but is also a highly
functional face that is still used frequently in
book publishing today.

Gutenberg's textura. Johannes Gutenberg
(and possibly Peter Schöffer), ca. 1450.
Used for the printing of Gutenberg's Bible
(often referred to as the 42-Line Bible), this
blackletter type was meant to mimic the
calligraphic style then practiced by scribes
in Germany. It has a steady rhythm, created
by the regularity of its vertical strokes,
and the shortness of both ascenders and
descenders. As a design, Gutenberg's
textura illustrates the extent to which
Gutenberg wanted his typographic shapes
to blend in with the aesthetic of existing
books on the market.

Haettenschweiler. Microsoft, ca. 1995.
Based on the typeface Schmalfette Grotesk
designed by Walter Haettenschweiler in
1954, this condensed, bold sans serif was
a style popular in the late '50s and 1960s.
Schmalfette Grotesk became a popular
typeface for magazine headlines in the '60s.
Microsoft designed a version of the face in
the mid-1990s and included it in its word
processing software. The typeface has
been used in psychological studies testing
the effects of disfluency on learning.

Helvetica. Max Miedinger and Eduard Hofmann, 1957. Based on Akzidenz Grotesk, a late nineteenth-century typeface that enjoyed newfound fame among the Swiss modernist designers in the mid-twentieth century. Helvetica, originally called Neue Haas Grotesk, was meant to be an updated version of the traditional European grotesk (sans serif). It is known for its expertly designed harmony between figure and ground, its clean, friendly appearance, and its legibility. Today the typeface is one of the most famous in the world, used frequently in corporate branding, government branding and documentation, and wayfinding systems. Some view Helvetica as the culmination of sans-serif design—perfect legibility and neutrality—while others view it as overused, lacking in creativity when used today, and lacking the necessary variation among characters that aids reading. Regardless of opinion, it remains among the most omnipresent typefaces in our daily lives.

Hypnopaedia. Zuzana Licko, 1997. This font (possibly better understood as a collection of ornaments) was designed to make a point about copyright law in the United States. In the US copyright system, typefaces are not eligible for protection, in large part due to a failure to distinguish between a typeface and the alphabet. To illustrate that typographic characters are shapes able to exist independent of language, Licko took characters from various Emigre typefaces and rotated and repeated them, transforming them into complex patterns. Distancing characters in this way from their ability to signify, Hypnopaedia argues and illustrates that type is shape first, and letter only second.

Glossary of Typefaces and Type Systems

Ionic. Mergenthaler Linotype, 1925. A newspaper typeface of a style (Ionic) first developed in the mid-nineteenth century, Ionic has a relatively high x-height, short ascenders and descenders, and sturdy, thick serifs partly inspired by the slab serifs of the nineteenth century. Ionic was included in Linotype's "legibility group," a number of typefaces marketed as maximizing legibility. This typeface was adopted by the *Newark Evening News* in 1926, and a similar typeface produced by Intertype was used by the *New York Times.*

ITSYLF. Harry Mergler and Paul Vargo, 1968. An early computer program for creating digital typefaces, ITSYLF had both an automatic version and a manual version. In the automatic version, a designer could input certain parameters for the character E, and the computer would generate two sets of twenty-four characters from that information (one with serifs, one without). The designer could then manually adjust any parameters of individual characters that they found problematic.

Jenson's Roman. Nicolas Jenson, 1470. Often considered the first fully roman typeface, Jenson's Roman would have a significant influence on most serifed typefaces that followed it. Like other early romans, its lowercase is modeled on Carolingian calligraphy, and the upper on Roman capitals. Though these two sets of forms are not fully integrated, the typeface overall is cleaner and more delicate than other romans of its time. Many of its forms still bear the influence of the pen in its curves.

Kabel. Rudolf Koch, ca. 1928. Similar to Edward Johnston's Railway Sans, Kabel is a sans serif designed by a man with calligraphic sensibilities. Rudolf Koch was a prominent calligrapher and teacher, and his sans-serif bears some details drawn from the history of that lettering art. The a and g are double story, the crossbar on the e is slanted (or smiling). Named in honor of industrial technologies, Kabel experiments with radical forms—such as an f with a unilateral crossbar and a radically unconventional g.

Keedy Sans. Jeffrey Keedy, 1989. A hybrid typeface designed by one of the most iconoclastic designers of the grunge design period, Keedy Sans breaks numerous conventions of typographic design. Most notably, it plays with the principle that a typeface is a set of alphanumerical characters united by repeating graphic elements. In this sans serif, some terminals are flat, others rounded, and still others are angular. Certain characters, like the t and f, seem to hover above the baseline rather than sitting firmly on it. A vigorous critic of the persistence of modernist design, Keedy takes aim with this typeface at the sanctity of the modernist sans serif.

Kombinationsschrift. Josef Albers, 1931. In this modular and stencil-inspired typeface designed by Bauhaus instructor Josef Albers, the characters are constructed out of ten basic forms (*Grundformen*): a dot, vertical rectangles of two sizes, three sizes of vertical strokes with two rounded corners, and four sizes of vertical strokes with one rounded corner. This is a reductive typeface inspired by the regularity of machine production, and intended to be used in and around physical constructions, rather than in books.

Glossary of Typefaces and Type Systems

M.O.L. Gerard Unger, 1974. A wayfinding typeface designed for Amsterdam's metro system, M.O.L. is a sans-serif typeface with relatively large counters to aid legibility. Its characters are also rounded to create harmony across printed signs and illuminated signs (where the light emerging through cutout characterforms tends to round corners).

Magneto. Leslie Cabarga, 1995. This is a display typeface based on streamlined lettering produced in industrial design of the 1940s or '50s (e.g., metal lettering on cars or refrigerators). Magneto has been referenced in arguments in favor of a relativistic application of copyright protection for typefaces, as a typeface that is notably designed (and therefore worthy of protection), rather than obvious.

Martin Luther. Harald Geisler, 2017. As with Geisler's previous typefaces—Sigmund Freud and Albert Einstein—this typeface, based on the handwriting of Martin Luther, contains numerous versions of each letter and numeral in order to better capture the natural variations in form that occur when humans write.

Meander. Maxim Zhukov, 1972. In this experimental typeface for both Latin and Cyrillic, meant to standardize the formation of the type family, each rounded (meandering) character is designed within a sixteen-unit grid and out of a number of stripes, depending on its weight. The lightest version of a character will be one stripe thick; the heaviest will be seven stripes thick.

METAFONT. Donald Knuth, ca. 1979. In this computer program for designing digital typefaces, a (metaphorical) elliptical pen defines the characters with a center line and contour. The user of METAFONT controls the design of the typeface by varying parameters (like pen angle or serif length). Knuth improved the program over time by adding more parameters, and he imagined that such a program would someday be able to create every imaginable typeface—an idea challenged by the cognitive scientist and philosopher Douglas Hofstadter, but which may be given new life by the recent development of variable font files.

Minuscule. Thomas Huot-Marchand, 2005. This type family explores the formal adjustments required for successful legibility at point sizes 6 and smaller. Basing the design on the pioneering legibility research of Émile Javal, Huot-Marchand designed characters that become increasingly angular as their sizes decrease. Counters and apertures are opened up as the sizes decrease, except for 2 point, where certain counters are entirely filled in.

Mister K. Julia Sysmäläinen, 2008. Designed by a philologist, Mister K is a typeface based on the handwriting of Franz Kafka, which takes advantage of OpenType's accommodation of large character sets by designing multiple versions of each character. This allows the typeface to vary which version of Kafka's e, or G, or f is used at any moment—allowing this handwriting typeface to capture more of the variability of how we write.

Mistral. Roger Excoffon, 1953. Designed for Fonderie Olive, Mistral is meant to mimic the fluidity with which people write. One of the challenges historically faced by handwriting-inspired typefaces is that they tend to fall into something akin to the uncanny valley found in robotics and AI. That is, they look more like handwriting than most type, but because they are mass produced, because every instance of e on the page looks identical, they are clearly not produced by a human hand. Mistral addresses this challenge a bit through the imperfect contours of its shapes and the asymmetrical length of strokes in a single character (like the M pictured here). It has been used in psychological disfluency studies.

Molecular Typography. Woody Leslie, 2015. This proposal was published in the form of an art book masquerading as a serious primer on the emerging field of "molecular typography." Attributed to the fictional author and scholar H. F. Henderson, the book lays out the systematic way in which typographic characters form out of atomic parts, and thanks to positive and negative charges—forming bonds similar to those in chemistry. Though it is not unlike modular typefaces, and the early digital programs that came before it, Molecular Typography does not approach its definition of typography's constituent parts with as much rigor as these other projects.

Monotype Corsiva. Patricia Saunders, 1991. This italic typeface is based on the calligraphy of Ludovico degli Arrighi, a late fifteenth- to early sixteenth-century scribe. It has been used in psychological studies exploring the effects of disfluency on learning.

Myriad. Robert Slimbach and Carol Twombly, 1992. According to Robert Slimbach, he and Carol Twombly set out to design a sans serif for Adobe that was likely to be completely overlooked. They wanted a clean, readable, Humanist sans serif, but with no exceptional features that would distract from its functionality. It makes sense, then, that this face was used in psychological fluency studies as a fluent typeface (one that would not impede reading in any way).

Neil Bold. Wayne Stettler, 1966. This display typeface, originally released by Typositor (a phototypesetting machine), enjoyed popularity primarily in designing album covers and book covers. It is a condensed bold sans serif, a style popular in the 1960s. The typeface has since been digitized and its character set expanded.

New Alphabet. Wim Crouwel, 1967. Troubled by the poor quality of early cathode ray tube typesetters, Crouwel set out to design a typeface that would better fit the technology, by following the logic of the digital technology's own display. The forms he designed were constructed within a grid using only vertical, horizontal lines, and 45° angles. Designed as roughly equilateral forms with no curves, they would experience less distortion when scaled up or down on a rasterized screen. It is a single-case typeface, with capitalization indicated with the addition of a horizontal line at the top of the character. Crouwel did not expect the typeface to gain wide use—given its lack of readability, and its unconventional forms for some characters—but it has found some use, and is a conceptually significant typeface.

Glossary of Typefaces and Type Systems

Noto. Google and Monotype, 2012–present. Shown here is Noto Sans, the sans-serif version of the Latin script in Google's massive Noto project. In a collaboration with Monotype, Google set out to design typefaces for every script currently supported by Unicode. In the interest of making more information and expression available to more people around the globe, the project has in some instances produced the first-ever typographic rendering of some scripts. The project has also come under scrutiny for the ways it has rolled out its typefaces, which scripts are and aren't included, and in some instances for the renderings themselves.

Oakland. Zuzana Licko, 1984. A typeface designed for the low resolution (72 dpi) of Apple's Macintosh 128k computer, Oakland embraces the aesthetic of the pixel—rather than trying to disguise it through a technique like anti-aliasing. It takes up the challenge of designing curves and diagonals out of a grid of pixels, and even explores nonessential design elements. In the d, for instance, the top of the bowl does not meet the stem, a design flourish that pushes the low-resolution type beyond mere utility.

OCR-A. ATF, 1965. Designed to meet the reading abilities of optical character recognition scanners as defined by the US Bureau of Standards, this is a mostly sans-serif typeface, with uniform stroke-widths. To eliminate ambiguity among its characters (for the sake of the computer reader), numerous characters must take on unconventional forms. For instance, the distinction between zero and O is established by making the zero a rectangle with rounded corners, and the O a diamond-shape, again with rounded corners.

OCR-B. Adrian Frutiger, 1968. Frutiger was tasked with designing a more aesthetically pleasing typeface than OCR-A that could still be used in optical character recognition. In the interest of avoiding ambiguity, he set out limitations—no character could appear within another (e.g., the I couldn't appear inside the T), and there could be no more than 7 percent agreement between two characters. It is monospaced, as was common for typewriter faces.

Optica Normal. Manolo Guerrero, 2010. This typeface uses orthographic lines to cloud the distinction between figure and ground. Its characters emerge from the ground thanks to the varying direction of the lines used. Though low in readability, the resulting typeface is still legible.

Patrona Grotesk. V. Kánsky, 1931. This modular typeface is made up of thirty-eight basic parts that can be combined to form numerous versions of each character (for instance, its type specimen shows five different versions of the P). These parts do not meet completely, producing instead a stencil-like character set that allows the constituent parts of each character to remain visible.

Peignot. A. M. Cassandre, 1937. Though Peignot is a typeface with two cases, the lowercase combines forms from both cases. Most notable is the use of an uppercase Q in the lowercase, and an h that combines the two vertical strokes of the uppercase H with the left ascender of the lowercase h. Like other sans serifs of its day, Peignot was meant to be a rational typeface that eliminated excesses of design in the interest of clarity and legibility.

Glossary of Typefaces and Type Systems

Prototype. Jonathan Barnbrook, 1997. A hybrid typeface, Prototype brings together elements from other typefaces into an unsettling set of characters. In this instance, two of Eric Gill's typefaces—Gill Sans (1928) and the serifed typeface Perpetua (1925)—are combined.

Putty Peeps. Richard Moore, 2008. In this novelty typeface, each character is made up of a lumpy cartoon figure. The legal scholar Jacqueline Lipton references this typeface as an example of obvious creativity in type design, and therefore as a typeface that challenges the current US attitudes toward not extending copyright to typefaces.

Qandus. Kristyan Sarkis, Laura Mesegeur, and Juan Luis Blanco, 2017. A multiscript type family developed as part of the Khatt Foundation's matchmaking project, this project brings designers and scholars together to design across the boundaries of language and script. In this instance designers collaborated on a type family that would serve Northern Africa—combining Arabic (which was the design's starting point), Latin, and Tifinagh (a script used for Berber languages). The influence of the Arabic script as the design's starting point can be seen most notably in the more fluid terminals that appear in the Latin and Tifinagh forms.

Railway Sans. Edward Johnston, 1916. Designed by famed calligrapher Edward Johnston for London's underground system; this typeface was intended to tie together the system's aesthetics, which varied from station to station. Its forms are based on the ideal proportions of Roman inscriptions, and the stroke width/height ratio of Ibn Muqlah. It is a sans serif, and helped to set the standard that sans are preferable to serifed faces for wayfinding.

Rattera. Jonathan Barnbrook, 2012. This strange typeface was designed for the experimental type magazine *Fuse*. Barnbrook, long a provocative type designer, based this typeface on the idea of a new philosophical alphabet, purportedly proposed by a schizophrenic artist, Alfred Rattera. This entirely new alphabet was meant not merely to stand in for existing letters, but to introduce to the public an entirely new way of thinking about, communicating, and organizing the world around us. Rattera allegedly imagined his philosophical alphabet would consist of many thousands of characters, and would be released to the public gradually to give them time to adjust to it. While Barnbrook's characters are not as numerous, and are not being rolled out in the fashion imagined, the typeface still raises important questions about the relationship between typography, language, and thought.

R

Romain du Roi. The Bignon Commission, Philippe Grandjean and Louis Simmoneau, ca. 1695. This typeface is generally seen as transitional between Old Style (or Garalde) typefaces and Modern (or Didone) faces. Designed by a committee for the French King Louis XIV, Romain du Roi was made for the exclusive use of the king's Imprimerie Royale. It was nonetheless influential in the future development of roman type. The nineteenth-century printer William Morris identified its design as the moment when the calligrapher was left behind as a model in favor of the engineer. The committee's assignment was to design the ideal typeface based on mathematic and scientific principles. The committee's designs were etched by Louis Simonneau, but in cutting the punches, Philippe Grandjean had to diverge from their idealized designs.

Safari Braille and Safari from A-to-B.
Underware, 2018. Variable fonts designed
by the type firm Underware (Akiem
Helmling, Bas Jacobs, and Sami Kortemäki).
In Safari Braille, the variable font is able to
slide between Latin characters and their
corresponding Braille character. In Safari
from A-to-B, users are able to slide
between individual Latin characters in
the font.

San Francisco. Susan Kare, 1984. Susan
Kare designed the first typefaces and icons
for Apple's Macintosh 128k computer. All
of her typefaces were named after American
cities, and San Francisco is a fanciful
typeface with wildly varying characters.
The aesthetic is meant to mimic the cutout
letters associated with ransom notes. In
recent years, Apple has designed another
typeface named San Francisco, but this new
face is a clean sans serif meant to replace
Helvetica Neue in Apple's operating system.

Shatter. Vic Carless, 1973. A typeface
designed to look like it's being read through
shattered glass, Shatter is based on
Helvetica. Douglas Hofstadter used it as
an example of a typeface that would not
be able to be formed simply by changing
the parameters of another typeface (like
Helvetica). Shatter involves more radical
changes to Helvetica (changes to the
contours, introduction of extra negative
spaces) than a computer parameterization
(like Knuth's METAFONT) would allow.

Sigmund Freud. Harald Geisler, 2013. Based on the handwriting of Sigmund Freud, this was the first of Geisler's large-scale handwriting-based typefaces (see also Albert Einstein, and Martin Luther). To capture more of the natural variation that occurs when humans write, Geisler designed numerous versions of each letter and numeral. As the user types, the software selects different versions, so in the end a page of text will show a variety of f's, Q's, and so on.

Snell Roundhand. Matthew Carter, 1966. Based on the seventeenth-century calligraphic work of Charles Snell, this script typeface took advantage of the technological capabilities of photo-typesetting. The flexibility of film (as compared to metal) allowed not only for more fluid, rounded forms, but also for seamless linking of adjacent characters in the lowercase.

Superunion blockchain type. Superunion, 2018. Superunion designed this typeface for the branding of the cybersecurity company Elliptic. What this design has to do with blockchain technology is unclear, but its play with the distinction between figure and ground does vaguely suggest the kinds of detective work Elliptic is involved in.

Sweynheym and Pannartz's Roman. Konrad Sweynheym and Arnold Pannartz, 1465. This was one of the first roman (rather than blackletter) typefaces cut. Sweynheym and Pannartz were German printers invited by a monastery to set up a printing press in Subiaco, Italy (this typeface is sometimes referred to as simply Subiaco). Diverging from the contemporary style in their native Germany, this typeface takes after the style of calligraphy practiced by scribes in Southern Europe—known as Carolingian. This style is generally rounder and more diverse in its forms than blackletter styles (like Gutenberg's textura).

Glossary of Typefaces and Type Systems

Systemschrift. Kurt Schwitters, 1927. Similar to Tschichold's universal and Bayer's later Fonetik Alfabet, this typeface was an attempt by Kurt Schwitters to create a more systematic alphabet. He produced a few versions, some more readily legible than others. An example of the most systematic and radical version can be seen on the left. He sought to create more symmetry between the relationship of characters phonetically, and their visual relationship—making all vowels rounded, for instance, to signify their phonetic relation to one another.

Template Gothic. Barry Deck, 1990. Inspired by a handmade sign Deck saw at a laundromat, Template Gothic was intended to be imperfect, to have human qualities rather than computer-produced perfection. It ended up being one of the most iconic typefaces of the 1990s.

Times New Roman. Stanley Morison, 1931. Morison created this typeface for a redesign of the *Times* of London, basing it on recent research into legibility and a set of "legibility typefaces" that Monotype advertised earlier in the twentieth century. It has a relatively high x-height and ascenders and descenders that stay close to the body of its characters. Though they only had exclusive right to use the typeface for one year, the *Times* used the face for forty years before beginning to make small adjustments to it. It has been digitized, and served as the default in Microsoft's word processing software for several years, contributing to its ubiquity in contemporary society as well. It should be noted, though, that the name is more recognizable to the general public than its design is.

Trebuchet. Vincent Connare, 1996. A typeface designed for screen-reading, Trebuchet is a Humanist sans serif designed for Microsoft. Inspired by numerous sans serifs before it—Akzidenz Grotesk, Gills Sans, and the highway lettering found in the United States (generally referred to as Highway Gothic)—this is a typeface focused on legibility at small sizes and on low-resolution screens. It has been bundled into Microsoft software and is one of the eleven core web fonts set out by Microsoft in 1996.

Tschichold universal. Jan Tschichold, 1929. Tschichold's universal typeface is a simplified, geometric, single-case sans serif similar to others like Bayer's universal. However, in addition to a regular universal typeface, Tschichold also designed a phonetic version. Here he eliminated redundant letters from words, expressed some sounds more literally (e.g., replacing the "eu" in "neu" with "oi"), and introduced a few new characters meant to stand in for letter combinations commonly found in German, like "sch."

Twin. Erik van Blokland and Just van Rossum, 2003. Designed for the city of Minneapolis, Twin is meant to be a graphic identity for the city, but also to be variable depending on the local weather. Designed with multiple versions of most characters, a cold day will be expressed with harsher characters with more pronounced, slab serifs; a warm day will be expressed with rounder, more playful, and more generally sans-serif characters.

Glossary of Typefaces and Type Systems

Typeface F, Dear John. Barbara Butterweck, 1992. A radically reductive typeface, Butterweck has reduced each character (in the uppercase) to a single essential form. In the B, that essential form is simply the section where the two bowls meet; in the S, it is only a section of the bottom curve. This design tests the limits of our ability to read characters when a significant amount of formal information has been removed.

Univers. Adrian Frutiger, 1957. A Swiss modernist sans serif designed for the French foundry Deberny & Peignot, Univers is inspired by Akzidenz Grotesk, a nineteenth-century sans-serif, but is a more stripped-down design. Still, with its high x-height and relatively open counters, it achieves a clean elegance. Used widely today in graphic design and wayfinding, it is perhaps best known for its systematic introduction not merely as a typeface, but as a type family. Frutiger released the design in twenty-one variations of weight, slant, and spacing, intending for this typeface to serve any need a designer might have in a single project—eliminating the need to mix typefaces.

Univers Revolved. Ji Lee, ca. 2004. This typeface takes the characters from Adrian Frutiger's Univers and revolves them around a central axis, creating the appearance of 3D forms. Apart from being an experiment with multidimensionality in type design, Univers Revolved was used by Ji Lee to publish a picture book. This suggests the possibility of learning to read an unconventional alphabet in the same ways we learn to read our current alphabet.

Universal. Herbert Bayer, 1925. A geometric sans serif typeface commissioned by Walter Gropius and designed by the Bauhaus's first director of "Printing and Advertising," Bayer's universal typeface has only one case; the uppercase is eliminated, because Bayer found it to be unnecessary. The forms of characters are similarly stripped of excesses and redundancies. As its name suggests, this stripping down of typographic forms was seen by Bayer as a means of achieving universality of design—a single typeface or type family that would possess universal applicability across languages.

Variex. Zuzana Licko and Rudy VanderLans, 1988. A typeface that experiments with the continued legibility of characters as they gain and lose weight, Variex is designed as a system that builds characters up with a series of concentric stripes. Around the single stripe of Variex light, each weight adds a stripe on either side (regular adds one stripe on either side of the central stripe, heavy adds two stripes on either side). As the weight increases and their contours change, the characters threaten to become illegible or ambiguous.

Von Speyer's Roman. Johann and Vindelin von Speyer, 1470. Johann von Speyer was granted a monopoly in printing when he set up shop in Venice in 1468—a monopoly that ended two years later when he died and his brother Vindelin took over his press's production. The typeface they used is among the first romans, modeled on Carolingian calligraphy; it gains more distance from the scribe's pen than Sweynheym and Pannartz's Roman, but is not nearly as open and delicate as Jenson's Roman. Though attractive, their Roman appears to be more of a work-horse typeface.

You Can Read Me. Phil Baines, 1995.
Initially designed as Can You Read Me? for *Fuse* magazine, this typeface experiments with the limits of legibility: it cuts out as much detail in a character as can be cut, while still allowing the character to be recognized. It is similar to Munari's Essential, but unlike his essentialist typeface or Barbara Butterweck's 1992 Typeface F, Dear John, Baines's typeface is serifed. In 2013, designer Sam Barclay used this typeface in a book designed to attempt to give nondyslexic readers an idea of what it's like to have dyslexia.

Zapf Dingbats. Hermann Zapf, 1978.
This font of symbols was originally released by International Typeface Corporation (ITC). Zapf designed about 1,000 symbols, of which ITC selected 360 for release. In 1985, Zapf Dingbats was included with Apple's LaserWriter printer and became a popular font for desktop publishing. The symbols are drawn from the history of printer's ornamentation and specialized symbols. Its most famous use was likely when David Carson used it to set an interview with the musician Bryan Ferry in *Ray Gun* magazine in 1994.

Notes

Chapter 1

1. George Orwell, "In Front of Your Nose," in *Facing Unpleasant Facts: Narrative Essays*, ed. George Packer (New York: Mariner Books 2009), 213.

2. This story is told, for instance, in Josiah Henry Benton, *John Baskerville: Type-founder and Printer, 1706–1775* (Boston: Marymount Press, 1914), 13–14; John Boardley, "History of Typography: Transitional. Part 3: Siècle des Lumières," *I Love Typography*, Jan. 17, 2008, http://ilovetypography.com/2008/01/17/type -terms-transitional-type/; Simon Garfield, *Just My Type* (New York: Gotham Books, 2011), 102; Simon Loxley, *Type: The Secret History of Letters* (New York: I.B. Tauris, 2004), 48–49; Philip B. Meggs, *A History of Graphic Design* (Hoboken, NJ: Wiley, 2012), 130; Errol Morris, "Hear, All Ye People; Hearken O Earth (Part 2)," *New York Times*, August 9, 2012; Talbot Baines Reed, *A History of the Old English Letter Foundries: With Notes Historical and Biographical* (London: Elliot Stock, 1887), 280. The story comes originally from Benjamin Franklin himself, who recounted it to Baskerville in a letter estimated to be from 1760. https:// founders.archives.gov/documents/Franklin/01-09-02-0085.

3. For more contemporary examples of this typographic passion, consider the IKEA font scandal of 2010, or the general ire that any mention of Comic Sans or Papyrus conjures up (for a humorous example, see Julio Torres's skit "Papyrus," *Saturday Night Live*, September 30, 2017).

4. The serifs in Baskerville are generally known to be more delicate than in Caslon, though because of ink spread, this can vary.

5. Ferdinand de Saussure, *Course in General Linguistics*, trans. Roy Harris (Chicago: Open Court, 2008), 118.

6. The French philosopher Roland Barthes greatly expanded de Saussure's idea of (linguistic) signification, arguing that everything—from photographs, to children's toys, to Einstein's brain—signifies. See Barthes's book *Mythologies*, trans. Annette Lavers (New York: Hill & Wang, 1972). It would follow from this that the design of type is involved in signification in some way as well. That being said, in his own analysis of the visual rhetoric in advertisements, Barthes ignores the signification involved in the design of advertising copy, focusing only on the verbal message there. See "Rhetoric of the Image," in *Image, Music, Text*, trans. Stephen Heath (New York: Hill & Wang, 1977), 32–51.

7. One of the recent and interesting trends in typographic branding involves organizations and companies (often, but not always tech) developing their own bespoke typefaces. For example: Nokia Pure (2011); Intel Clear (2013); Google's

Robot, and Product Sans, and Apple's San Francisco (2015; not to be confused with Susan Kare's earlier San Francisco, 1984); Samsung One (2016); BBC Reith, HP Simplified, IBM Plex, Sony SST, and YouTube Sans (2017); Airbnb Cereal, Coca-Cola's TCCC Unity, Netflix Sans, and Uber Move (2018); Alibaba Sans, PBS Sans (2019); Durex's One Night Sans, and Goldman Sans (2020); and poking fun at all of these faces, Arby's Saucy_AF (2018).

8. The designer Rudy VanderLans argues this point in his writing on copyright. He notes that the "alphabet is a system, but it's an idea that exists without a single fixed expression. It materializes only after the letters have been fully rendered." See VanderLans, "The Trouble with Type," in *Texts on Type: Critical Writings on Typography*, ed. Steven Heller and Philip B. Meggs (New York: Allworth Press, 2001), 226.

9. Vilém Flusser, "On Typography," unpublished essay, n.d. (Flusser Archiv, Universität der Künste Berlin), 1; Walter Ong, *Orality and Literacy: The Technologizing of the Word* (London: Routledge, 2000), 118.

10. While both China and Korea had movable type printing long before Gutenberg developed his method, it did not, for various reasons, set off a comparable revolution in these countries. Neither did print in Asia have a direct influence on the development of print in Europe. So, there may be reason to measure the medium's daily social influence starting from the mid-fifteenth century. It did, however, also take typography a long while to become a center of daily life for the majority of society, even in the West.

11. In interviews, Massimo Vignelli and Ken Garland have independently argued that they have a handful of typefaces they use, and need no more. See Gary Hustwit, dir., *Helvetica* (2007; Brooklyn, NY: Plexifilm, 2010), DVD; and Briar Levit, dir., *Graphic Means A History of Graphic Design Production* (Austin, TX: Tugg, 2018), DVD, respectively. The design of ever more typefaces is, for them, unnecessary.

12. Concerning the idea of values in typographic designs: Stanley Morison's *Politics and Script* (Oxford: Clarendon Press, 1972) is an exploration of the force exerted on characterforms (both typographic and pretypographic) by different forms of authority—state, religious, class, and so on.

13. N. Katherine Hayles, a critical theorist working at the intersection of literature and technology, has argued that there is an increased need for the teaching of "deep attention," as opposed to the "hyper attention" frequently demanded by our contemporary technologies. She makes this argument without vilifying hyper attention, merely arguing that while previously a balance of these two forms of attention could be assumed, today extra work is required to maintain the capacity for deep attention. See Hayles's "Hyper and Deep Attention," *Profession* (2007): 187–199.

14. Orwell writes about this struggle in "In Front of Your Nose." But he also links the importance of thinking for oneself to the formal (though not typographic) concerns of writing in his essay "Politics and the English Language," in *Why I Write* (New York: Penguin, 2004), 102–120. He maintains, as does this book's view of typography, that how an idea is expressed can be as important (or as politically significant) as what that idea is.

15. The infinite possibility of typographic variations exists within the limits of technological capabilities and, to a lesser extent, the limits of legibility. But this will be discussed in more depth later.

16. On history, the following are a good starting place: Lewis Blackwell, *20th Century Type* (New Haven: Yale University Press, 2004); Robin Kinross, *Modern Typography: An Essay in Critical History* (London: Hyphen Press, 2004); Alexander Lawson, *Anatomy of a Typeface* (Boston: David R. Godine, 1990); Paul McNeil, *The Visual History of Type* (London: Laurence King Publishing, 2017); Daniel Berkeley Updike, *Printing Types: Their History, Forms, and Use* (New Castle, DE: Oak Knoll Press, 2001). On technique, the following are a good place to start: Robert Bringhurst, *Elements of Typographic Style* (Point Roberts, WA: Hartley & Marks, 2004); Jost Hochuli, *Detail in Typography* (London: Hyphen Press, 2008). Steven Heller has also compiled copious amounts of typographic examples in the approximately 50 billion books he's authored and edited.

17. The field of bibliography is expansive and works tend to be highly specific. For an introductory glance, see Philip Gaskell's *A New Introduction to Bibliography* (New Castle, DE: Oak Knoll Press, 1995); or D. F. McKenzie, *Bibliography and the Sociology of Texts* (New York: Cambridge University Press, 1999).

18. The work of Jerome McGann is key here. See, e.g., *Black Riders: The Visible Language of Modernism* (Princeton: Princeton University Press, 1993) and *The Textual Condition* (Princeton: Princeton University Press, 1991). The theoretical basis of this work is oftentimes Jacques Derrida, *Of Grammatology*, trans. Gayatri Chakravorty Spivak (Baltimore: Johns Hopkins University Press, 1997). More typographically centered work includes Johanna Drucker, *The Visible Word: Experimental Typography and Modern Art* (Chicago: University of Chicago Press, 1994); Mary Ellen Solt, ed., *Concrete Poetry: A World View* (Bloomington: Indiana University Press, 1970); and Stefan Themerson, "Idéogrammes lyriques," in *The Liberated Page: A Typographica Anthology*, ed. Herbert Spencer (San Francisco: Bedford Press, 1987), 68–90. On the related field of typewriter art, see Nicola Simpson, *Notes from the Cosmic Typewriter: The Life and Work of Dom Sylvester Houédard* (London: Occasional Papers, 2012); Barrie Tullett, *Typewriter Art: A Modern Anthology* (London: Laurence King Publishing, 2014).

19. See Harold Innis, *Empire and Communications* (Toronto: Dundum, 2014); Marshall McLuhan, *The Gutenberg Galaxy* (Toronto: University of Toronto Press, 2011); Ong, *Orality and Literacy*.

20. See, e.g., Charles Bigelow and Donald Day, "Digital Typography," *Scientific American* (August 1983): 106–119; Warren Chappell and Robert Bringhurst, *A Short History of the Printed Word* (Point Roberts, WA: Hartley & Marks, 1999); James Craig, *Phototypesetting: A Design Manual* (New York: Watson-Guptill Publications, 1978); Thomas Drier, *The Power of Print and Man* (New York: Mergenthaler Linotype Company, 1936); David Jury, *Reinventing Print: Technology and Craft in Typography* (New York: Bloomsbury, 2018); Luciene Alphonse Legros and John Cameron Grant, *Typographical Printing Surfaces* (London: Longmans, Green & Co., 1916); Levit, dir., *Graphic Means*; James Moran, *Printing Presses* (Berkeley, CA: University of California Press, 1973); Thomas Mullaney, *The Chinese Typewriter: A History* (Cambridge, MA: MIT Press, 2017); Doug Wilson, dir., *Linotype: The Film* (Colorado Springs, CO: Ikonik Media, 2012), DVD.

21. This book also offers a glossary of most of its discussed typefaces at the end. Where typefaces mentioned in the body of this text aren't accompanied by illustrations, an illustration can be found in that glossary.

22. One aspect of the medium that is not explored in the following pages in as much detail as it deserves is non-Latin typography. This is partly due to the historical trajectory of typographic technologies (much of typographic history is filled with Latin text because this is the linguistic community in which print proliferated most quickly and forcefully). But it also has a good deal to do with technological colonialism. Western typographic technologies have dominated globally and are designed primarily for the Latin alphabet, causing challenges for non-Latin scripts. For more on this, see chapter 3.

23. In typography, "roman" refers to the style of typeface that developed in Southern Europe (around Rome and Venice), as distinct from the "blackletter" styles that developed in Northern Europe (first in Germany, but also in fifteenth- and sixteenth-century Belgium, among other places). The style read by most people who use the Latin alphabet today is roman.

24. Tobias Frere-Jones's typeface Retina (1999) is of a similar sort—designed for stock reports printed in the *Wall Street Journal* at sizes of 7 point and below. The issue of spread is also significant in the design of typefaces for cathode-ray-tube television screens. CBS News 36 (Rudi Bass and CBS Graphic Arts Dept., 1968) similarly uses notches where strokes meet in order to reduce halation.

25. Dry-transfer type was also more accessible commercially, introducing a new DIY ethos into typography and graphic design.

26. We'll discuss the requirements of MICR and OCR (optical character recognition) typefaces in chapter 5.

27. We'll see in related experimental typefaces, like the Epps Evans Alphabet and Wim Crouwel's New Alphabet (the latter of which Zhukov cites as an influence), that grid-based experiments from this period generally eliminated curves and diagonals (see chapter 5). So Zhukov's face is unusual for this reason, but it still fits nicely in the long tradition of grid-based designs (see chapter 4). Each Cyrillic and Latin character is designed in a sixteen-unit grid, though some characters exceed this grid with a descender or ascender.

28. Maxim Zhukov, email messages to the author, August 22–28, 2018. Even if Zhukov's ambitions were limited to the development of a single type family, the systematic way in which that family is produced suggests the possibility of systematizing typographic design more broadly.

29. Here we might think of the paintings of Piet Mondrian, Malevich's *Black Square*, or Clement Greenberg's theories of the flatness of Abstract Modernist painting.

30. Ludwig Wittgenstein, *Philosophical Investigations*, trans. G. E. M. Anscombe (Oxford: Blackwell, 2001), 31e–34e. We'll discuss Wittgenstein's philosophy further in chapter 6.

31. Gottlob Frege, "Sense and Reference," *Philosophical Review* 57, no. 3 (May 1948): 209–230. "Mode of presentation" is a translated phrase. Frege's own words are "*der Art des Gegebenseins*," that is, the way of being given or of being present.

For the German, see Gottlob Frege, "Über Sinn und Bedeutung," in *Funktion, Begriff, Bedeutung: Fünf logische Studien*, ed. Günther Patzig (Göttingen: Vandenhoeck & Ruprecht, 2008, 1962), 24. Frege argues that the truth-value, or meaning, of a statement depends not merely on what a word or phrase refers to, but also on the sense of that word or phrase. It's worth noting that though he produced some useful concepts—in the highly abstract worlds of language, logic, and math—Frege was also an anti-Semite and disparaged the French and supporters of democracy, among others. Richard L. Mendelsohn, trans. "Diary: Written by Professor Dr Gottlob Frege in the Time from 10 March to 9 April 1924," *Inquiry* 39, no. 3–4 (1996): 303–342.

32. To illustrate the difference between reference and sense, Frege uses two different names for the same object, "the morning star" and "the evening star." See Frege, "Sense and Reference," 210. Though these names both *refer* to the same object, a statement such as "the morning star = the evening star" is not an uninformative statement, as reference would suggest. If we look at this statement merely with reference in mind, we could reduce it to "Venus = Venus." But because these two names have two different senses, the identity statement between them allows us to learn something about the names themselves (e.g., that, though they refer to a heavenly body prominent in the sky at two different times, the referent they name is identical). Their differing senses allow Frege's identity statement to be informatively, rather than uninformatively, true.

33. Frege, "Sense and Reference," 213.

34. Wolfgang Ernst, "Experimenting with Media Temporality: Pythagoras, Hertz, Turing," in *Digital Memory* (Minneapolis: University of Minnesota Press, 2013), 184–185; "Media Archaeology—Method & Machine." Lecture given at Anglia Ruskin University, Cambridge, UK, November 18, 2009; "Media Archaeography," in *Media Archaeology*, ed. Erkki Huhtamo and Jussi Parikka (Berkeley: University of California Press, 2011), 242.

35. In "Signals versus Symbols" (extended version of lecture given at Yale University, March 29, 2012), 3, Wolfgang Ernst critiques the humanities for favoring the hermeneutic over the reality of smell and noise; this wide-ranging field has looked for meaning in symbols, while ignoring the accounting carried out by signals. As a result, Ernst's Berlin school of media archaeology focuses on signal processing over symbol processing.

36. Ernst, "Media Archaeology—Method & Machine," 6–7. Across typographic technologies, we could say that this transubstantiation applies to other keyboards as well—the semantic symbols become mechanical operations in the typewriter and typecasting machines, and become signals and instructions in phototypesetting and digiset machines. For more on the idea of indexicality, see Charles Sanders Peirce, "What Is a Sign?" in *The Essential Peirce*, vol. 2 *(1893–1913)* (Bloomington: Indiana University Press, 1998), 4–10. In his semiotics, an "index" is a kind of sign that maintains a physical connection to the thing it is a sign for—so seeing smoke as a sign for fire, or a photograph as a sign of the light that was present when the shutter was opened.

37. Ernst, "Media Archaeography," 249. I note that this subsemantic level is "largely inaccessible," given that we can think of scenarios in which we are able to process symbolic media without concerning ourselves with semantics. As an example from philosophy, in John Searle's Chinese Room thought experiment, a human with no knowledge of the Chinese language is sitting inside a room, following instructions that guide their processing of Chinese characters passed to them from outside. He concludes that the person inside the room, though able to accurately manipulate symbols, has no understanding of the semantic content they are processing. See Searle's *Minds, Brains, and Science* (Cambridge, MA: Harvard University Press, 1984), 32–35. Searle's thought experiment is also an argument against the possibility of media being able to work at the semantic level—that is, he is making the case that while (what we call) "weak AI" may be able to be developed, "strong AI" will not be possible.

38. Wolfgang Ernst, "Telling versus Counting? A Media-Archaeological Point of View," *Intermédialités* 2 (Autumn 2003): 33–34.

39. Ernst, "Telling versus Counting," 34.

40. Vilém Flusser, *Into the Universe of the Technical Image*, trans. Nancy Ann Roth (Minneapolis: University of Minnesota Press, 2011), 28. See also "Why Do Typewriters Go 'Click'?" in *The Shape of Things* (London: Reaktion Books, 1999), 62–65. In Flusser's philosophy, the line between type and writing is somewhat murky. For him, writing is a means of recording the world that imposes on us a certain way of thinking—a linear, historical means of thinking. In his own practice, the gesture of writing was intimately tied to the materiality of the typewriter, the pushing of keys, the changing of ribbons and sheets of paper, etc. (See Flusser, "The Gesture of Writing." *Flusser Studies* 8 [May 2009]: 1–18, http://www.flusserstudies.net/pag/archive08.htm.) However, when he writes specifically on the technologies of type, those technologies do seem to exist in a slightly different worldview than writing does. Rather than being predominantly linear, they stutter and skip, and treat letters as individual (and significantly three-dimensional) units. See also Flusser, "On Typography."

41. Plato wrote about writing as an (unfortunate) extension of the memory and voice in "Phaedrus," in *The Collected Dialogues of Plato*, trans. R. Hackforth, ed. Edith Hamilton and Huntington Cairns (Princeton, NJ: Princeton University Press, 1989), 496–497.

42. See Flusser, "On Typography." In "On Memory (Electronic or Otherwise)," *Leonardo* 23, no. 4 (1990): 397–399, Flusser also characterizes the technologies of writing as a means of extending memory.

43. McLuhan, *The Gutenberg Galaxy*, 144–146. McLuhan discusses moveable type printing specifically, rather than type as a whole.

44. This would also be a view that might extend Socrates's critique of writing in "Phaedrus" to typography—casting it as a crutch for our memory, an unfaithful communicator, a repetitive conversationalist; see Plato, "Phaedrus." Or it might support Beatrice Warde's view of (good) type as a "crystal goblet"—an unobtrusive vessel conveying the author's beautiful ideas to the reader. We will discuss the goblet in chapter 2. Beatrice Warde, "The Crystal Goblet, or

Printing Should Be Invisible," in *Looking Closer 3*, ed. Michael Bierut, Jessica Helfand, and Steven Heller (New York: Allworth Press, 1999), 56–59.

45. As one small example of what it could mean for the typographic medium to have its own operational logic, we might consider the way in which Manuel Krebs discusses Helvetica (in Gary Hustwit's documentary on the typeface, *Helvetica*). There, Krebs suggests that Helvetica contains its own design program, meaning that you as a designer (and even as an amateur "designer") will use the typeface the way *it* wants you to use it.

46. "To the things themselves" became the slogan for the branch of philosophy that Husserl started, phenomenology. It originates from Husserl's argument that his phenomenological research, "actually reaches up to the things themselves, [it] orients itself towards their intuitive self-givenness." See Edmund Husserl, *Logical Investigations*, vol. 2, trans. J. N. Findlay (New York: Routledge, 2001), 178.

47. Edmund Husserl, *General Introduction to Pure Phenomenology*, trans. F. Kersten (Dordrecht: Springer Netherlands, 1982), 65–66.

48. Husserl, *General Introduction to Pure Phenomenology*, 61.

49. Husserl, *General Introduction to Pure Phenomenology*, 61, n. 30.

50. For an introductory view of research into the connotative or emotional effects of type see Sarah Hyndman, *Why Fonts Matter* (Berkeley, CA: Gingko Press, 2016).

51. Hannah Arendt, *The Origins of Totalitarianism* (New York: Harcourt Brace, 1973), viii.

52. Arendt, *The Origins of Totalitarianism*; and Arendt, *Eichmann in Jerusalem* (New York: Penguin, 1964).

53. On typography's relation to German totalitarianism see Peter Bain and Paul Shaw, eds., *Blackletter: Type and National Identity* (New York: Princeton Architectural Press, 1998). There are some connections between Italian futurist poetry (which made active use of typography) and the rise of fascism in that country, but these links are more complicated than the German story captured by the authors in Bain and Shaw's book.

54. Laszlo Moholy-Nagy, "The New Typography," in *Texts on Type*, ed. Steven Heller and Philip B. Meggs (New York: Allworth Press, 2001), 108.

55. Claude Shannon, "Mathematical Theory of Communication," *Bell System Technical Journal* 27 (July 1948), 379.

56. John Durham Peters, *Speaking into the Air* (Chicago: University of Chicago Press, 1999), 25.

57. Shannon, "Mathematical Theory of Communication," 379.

58. Peters, *Speaking into the Air*, 21.

59. Stuart Hall, "Encoding and Decoding in the Television Discourse," *CCCS Stencilled Occasional Papers*, no. 7 (1973), 16.

60. Hall, "Encoding and Decoding in the Television Discourse," 9.

61. Hall, "Encoding and Decoding in the Television Discourse," 12.

62. Quoted in Friedrich Kittler, *Gramophone, Film, Typewriter*, trans. Geofrey Winthrop-Young and Michael Wutz (Stanford, CA: Stanford University Press, 1999), 200.

63. Kittler, *Gramophone, Film, Typewriter*, 203. The shift to aphorism may also be related to Nietzsche's failing health, or to his preference for working while walking. On Nietzsche's walking, see Frédéric Gros, *Philosophy of Walking* (New York: Verso, 2014), 11–29.

64. Flusser explores this idea of shifting ways of thinking in several texts. See, for instance, "Line and Surface" and "The Codified Word," both in *Writings*, ed. Andreas Ströhl (Minneapolis: University of Minnesota Press, 2002), 21–34; 35–41. Flusser didn't live long enough to say for certain what kind of thinking the techno-image would introduce.

65. Johanna Drucker, *Graphesis: Visual Forms of Knowledge Production* (Cambridge, MA: Harvard University Press, 2014), 10. Italics in original.

66. Susan Buck-Morss, "Envisioning Capital," *Critical Inquiry* 21 (Winter 1995): 434–467.

Chapter 2

1. Jan Tschichold, *The New Typography*, trans. Ruari McLean (Berkeley: University of California Press, 1995), 47.

2. One could argue that form is a more pressing concern in certain non-Latin typographic traditions, given the difficulties of fitting a script's traditional forms into technologies designed for Latin typography—allowing those forms to function typographically. For instance, in Chinese, both common use limitations on how many characters are included within these technologies and design challenges standing in the way of the development of divisible type are formal considerations that overshadow, or at least precede, function. See Mullaney, *The Chinese Typewriter*, 89–103. Other non-Latin scripts such as Greek and Cyrillic have a typographic history largely parallel to that of Latin, and similarly appear to favor function over form.

3. Louis Sullivan, "The Tall Office Building Artistically Considered," *Lippincott's Monthly Magazine* (March 1896): 408. Victor Papanek argues that the idea that "form follows function" originated in 1739, in the work of the American sculptor Horatio Greenough. See Papanek's *Design for the Real World*, 2nd ed. (Chicago: Academy Chicago Publishers, 2000), 6.

4. Adolf Loos, "Ornament and Crime," in *Programs and Manifestoes on 20th-Century Architecture*, ed. Ulrich Comrads, 19–24 (Cambridge, MA: MIT Press, 1970). Even an absurdist artist like Paul Klee argued that what was desired was not form, but function. See Emil Ruder, *Typographie* (New York: Visual Communications Books, 1981), 202.

5. Walter Gropius, "The Theory and Organization of the Bauhaus," in *Art in Theory 1900–1990*, ed. Charles Harrison and Paul Wood (New York: Blackwell, 1999), 338–343. Of course, despite its best efforts, the Bauhaus did end up developing an aesthetic that would go on to have a profound influence on numer-

ous areas of design, including typography. The Bauhaus was founded as an institution opposed to traditional academies and dedicated to the unity of all arts—fine and industrial. Shortly after its founding, it rejiggered its mission to be the unification of art and technology.

6. Tschichold, *The New Typography*, 11.

7. See Tschichold, *The New Typography*, for examples of this design aesthetic.

8. Moholy-Nagy developed a concept he called typophoto, which involved the combination of typography's clarity and photography's objectivity to arrive at a clearer means of communicating in the public sphere. See Laszlo Moholy-Nagy, "Typophoto," in *Looking Closer 3*, ed. Michael Bierut, Jessica Helfand, and Steven Heller (New York: Allworth Press, 1999), 24–26.

9. Warde, "The Crystal Goblet, or Printing Should Be Invisible," 57. Keep this language of type as type in mind, as it will reappear in the debate about extending US copyright to typefaces.

10. Stanley Morison, "First Principles of Typography," in *Typographers on Type*, ed. Ruari McLean (New York: W. W. Norton, 1995), 63.

11. Though not strictly defined categories, text type includes those typefaces that are usually used to set large amounts of text (books, magazines, newspapers, some websites, etc.), while display type refers to those typefaces that are more often used for small amounts of often attention-seeking text (advertising, headlines, signage, some product packaging, etc.). Although display faces are generally meant to attract attention to themselves, the case for transparency in display faces can be seen in an example like Helvetica, where its perceived transparency or neutrality is seen as making it amenable to contradictory brand identities. See Gary Hustwit's documentary *Helvetica*, for a discussion of how this quality of Helvetica's design has contributed to its ubiquity in the corporate world and the government. Wayfinding systems often turn to sans-serif display faces for transparency as well.

12. There are many contexts in which transparency can be dangerous. Philip Ball has explored some of these in his book *Invisible: The Dangerous Lure of the Unseen* (Chicago: University of Chicago Press, 2015). Consider, for example, ideas that have held back techno-scientific progress, such as the belief in occult forces or in the ether; or the sociopolitical figure of the "invisible man" that Ralph Ellison analyzed and immortalized in his novel of the same name. In his book *In the Swarm: Digital Prospects* (Cambridge, MA: MIT Press, 2017), Byung-Chul Han argues that, even as people today call for more transparency in politics, the always-on transparency offered by digital media and 24/7 news outlets is a threat to a government's ability to deliberate in private and take risks in thinking up new solutions to entrenched problems.

13. Patricia Crain, *The Story of A* (Stanford: Stanford University Press, 2000), 7.

14. In chapter 5, we will discuss the distinction between legibility and readability.

15. There are even studies, which we will discuss in chapter 7, that suggest disfluency in reading (a moderate amount of difficulty in deciphering the text) may make a reader more open to considering the ideas they read, or may make it easier for them to retain the information they consume. See Adam Alter,

Daniel M. Oppenheimer, Nicholas Epley, and Rebecca N. Eyre, "Overcoming Intuition: Metacognitive Difficulty Activates Analytic Reasoning," *Journal of Experimental Psychology: General* 136, no. 4 (2007): 569–576; Connor Diemand-Yauman, Daniel M. Oppenheimer, and Erikka B. Vaughan, "Fortune Favors the **Bold** (*and the Italicized*): Effects of Disfluency on Educational Outcomes," *Cognition* 118 (2011): 111–115.

16. Isobel Armstrong, *Victorian Glassworlds* (New York: Oxford University Press, 2008), 11. The push and pull of visible invisibility is seen as central to the shop window's own dual role of inspiring desire and restricting access. Robert Bringhurst also uses the phrase "visible invisibility" in his *Elements of Typographic Style*, 77. In this case he is referring to the peculiar quality of punctuation marks as visible shapes that are overlooked (presumably more overlooked than other kinds of characterforms).

17. György Kepes, *Language of Vision* (Chicago: Paul Theobald, 1964), 77. Kepes's definition of transparency may have been influenced by his work with the Bauhaus's Laszlo Moholy-Nagy. Kepes began his career working as an assistant to this giant of the Bauhaus, who experimented with photography and Plexiglas, finding new ways to play with new materials, light, shadow, and transparency. For more on Kepes's relation to post-WWII science like cybernetics (and to the military-industrial-complex) see John R. Blakinger, *Gyorgy Kepes: Undreaming the Bauhaus* (Cambridge, MA: MIT Press, 2019).

18. As we'll see, the primary weak point in protection for typefaces is where copyright is concerned—US designers cannot copyright their typeface designs. On this point, the United States is out of step with the rest of the Western world. Though Japan, at least, maintains a similar position to that of the United States, for much the same reason. Dennis S. Karjala and Keiji Sugiyama, "Fundamental Concepts in Japanese and American Copyright Law," *American Journal of Comparative Law* 36, no. 4 (Autumn 1988), 625–626.

19. This was the case in Keystone Type Foundry v. Portland Publishing Co. 186 Fed. 690, 907 (1st Cir. 1911). Given how long it takes for most typefaces to achieve popularity (even in a sped-up digital age), this lack of protection can have significant negative consequences.

20. The patents and copyright clause of the US Constitution is in art. I, sec. 8: "Congress shall have the power to . . . promote the progress of science and useful arts, by securing for limited times to authors and inventors the exclusive right to their respective writings and discoveries." The general belief in IP law is that the promotion of progress is best achieved by ensuring private, financial incentives for authors. It should not be assumed, however, that without monetary incentives creativity languishes. There are plenty of examples of other kinds of incentives leading to significant amounts of creativity and progress. See James Boyle, "Fencing off Ideas: Enclosure and the Disappearance of the Public Domain," *Daedalus* 131, no. 2 (Spring 2002), 20–23; and Kate Darling and Aaron Perzanowski, eds., *Creativity without Law: Challenging the Assumptions of Intellectual Property* (New York: NYU Press, 2017).

21. Blake Fry, "Why Typefaces Proliferate without Copyright Protection," *Journal on Telecommunication and High Technology Law* 8, no. 2 (2010): 425–490; Eliza-

beth L. Rosenblatt, "A Theory of IP's Negative Space," *Columbia Journal of Law & the Arts* 34, no. 3 (2011): 317–365.

22. See Dan L. Burk, "Expression, Selection, Abstraction: Copyright's Golden Braid," *Syracuse Law Review* 55, no. 3 (2005): 615. For examples of those who argue for IP protection, see Terrence J. Carroll, "Protection for Typeface Designs: A Copyright Proposal," *Computer & High Technology Law Journal* 10 (1994): 139–194; Jacqueline Lipton, "To © or Not to ©? Copyright and Innovation in the Digital Typeface Industry," *University of California, Davis Law Review* 43 (2009): 143–192; Rudy VanderLans, "The Trouble with Type"; Hermann Zapf, "New Typeface Designs in the Shadow of Protection," in *Hermann Zapf & His Design Philosophy* (Chicago: Society of Typographic Arts, 1987), 78–84.

23. Francis Bailey, Forming punches, US Patent X-4, January 1791. Unfortunately, this patent doesn't specify what that method was.

24. George Bruce, Letters Patent No. 1, US Design Patent 1, November 19, 1842. This text is transcribed from the "best available copy" of the original patent; any errors in transcription are my own.

25. Others in the copyright debate have made this argument as well, some likening a typeface to a foundry's trademark—a face that is uniquely associated with their business. Travis Manfredi makes this point, and notes that some designers, like Goudy or Rogers, received commissions based on the particular qualities of their previous work. See Manfredi, "Sans Protection: Typeface Design and Copyright in the Twenty-First Century," *University of San Francisco Law Review* 45, no. 3 (Winter 2011): 841–871.

26. Waldon Fawcett, "Is There Need for More Protection for Type-Faces?" *Inland Printer* 60, no. 6 (Mar. 1918): 798–800.

27. Feist Publications Inc. v. Rural Telephone Service Co., 499 U.S. 340 (1991). For a broader picture of different definitions of originality in IP law, see Elizabeth Judge and Daniel Gervais, "Of Silos and Constellations: Comparing Notions of Originality in Copyright Law," *Cardozo Arts & Entertainment* 27 (2009): 375–408.

28. Ralph Oman and Daniel J. Boorstin, "Notice of Inquiry: Copyrightability of Digitized Typefaces," *Announcement from the Copyright Office, Library of Congress, Washington, D.C. 20559*. Excerpt from *Federal Register* 51, no. 197 (Oct. 10, 1986): 36410–36412.

29. The existential or essentialist nature of these questions is likely true of most copyright debates. Rudy VanderLans has made this argument in his essay, "The Trouble with Type." In his history of copyright, Mark Rose similarly argues that in the literary IP debate it is impossible to tell the difference between aesthetic and legal questions. See Mark Rose, *Authors and Owners: The Invention of Copyright* (Cambridge, MA: Harvard University Press, 1993).

30. Goudy v. Hansen, 247 Fed. 782, 1264 (1st Cir. 1917).

31. Goudy v. Hansen, 247 Fed. 782, 1264 (1st Cir. 1917). In his decision on the metal type/ punches, Judge Hale dismisses them as being neither inventive nor beautiful, suggesting that utility is not his only consideration when it comes to patentability.

32. At times, there have been differences between the design and the punches cut, but these are rare, or minor—for instance, in the case of Romain du Roi, in which the precise drawings made by a committee for King Louis XIV were altered when they were actually cut into punches by Grandjean. More commonly, as Charles Babbage pointed out, the process of producing the impress of type is a multistage process of copying. In his description of printing by stereotype, he identified "six successive stages of copying." The design gets copied in the punch (which, depending on the character, can involve multiple counterpunches), the punch gets copied in the matrix, the matrix in the metal type, the metal type in plaster, the plaster in the stereotype plate, and the stereotype plate gets copied onto the page in printing. See Babbage, *The Works of Charles Babbage*, vol. 8: *The Economy of Machinery and Manufactures*, ed. Martin Campbell-Kelly (New York: NYU Press, 1989), 78.

33. Goudy v. Hansen, 247 Fed. 782, 1264 (1st Cir. 1917).

34. Keystone Type Foundry v. Portland Publishing Co. 186 Fed. 690, 907 (1st Cir. 1911). It was suggested in the case that Portland should change the name of the type they were selling, but this was the extent of their reprimand.

35. On the *Adobe* decision as a means of production argument, see Jonathan L. Mezrich, "Extension of Copyright to Fonts—Can the Alphabet Be Far Behind?" *Computer Law Review and Technology Journal* (Summer 1998): 61–67.

36. 17 U.S.C. §202.10(e). Initially Oman's Copyright Office decided that it would not grant protection to digital typefaces, but it reopened the issue in 1991, and in 1992 decided that it would register the underlying computer programs.

37. Ralph Oman and James H. Billington, "Final Regulation; Registrability of Computer Programs that Generate Typefaces," *Announcement from the Copyright Office, Library of Congress, Washington, D.C. 20559*. Excerpt from *Federal Register* 57, no. 35 (Feb. 21, 1992): 6201.

38. In their 1992 final regulation, the Copyright Office advises applicants on how to approach the application process in light of this distinction. Because referring to the proposed work as an "entire work" would lead to confusion over whether they're trying to copyright the program or the typeface, they advise them to frame the application as being for a computer program. Oman and Billington, "Final Regulation; Registrability of Computer Programs That Generate Typefaces," 6201.

39. It's worth noting that not all font-generating code has been found to be copyrightable. Apart from the general requirements of originality, fixation, and human authorship, there's a recent disagreement between the Copyright Office and The Martinez Group PLLC about what kinds of digital language can be copyrighted. At time of writing, the Copyright Office has refused registration to an application filed by designer-turned-lawyer Frank Martinez, arguing that as XML, the proposed article is markup language rather than a computer program. See copyright examiner C. DiFolco's letter to Frank Martinez, reproduced on Luc Devroye's website, http://luc.devroye.org/fonts-95584.html.

40. Several legal scholars have pointed out why these protections are not sufficient or well fitted to the protection of typefaces. For instance, Manfredi and

Lipton argue that design patents are expensive, and do not provide enough time for a typeface to establish itself before its protection runs out. Lipton has also noted that because many designers use widely available font design software to design their typefaces, much of the code behind these typefaces is not eligible for copyright protection. Because of these shortcomings, the most common form of protection for new typefaces in the US today is the click-wrap agreement. Lipton, "To © or Not to ©?"; Manfredi, "Sans Protection."

41. See Barbara Ringer, "Letter to Representative Kastenmeier, June 6, 1975," reprinted in "Registration of Original Typeface Designs, Legislative Consideration," *Announcement from the Copyright Office, Library of Congress, Washington, D.C. 20559*; Oman and Billington, "Final Regulation; Registrability of Computer Programs That Generate Typefaces," 6201; Gloria C. Phares, "An Approach to Why Typography Should Be Copyrightable," *Columbia Journal of Law & The Arts* 39, no. 3 (2016): 417–420.

42. Barbara Ringer and L. Quincy Mumford, "Registration of Original Typeface Designs," *Announcement from the Copyright Office, Library of Congress, Washington, D.C. 20559*, excerpted in *Federal Register* 39, no. 176 (Sept. 10, 1974). Ringer was moved to open this public debate in 1974 by a combination of technological developments and the 1973 Vienna Agreement, which granted signatories international protection for typefaces. It is also worth noting that in US copyright law, creativity is one of the key means of defining originality—so there is a near-equivalence in the terms Ringer uses in this question.

43. Some of the most famous cases of one design cleaving too closely to another (and yet getting away with it) involve Microsoft and typefaces that were designed to resemble (and generally take up the same space as) existing typefaces. Arial (Robin Nicholas and Patricia Saunders, 1982) is a typeface that is, today, nearly as ubiquitous as the typeface it mimics—Helvetica. It has been rumored Microsoft chose Arial to avoid paying Helvetica's licensing fees. Though the two typefaces have the same dimensions and share quite a few shapes, there are differences that can be perceived by the naked eye. The more egregious example of creating a "new" typeface by changing one or two minor details from an existing face is Microsoft's own Book Antiqua, which is a copy of Hermann Zapf's Palatino (1950). In this case, the differences appear nonexistent to the naked eye, though overlaying the two faces reveal barely perceptible variations in the ends of strokes (or terminals) in the f, k, x, t, g, and slight differences in the W and Q.

44. Schmohl's typeface took an outline from Herman Ihlenburg's type and applied it to a typeface designed by Daniel Berkeley Updike and Bertram Gosvenor Goodhue. "Ex Parte Schmohl," *Official Gazette of the United States Patent Office* 140 (Mar. 7–Apr. 25, 1905): 505.

45. "Ex Parte Schmohl," 505.

46. Courts and legislative bodies have debated whether that difference ought to be visible to typographic experts, or if it should be apparent to non-experts as well. See, for instance, the disagreement between the judges in Goudy v. Hansen, 247 Fed. 782, 1264 (1st Cir. 1917). In copyright infringement cases, this

question of the perception of expert vs. lay audiences has generally been settled in favor of the lay population. See Arnstein v. Porter 154 F2d 464 (2nd Cir. 1946).

47. American Type Founders' Co. v. Damon & Peets 140 Fed. 715, 9,030 (S.D.N.Y. 1905). This language of "peculiar configuration" and ornamentation also appears in the decision for Goudy v. Hansen, 247 Fed. 782, 1264 (1st Cir. 1917).

48. Hermann Zapf, "A Plea for Authentic Type Design," in *Texts on Type*, ed. Steven Heller and Philip B. Meggs (New York: Allworth Press, 2001), 34–35; Zapf, "New Typeface Designs in the Shadow of Protection," 78–84; Zapf, "Is Creativity in Alphabet Design Still Wanted?" *Visible Language* 24, no. 3 (Summer 1990): 254–261. It's worth noting that this question of hard work expended on creation holds more weight as an argument for intellectual property protection in countries other than the United States. The UK system, for instance, favors a "sweat-of-the-brow" definition for what constitutes originality—if you've spent intellectual labor on something it can be seen as having originality. Judge and Gervais, "Of Silos and Constellations," 394–399.

49. The committee consisted of "Dr. Walke Greisner, Managing Director, D. Stempel AG, Chairman; graphic designer Max Caflisch; Edward Gottschall, Executive Vice President, ITC; Professor G. W. Ovink and Professor Hans Peter Willberg." See Edward Gottschall, "The State of the Art in Typeface Design Protection," *Visible Language* 19, no. 1 (Winter 1985), 152. According to Gottschall, this definition was made and the committee was formed at a particular moment in type history, when the US copyright debate was being reignited. Most other Western countries had already provided copyright or copyright-like protection for typefaces, and several international agreements also existed. However, even the mostly European members of ATypI who comprised the committee discussing IP protection were concerned about the gap in protection in the United States. They feared the rise of corporations in America (mainly computer hardware and software corporations) that would be unfamiliar with existing design ethics. One might be able to trust an American graphic designer to respect the legal protections of designers in other countries, but the same respect couldn't be assumed of these young corporations.

50. Gottschall, "The State of the Art in Typeface Design Protection," 153.

51. Skill appears as a measure of originality in a number of legal traditions. For an introduction on the role of skill in different definitions of originality in copyright see Judge and Gervais, "Of Silos and Constellations: Comparing Notions of Originality in Copyright Law."

52. Goudy v. Hansen, 247 Fed. 782, 1264 (1st Cir. 1917).

53. Goudy v. Hansen, 247 Fed. 782, 1264 (1st Cir. 1917).

54. The court decision mentions the cost of the face, but doesn't mention that the well-known designer was Zapf, that information comes from Phares, "An Approach to Why Typography Should Be Copyrightable," 418.

55. As the Circuit Court Judge Russell noted, Eltra would have been aware that their attempt to gain copyright was likely to fail. Eltra Corp. v. Ringer, 579 F2d 294, 301 (4th Cir. 1978). They were involved in lobbying Congress for a change

to this policy for some time, and so knew perfectly well that the Copyright Office would not register their typeface when they applied. The Eltra case, then, appears to be a move to force the debate over the copyright of typefaces.

56. *Eltra*, 579 F.2d 294. The court has also made a second ruling concerning the powers available to the Register of Copyrights, which is more a legislative matter, than being relevant to the question of copyrighting typefaces.

57. Quoted in *Eltra*, 579 F.2d 294.

58. See Carroll, "Protection for Typeface Designs: A Copyright Proposal." This idea of conceptual separability was made more explicit five years later in Carol Barnhart v. Economy Cover Corp. 773 F.2d 411 (2d Cir. 1985), a case involving partial torso mannequins.

59. Circuit Judge Oakes of the US Court of Appeals, Second Circuit, quoted in Carroll, "Protection for Typeface Designs: A Copyright Proposal," 153. See Carroll for the full narrative of this series of cases (from *Mazer* to *Brandir International*). For more on the Denicola test, see Robert C. Denicola, "Applied Art and Industrial Design: A Suggested Approach to Copyright in Useful Articles," *Minnesota Law Review* 67 (1983): 707-748.

60. Star Athletica, L.L.C. v. Varsity Brands, Inc., et al. 580 U.S. (2017). From the perspective of fashion, this decision was not groundbreaking; it upheld the existing standards in fashion IP. Thomas's characterization of the artistic element being incorporated "into" the useful article is particularly useful language when thinking about eligible separability in relation to type. It seems to suggest the artistic element could inhere in the physical useful article, rather than simply adorning or being attached to it.

61. Rep. Robert Kastenmeier, "Copyright Law Revision" (U.S. House of Representatives Report No. 94-1476, September 3, 1976), 55.

62. Kastenmeier, "Copyright Law Revision," 55.

63. Phares, "An Approach to Why Typography Should Be Copyrightable," 419.

64. While I've used the idea that typeface designs are shapes and therefore exhibit qualities of pictorial, graphic, or sculptural works, it should also be noted that basic shapes themselves (circle, star, etc.) are not eligible for copyright. Were typefaces eligible for copyright, one requirement would likely be that a particular typeface would have to exhibit its distance from basic shapes (perhaps defined in this case as the "characteristic lines" that Bruce wrote about). Such a requirement would be a bulwark against any remaining concerns over copyrighting the alphabet.

65. *Star Athletica*, 580 U.S. (2017). Here Justice Thomas is responding to an argument made by Star Athletica LLC that if the decorative elements of a cheerleading uniform were removed, all that would be left would be a white uniform, and this is no longer able to function as a cheerleading uniform (since it exhibits no cheer). Thomas rejects this argument.

66. Carroll, "Protection for Typeface Designs: A Copyright Proposal," 171.

67. Lipton, "To © or Not to ©?," 161.

68. VanderLans, "The Trouble with Type," 225. Deconstructivist design was an experimental period that openly challenged the conventions of writing and signification—we will discuss it further in chapter 5.

69. Carroll, "Protection for Typeface Designs," 153; Lipton, "To © or Not to ©?," 155. Manfredi argues that the relativity problem can be avoided by incorporating typeface into copyright regulations as its own special category, rather than trying to fit it into existing standards of separability. See Manfredi, "Sans Protection."

70. Lipton, "To © or Not to ©?," 155.

71. Lipton, "To © or Not to ©?," 156, 159.

72. Apart from these extremes, Carroll also notes that the originality in certain typefaces, like Koch Antiqua (Rudolf Koch, 1922), would be open to subjective interpretation. Carroll, "Protection for Typeface Designs," 153.

73. Lawson, *Anatomy of a Typeface*, 270–276.

74. Stanley Morison, quoted in Lawson, *Anatomy of a Typeface*, 274.

75. Times New Roman was similarly positioned in the digital era, serving as the default in Microsoft Word for many years, but it had also proved its utility decades before the development of computers.

76. "Hypnopaedia," *Emigre Fonts*, https://www.emigre.com/Fonts/Hypnopaedia. See also Licko's interview with Rhonda Rubenstein in *Eye* 11, no. 43 (Spring 2002), http://www.eyemagazine.com/feature/article/reputations-zuzana-licko.

77. To be copyrighted, a work must be fixed in a tangible medium of expression—it cannot be an idea.

78. Larry List, *The Imagery of Chess Revisited* (New York: Noguchi Museum, 2005), 57–59.

79. Colleen Schafroth. *The Art of Chess* (New York: Harry N. Abrams, 2002), 95.

80. Schafroth. *The Art of Chess*, 31–32.

81. Oftentimes in chess fonts, the standards around relative height of the pieces disappears—all pieces taking on the same height.

82. D'Arcy Thompson, *On Growth and Form* (Cambridge: Cambridge University Press, 1952), 231–234.

Chapter 3

1. Eric Gill, *Autobiography* (New York: Biblo & Tannen, 1969), 120. Eric Gill is quoted here, and will be referenced in more depth later in this book. He was an important figure in early twentieth-century typography, design, and art. However, it should be noted that in his personal diaries he documented sexual experimentation with his own pubescent daughters, and a dog. Fiona MacCarthy discovered this information while researching her 1989 biography of Gill. See MacCarthy's *Eric Gill: A Lover's Quest for Art and God* (New York: Dutton, 1989), 155–156. She notes Gill's own conflicted view of what he was doing, and in recent years has noted she intended this information to be

a (admittedly difficult) sign of a complicated and multifaceted artist—rather than as a reason to dismiss his influence entirely. See Rachel Cooke, "Eric Gill: Can We Separate the Artist from the Abuser?" *Guardian*, Apr. 9, 2017, https://www.theguardian.com/artanddesign/2017/apr/09/eric-gill-the-body-ditchling-exhibition-rachel-cooke.

2. Phil Baines and Andrew Haslam, *Type and Typography* (New York: Weston Gutill Publications, 2005), 7; Alan Bartram, *Typeforms: A History* (New Castle, DE: Oak Knoll Press, 2007), 125; Bringhurst, *Elements of Typographic Style*, 20; Karen Cheng, *Designing Type* (New Haven: Yale University Press, 2005), 7; Ellen Lupton and J. Abbott Miller, *Design Writing Research* (New York: Phaidon, 2006), 17.

3. Gerrit Noordzij, *The Stroke Theory of Writing*, trans. Peter Enneson (London: Hyphen, 2005), 41.

4. For instance, Bror Zachrisson did a series of studies in the 1960s that showed that readers have very little memory of the typeface they were just reading, and are unable to recreate from memory the details of typographic characters like the lowercase (double story) a. See Zachrisson, *Studies in the Legibility of Printed Text* (Stockholm: Almqvist & Wiksell, 1965). Today, the art historian Jennifer Roberts makes a compelling argument that attention to visual detail is a skill in decline, and it needs to be taught if we are to avoid a society that takes the world as it appears rather than as it is. Jennifer Roberts, "The Power of Patience," *Harvard Magazine*, Nov.–Dec. 2013, https://www.harvardmagazine.com/2013/11/the-power-of-patience.

5. To have a necessary quality means that a thing is a certain way and could not possibly be any other way. The philosopher Saul Kripke notes that necessity (or at least one of its definitions) has to do with metaphysics rather than epistemology. That is, a necessary quality of a thing does not rely on our knowing that it is necessary—it will be true whether there is anyone to know it is true or not. Saul Kripke, *Naming and Necessity* (Cambridge, MA: Harvard University Press, 1980), 35–36.

6. Saussure, *Course in General Linguistics*, 118.

7. Friedrich Nietzsche, "On Truth and Lies in Non-Moral Sense," in *On Truth and Untruth: Selected Writings*, ed. and trans. Taylor Carman (New York: HarperCollins, 2010), 15–49.

8. Most of those in type theory who have used Saussure's theories have taken up the first option, whether consciously or not, choosing to build on certain parts of Saussure's theory (like the arbitrary relationship between signifier and signified), while ignoring his own disregard for the physical details of the signifier. See, for instance, Drucker, *Visible Word*; Lupton and Miller, *Design, Writing, Research*.

9. According to Lucille Chia, woodblock printing remained dominant in China until the late nineteenth century. Neither the Chinese nor Korean movable type printing systems spread to the same degree Gutenberg's would in Europe in the fifteenth century. (Though Chinese movable type did spread at least as far West as Uyghur Turkish communities in the early 1300s.) See Thomas Fran-

cis Carter, *The Invention of Printing in China* (New York: The Ronald Press Company, 1955). Chia has argued this limited spread of movable type in Asia had less to do with the apparent complexity of the Chinese script, and more to do with the economy and ease of woodblock printing. See Chia, *Printing for Profit: The Commercial Publishers of Jianyang, Fujian (11th–17th Centuries)* (Cambridge, MA: Harvard University Press, 2002), 361, n. 122. It's also worth remembering that in China, Korea, and Japan, movable type printing depended heavily on state funding; in fifteenth-century Germany, Gutenberg depended on private funding. This ruined Gutenberg's later years, but he was also less susceptible to shifts in political power.

10. Frederic W. Goudy, "I Am Type," in *Texts on Type*, ed. Stephen Heller and Philip B. Meggs (New York: Allworth Press, 2001), 218.

11. Michael Middleton, *Soldiers of Lead: An Introduction to Layout and Typography for Use in the Labour Party* (London: Pelican Press, 1943).

12. Quoted in Middleton, *Soldiers of Lead*, 3. Also quoted in Herbert Spencer, *The Visible Word* (London: Lund Humphries, 1968), 10. At the time this printer worked, there were only twenty-five letters in the Latin alphabet, so this assumes only one case (upper or lower).

13. Elizabeth Eisenstein's *The Printing Revolution in Early Modern Europe* (New York: Cambridge University Press, 1983) explores the ways in which print affected labor and social relations, the Protestant Reformation, and the Copernican Revolution. The idea that print helps to standardize and vernacularize the printed word is also discussed by Eisenstein, and by Harold Innis in *Empire and Communications*; and William Kuskin, ed., *Caxton's Trace: Studies in the History of English Printing* (Notre Dame: University of Notre Dame Press, 2006). The idea that print is essential to the modern nation is discussed by Benedict Anderson's *Imagined Communities* (New York: Verso, 2003); and David M. Henkin's *City Reading* (New York: Columbia University Press, 1998) explores a similar theme at the level of the city (New York City in the Antebellum period).

14. McLuhan, *Gutenberg Galaxy*; see also Norbert Bolz's characterization in "Goodbye to the Gutenberg Galaxy," *New German Critique*, no. 78 (Autumn 1999): 109–131. Lewis Mumford focuses on the importance of print's standardizing influence on culture, but also claims that the development of paper was of equal importance with the press itself; see Mumford, *Technics and Civilization* (New York: Harcourt & Brace, 1962), 134–137.

15. Flusser, "On Typography."

16. Flusser, "On Typography," 1. A literal manifestation of Flusser's idea that Gutenberg's revolution involved treating letters as though they were three-dimensional objects can be seen in dimensional typefaces, like Ji Lee's Univers Revolved (ca. 2004). Recent experiments in 3D-printed typefaces also present useful examples.

17. Philip Meggs identifies the mold as the key to the success of moveable type printing in his *History of Graphic Design*, 72–73. Anthony Froshaug's "Typography Is a Grid," and "Typographic Norms," both in *Anthony Froshaug Texts & Type*, ed. Robin Kinross (London: Hyphen Press, 2000), likewise identify the type mold as central. The strongest view on the type mold may belong to Theo-

dore L. De Vinne, who argues that the inventor of the type mold (whoever this may have been) is the inventor of typography. See De Vinne's *The Invention of Printing* (New York: Francis Hart, 1876), 67. Abbott Payson Usher makes a more measured claim, arguing that the type mold's careful development was the key problem to be solved in casting type. See Usher, *A History of Mechanical Inventions* (Cambridge, MA: Harvard University Press, 1954), 251.

18. In this sense, I would argue that the "Gutenberg galaxy" actually introduces simultaneity, not sequentiality. Marshall McLuhan characterizes print culture as being sequential—one letter following another, one word following another, one historical record following another. See McLuhan, *Gutenberg Galaxy*, 273-276. However, from the perspective of the production of a typographic text, the simultaneity involved in the production of a single page of text is more revolutionary than the sequentiality of writing or setting a line of text, since that linear quality existed prior to movable type printing as well.

19. Mullaney, *The Chinese Typewriter*, 89–103.

20. Erik Spiekermann and E. M. Ginger, *Stop Stealing Sheep and Find Out How Type Works* (Berkeley, CA: Adobe Press, 2003), 125.

21. I don't believe this is a disagreement with Spiekermann's view. Given his affection for the details of typographic characters, shape constrained by technology is what I take Spiekermann's statement on typographic history to mean. He discusses, for instance, the way in which typewriters led to monospaced typefaces; Spiekermann and Ginger, *Stop Stealing Sheep and Find Out How Type Works*, 125.

22. Charles Bigelow and Donald Day note this pattern in their article, "Digital Typography," 110.

23. Cited in Meggs, *A History of Graphic Design*, 122.

24. Meggs, *A History of Graphic Design*, 128.

25. Raymond Williams, "Base and Superstructure in Marxist Cultural Theory," in *Media and Cultural Studies*, ed. Meenakshi Gigi Durham and Douglas M. Kellner (Oxford: Blackwell, 2006), 131.

26. Drier, *The Power of Print and Man*, 97.

27. In typography, a "point" is a measure of the size of the type (not of the character itself), which is equivalent to 1/72 of an inch (in the Didot point system, each inch has 67.5 points). I'm indebted to Davin Kuntze for numerous conversations about the Linotype, which is a truly glorious machine.

28. See Wilson's documentary *Linotype* for more on the influence the machine had on the typographic design industry—in particular, Nadine Chahine's contributions to the documentary.

29. For more on the history and technology of phototypesetting, see Bigelow and Day, "Digital Typography," 115; Craig, *Phototypesetting: A Design Manual*, 161–193; Gerard O. Walter, "Typesetting," *Scientific American* 220, no. 5 (May 1969), 65.

30. Adrian Frutiger, *Type Sign Symbol*, trans. Andrew Bluhm (Zurich: ABC Verlag, 1980), 20.

31. Another reason often offered for the relatively slow development of typographic arts in the Arabic-speaking world is the idea that movable type printing was banned in the Ottoman Empire. However, Kathryn Schwartz has argued the historical evidence suggests no such ban, but that the longevity of this narrative is a result of historians expecting to find a typographic revolution in the Arabic-speaking world comparable to that in the Latinate. See Schwartz, "Did Ottoman Sultans Ban Print?" *Book History* 20 (2017): 1–39.

32. Huda Smitshuijzen AbiFares, *Arabic Typography* (London: Saqi Books, 2001), 93; Seyyed Hossein Nasr, *Islamic Art and Spirituality* (Albany: SUNY Press, 1987), 21. Hebrew writing has similarly holy connections; that script's twenty-two characters similarly being viewed as the means by which God brought everything else into being. See Johanna Drucker, *The Alphabetic Labyrinth* (London: Thames & Hudson, 1995), 129.

33. AbiFares, *Arabic Typography*, 65; Mourad Boutros, *Arabic for Designers* (New York: Mark Batty, 2006), 41. Printing presses existed in Egypt prior to this, having been brought in by Napoleon's invading forces at the end of the eighteenth century.

34. For more on the challenges of fitting the Chinese character set into Western typographic technologies, see Thomas Mullaney, "The Moveable Typewriter: How Chinese Typists Developed Predictive Text during the Height of Maoism," *Technology and Culture* 53 (Oct. 2012): 777–814.

35. The Ta'liq or nastaliq style means "hanging," describing the way its strokes swoop and hang below the baseline. One of the few calligraphic styles that minimizes curves and swooping lines is Kufic, a style developed in the eighth century that is heavily angular and has shorter vertical strokes than other styles. See Boutros, *Arabic for Designers*, 24–26. Yasmine Nachabe Taan characterizes Arabic typography as having multiple baselines, rather than as crossing one baseline. See Taan's *Abdulkader Arnaout: Designing as Visual Poetry* (Amsterdam: Khatt Books, 2017), 115–116.

36. Boutros, *Arabic for Designers*, 44–45.

37. Drawn from "Arabic at Stanford," *Stanford University*, http://web.stanford.edu/dept/lc/arabic/alphabet/incontextletters.html.

38. This number is still not far from the requirements of a Latin typeface, once you factor in both cases, numerals, and punctuation.

39. "Tobias Frere-Jones: Fibonacci," in *Fuse 1–20: From Invention to Antimatter*, ed. Neville Brody and Jon Wozencroft (Cologne: Taschen, 2012), 186.

40. Froshaug, "Typography Is a Grid," 187.

41. The most likely exception to this difficulty of modularity is in the Kufic style of Arabic. Jean Joseph Marcel presents some semimodular Arabic typography in his 1819 book *Leçons de langue Arabe* (Paris: Éberhart, Imprimeur du Collége Royal de France), 69–70 (or pages 15–16 of the section "Du Caractère Koufique Quadrangulaire"). Here, Square Kufic representations (made after wooden carvings Marcel observed in Cairo) are constructed out of uniform squares of metal. Thanks to Borna Izadpanah for bringing these to my attention.

42. The basic proportion that Ibn Muqlah worked out for the first letter of the Arabic alphabet, Aleph, is 1 to 7, the same ratio used by Edward Johnston in designing his Railway Sans. See Walter Tracy, *Letters of Credit: A View of Type Design* (Boston: David R. Godine, 1986), 89.

43. See, for instance, the 1537 Venice Qu'ran, which according to Mourad Boutros is full of errors—see Boutros, *Arabic for Designers*—or William Caslon's Arabick typeface, which looks like a halting Latin interpretation of Arabic characters.

44. Arnaout's typographic design was motivated by his own frustration with the lack of casual typefaces to use in poster design. Letraset's adoption of Arnaout's type in the mid-1970s played an important role in making these more experimental Arabic typefaces accessible to more designers. See Taan, *Abdulkader Arnaout*, 113–126. For a contemporary example of modernist experimentation in Arabic typography, see for instance AYNA, the typeface Tarek Atrissi designed for an Arabic web portal. He based the typeface on the square Kufic script, taking that style's rectangular qualities to an extreme, not unlike work done by European modernists like Theo van Doesburg or Wim Crouwel (see chapters 4 and 5). Tarek Atrissi, "Arabic Type Design," *Tarek Atrissi Design*, Nov. 19, 2006, https://www.atrissi.com/arabic-type-design/.

45. Laura Meseguer, "Qandus, a Triscript Typeface Family," *Laura Meseguer*, http://www.laurameseguer.com/project/qandus.

46. Ali Eteraz, "The Death of Urdu Script," *Medium*, October 7, 2013, https://medium.com/@eteraz/the-death-of-the-urdu-script-9ce935435d90.

47. See Kuskin, "'Onely Imagined': Vernacular Community and the English Press," in *Caxton's Trace: Studies in the History of English Printing*, 199–240. There is a similar but more peculiar attempt to standardize a language in Geofroy Tory's sixteenth-century book *Champ Fleury*, trans. George B. Ives (Mineola, NY: Dover, 1967), in which Tory, frustrated with the variation in French pronunciation he saw around him, proposed that the design of characters should illustrate to the reader the proper pronunciation of each character. This project is challenged by any proponent of the adoption of shorthand as a response to the fact that the Latin alphabet is no longer a truly phonetic alphabet. See Eric Gill, *An Essay on Typography* (Boston: David R. Godine, 1988).

48. Elizabeth Eisenstein has argued that the production of vernacular and polyglot Bibles brought together not only different languages, but also people from different trades and from different strata of society in ways that were socially novel. See Eisenstein, *The Printing Revolution in Early Modern Europe*, 182–183.

49. Herbert Bayer, "Toward a Universal Type," in *Looking Closer 3*, ed. Michael Bierut, Jessica Helfand, and Steven Heller (New York: Allworth Press, 1999), 62.

50. Tschichold, *The New Typography*, 74–75. The debate over the use of blackletter or roman type would, soon after Tschichold first published his book (1927), take on a more loaded political dimension with the adoption of blackletter as the official type style of the Third Reich. See Bain and Shaw, eds., *Blackletter: Type and National Identity*.

51. See Eteraz, "The Death of the Urdu Script"; and Tanvi Misra, "Can Google Build a Typeface to Support Every Written Language?" *NPR: Code Switch*, August 3, 2014. https://www.npr.org/sections/codeswitch/2014/08/03/337168933/-no-tofu-doesn-t -equate-to-no-problem-for-google-universal-typeface.

52. Google has taken up Unicode's controversial method of Han unification (which assigns the same code point to characters in Chinese, Japanese, and Korean that are perceived as being the same). However, in their CJP Sans group of Noto typefaces, they also offer regional variations. In response to frequently asked questions about their use of Han unification, they argue that they are working within the system as it exists—as long as Unicode maintains Han unification, Google's Noto fonts will as well. See Google, "Google Noto Fonts: FAQ," accessed April 15, 2018, https://www.google.com/get/noto/help /faq/.

53. Stanislas Dehaene has argued that the arbitrariness of writing systems merely appears arbitrary—that these systems are in fact sculpted over time to fit the brain most efficiently. See Dehaene's "Natural Born Readers," *New Scientist*, July 5, 2003, 33. He also argues that the arbitrariness goes away when one learns a language in *Reading in the Brain* (New York: Penguin, 2009), 113. We might consider, however, whether Dehaene's meaning of "arbitrary" is different from Saussure's.

54. See Dehaene, *Reading in the Brain*. There are cases of pure alexia in which patients who have lost the ability to read, because of damage to the left occipitotemporal region, are still able to handle numerals.

55. For more on the neurological aspects of reading and typography, see chapter 7.

Chapter 4

1. Edward Johnston, *Writing & Illuminating, & Lettering* (New York: Pitman Publishing, 1954), 239.

2. Plato's ideal form and Kant's noumenon are both philosophical concepts that maintain there are immutable truths that are beyond us, indifferent to us and for Kant, beyond our ability to know. Marx and Freud both maintained that the reality of a thing is not found on its surface, but by digging down and revealing the hidden layers (the social conditions that emerge from an industrial capitalist means of production in Marx's case, and buried traumas and memories in Freud's case).

3. Other notable treatises include: Andrea Mantegna, 1456–1457; Domianus Moyllus, ca. 1480; Luca Pacioli, 1509; Sigismondo de' Fanti, 1514; Francesco Torniello, 1517; Albrecht Dürer, 1525; Giovanni Battista Verini, ca. 1527; Geofroy Tory, 1529; Vespasiano Amphiareo, 1554; Giambattista Palatino, 1543–1575; Joseph Moxon, 1676; Jacques Jaugeon et al., ca. 1693. See Millard Meiss, "The First Alphabetical Treatises in the Renaissance," *Journal of Typographic Research* 3, no. 1 (Jan. 1, 1969): 3–30; Robin Rider, "Shaping Information: Mathematics, Computing & Typography," in *Inscribing Science*, ed. Timothy Lenoir (Stanford, CA: Stanford University Press, 1998), 39–54.

4. Luca Pacioli, quoted in Meiss, "The First Alphabetical Treatises in the Renaissance," 8.

5. See Meiss, "The First Alphabetical Treatises in the Renaissance." Pacioli's ratio for a letter with a crossbar, such as A or H, was 1:3:9, a ratio that appears in Plato's *Timaeus*.

6. Quoted in Rider, "Shaping Information," 41. On Feliciano's attitude toward R as a second-class character, see Meiss, "The First Alphabetical Treatises in the Renaissance," 15.

7. Rider, "Shaping Information," 41.

8. Meiss, "The First Alphabetical Treatises in the Renaissance," 21.

9. Albrecht Dürer, *Of the Just Shaping of Letters: From the Applied Geometry of Albrecht Dürer* (Mineola, NY: Dover, 1965). Meiss attributes the opening up of proportional ideals to an apparently unnamed manuscript by an unknown author, which in turn influenced Dürer's definition of characters. See Meiss, "The First Alphabetical Treatises in the Renaissance," 25.

10. Meiss notes that Sigismondo de' Fanti's treatise began not with Roman capitals, but with blackletter. While Meiss mentions this as a sign of the changing times (Fanti published in 1514), blackletter is also a style of lettering that, while it has a lowercase, is roughly as uniform from shape to shape, and so would be expressible in this kind of definition. See Meiss, "The First Alphabetical Treatises in the Renaissance," 25. Albrecht Dürer's treatise similarly includes a lowercase, but it is for blackletter only. See Dürer, *Of the Just Shaping of Letters*.

11. Quoted in Kinross, *Modern Typography*, 24.

12. Updike, *Printing Types*, 242.

13. The nineteenth century, and its explosion of outdoor advertising and signage, saw the development of numerous styles of type including the sans-serif, slab-serif, Tuscan, fat-face, typefaces that attempted to mimic three-dimensional qualities, highly ornamented faces, and more subdued styles like Clarendons. Often advertisements would use as many of these styles as possible, making for a particularly cluttered aesthetic that mimics the expanding cities in which these ads appeared.

14. Linda Dalrymple Henderson, *The Fourth Dimension and Non-Euclidean Geometry in Modern Art* (Cambridge, MA: MIT Press, 2013). The belief in the vertical and horizontal was so strong that Theo van Doesburg's divergence from it (allowing diagonals into some of his works) led to a schism in the movement between him and Piet Mondrian.

15. Tschichold, *The New Typography*, 73. While Tschichold wrote the book on New Typography, the name appears earlier in an essay by Laszlo Moholy-Nagy, a key figure at the Bauhaus—see Moholy-Nagy, "The New Typography." Tschichold identified the sans serif as the "logical development from Didot" (see *The New Typography*, 20), connecting the late eighteenth- and early nineteenth-century modernist style to nineteenth-century sans serifs.

16. Tracy, *Letters of Credit*, 89.

17. There is still some debate around what typefaces work best in wayfinding (signs for navigation, whether in subways or on the highway), but most often the faces designed for this purpose are sans serifs. In addition to Johnston Sans, see DIN 1451 (ca. 1931); Highway Gothic (ca. 1950); Transport (1963); Frutiger (1976); Clearview (1990s); and the application of Akzidenz Grotesk (1896) and Helvetica (1957) to the New York City subway system. One of the few serifed typefaces that has passed American wayfinding visibility tests is NPS Rawlinson (2000), used by the National Parks Service. Gerard Unger's Capitolium (1998), designed for the city of Rome, is also serifed.

18. Paul Renner, quoted in Christopher Burke, *Paul Renner: The Art of Typography* (New York: Princeton Architectural Press, 1998), 96.

19. In the early years of legibility studies, the idea that serifs are nonessential would have been contested by scholars like Émile Javal and those who followed his work. While more contemporary legibility studies tend to find little difference brought about by the serif, to identify it as nonessential is not to suggest it is entirely without purpose.

20. Edward M. Catich, *The Origin of the Serif: Brush Writing and Roman Letters* (Davenport, IA: St. Ambrose University Press, 1991).

21. See Warren Chappell, *The Anatomy of Lettering* (Pelham, NY: Bridgeman, 1940); Raymond A. Ballinger, *Lettering in Modern Use* (New York: Reinhold, 1952).

22. Henry Lewis Bullen, "Notes Toward the Study of Types: 1. The Power of the Serif; Evolution of Type Faces by Change of Serifs," *Graphic Arts* 1, no. 1 (Jan. 1911): 33–37.

23. Bullen, "Notes Toward the Study of Types," 34. In different times and places, the sans serif has had a wide variety of names, including gothic, grotesque/grotesk, and lineal(e).

24. The computer scientist Donald Knuth, for instance, argues that a computer-scientific way of thinking is a more natural fit for mathematicians skilled at logic rather than geometry. In an interesting nod to visual thinking, he once sought to observe the visual differences in these ways of thinking by comparing page 100 of several mathematical texts. See Knuth's "Donald Knuth interviewed by Donald J. Albers and Lynn A. Steen," in *Mathematical People: Profiles and Interviews*, ed. D. J. Albers and G. L. Alexanderson (Boston: Birkhäuser, 1985).

25. H. W. Mergler and P. M. Vargo, "One Approach to Computer Assisted Letter Design," *Journal of Typographic Research* 2, no. 4 (Oct. 1968): 299–322.

26. ITSYLF also has a nonautomatic version, in which the designer does more than the computer in generating typographic forms.

27. Mergler and Vargo, "One Approach to Computer Assisted Letter Design," 307. This is not a direct quote from Mergler and Vargo's text; it is my own summary of their categories.

28. Mergler and Vargo, "One Approach to Computer Assisted Letter Design," 307.

29. Mergler and Vargo, "One Approach to Computer Assisted Letter Design," 322.

30. Mergler and Vargo, "One Approach to Computer Assisted Letter Design," 301.

31. Hustwit, dir., *Helvetica*.

32. See Liz Stinson, "Two Legends Dish on How to Design a Typeface," *Wired*, June 5, 2013, https://www.wired.com/2013/06/typefaces/.

33. Martin Mendelsberg, "Alef-Beit: A Typographic Journey," in *The Education of a Typographer*, ed. Steven Heller (New York: Allworth Press, 2004), 143.

34. Philippe Coueignoux, "Approche Structurelle De La Lettre," *Langue Française*, no. 59 (Sept. 1983), 54. I've added "technically 5," because Mergler and Vargo's class 5 is not solidly a group of its own, it consists of characters that should belong to other groups, but which have been rejected because they have tails. See Mergler and Vargo, "One Approach to Computer Assisted Letter Design," 307.

35. Coueignoux, "Approche Structurelle De La Lettre," 54. All translations of Coueignoux's essay are my own.

36. Coueignoux, "Approche Structurelle De La Lettre," 55. Coueignoux provides as another example the rule that a turn cannot be attached to a stem, but can be attached to a bow. It would seem, however, that the lowercase f disproves this rule.

37. Coueignoux, "Approche Structurelle De La Lettre," 53.

38. Coueignoux, "Approche Structurelle De La Lettre," 53.

39. Like the modernist theorists discussed above, Coueignoux and Mergler and Vargo all identify the serif as secondary, or expendable. This may be attributed to the work that modernists did to separate the serif from our notions of what a typographic form is. Or it may simply be an attempt to make the work of programming characters digitally more manageable.

40. C. H. Cox., P. Coueignoux, B. Blesser, and M. Eden, "Skeletons: A Link between Theoretical and Physical Letter Descriptions," *Pattern Recognition* 15, no. 1 (1982), 11.

41. Cox et al., "Skeletons," 13.

42. In typographic circles, Donald Knuth is also known as the developer of T$_E$X, an early program for digital typesetting or page layout.

43. Knuth had originally thought he would construct his typographic shapes by setting lines around the edges of existing typefaces, as he had seen John Warnock at Xerox PARC doing. He found, however, that he wasn't interested in simply recreating existing typefaces, and that it was easier to describe a line traced by an imaginary pen than to describe the contour of a typographic shape. See Knuth, "Digital Typography," in *Digital Typography* (Stanford, CA: CSLI Publications, 1999), 8; and "Lessons Learned from Metafont," *Visible Language* 19, no. 1 (Winter 1985): 36.

44. Donald Knuth, "The Concept of a Meta-Font," in *Digital Typography* (Stanford, CA: CSLI Publications, 1999), 299.

45. Donald Knuth, "Conversations, 1996: Printing," in *Companion to the Papers of Donald Knuth* (Stanford, CA: CSLI Publications, 2011), 60.

46. Donald Knuth, "Mathematical Typography," *Bulletin (New Series) of The American Mathematical Society* 1, no. 2 (Mar. 1979): 352–353. He favored Francesco Torniello, because his descriptions were unambiguous. He even uses Torniello's

instructions for the construction of an S (the most difficult letter for Knuth to construct) as a stepping stone to his own equation. See Knuth's essay, "The Letter S," in Digital Typography (Stanford: CSLI Publications, 1999), 264–266.

47. Knuth, "Lessons Learned from Metafont," 37.

48. Knuth, "The Concept of a Meta-Font," 290.

49. Charles Bigelow, "Other Replies to Donald E. Knuth's Article 'The Concept of A Meta-Font,'" *Visible Language* 16, 4 (Fall 1982): 339–343; Gerard Unger, "Other Replies to Donald E. Knuth's Article 'The Concept of a Meta-Font,'" *Visible Language* 16, no. 4 (Fall 1982): 353–356.

50. Knuth, "Mathematical Typography," 351.

51. See, for instance, Henri-Paul Bronsard, "Other Replies to Donald E. Knuth's Article," 342.

52. Knuth, "Lessons Learned from Metafont," 36.

53. Knuth, "The Concept of a Meta-Font," 303.

54. Mergler and Vargo note that for some characters, the set of possible parameters is obvious (such as E), but that for others there is more than one possible way in which it could be parameterized (such as A). See Mergler and Vargo, "One Approach to Computer Assisted Letter Design," 308–309.

55. Hofstadter uses Shatter (Vic Carless, 1973) and its relation to Helvetica as an example of a variation on a theme that cannot be produced simply by altering parameters. Shatter is a typeface that takes Helvetica's shapes, slices through them, and then staggers the resulting shapes, mimicking the distortion created by shattered glass. Douglas R. Hofstadter, "Metafont, Metamathematics, and Metaphysics: Comments on Donald Knuth's Article 'The Concept of a Meta-Font,'" *Visible Language* 16, no. 4 (Fall 1982): 309–338.

56. Hofstadter, "Metafont, Metamathematics, and Metaphysics," 329.

57. Hofstadter, "Metafont, Metamathematics, and Metaphysics," 331. Hofstadter does note that at least one of Knuth's parameters is equally spread across multiple characters, namely, serif length. As this parameter is adjusted it affects all characters in the type family.

Chapter 5

1. Zuzana Licko, "Zuzana Licko Answers Frequently Asked Questions," *Emigre Fonts*, 2000, https://www.emigre.com/Essays/ZuzanaLicko/FAQ.

2. Burke, *Paul Renner: The Art of Typography*. The primary model for the uppercase Latin characters was not the calligrapher's pen (as it was for the lowercase), but was rather Roman inscriptions like the Trajan Column.

3. Paul Renner, quoted in Burke, *Paul Renner: The Art of Typography*, 99.

4. Spencer, *The Visible Word*, 10.

5. Tory, *Champ Fleury*.

6. Gill, *An Essay on Typography*, 120.

7. Kurt Schwitters, "Proposal for a Systemschrift (Anregungen zur Erlangung einer Systemschrift)," *International Revue 1927–1929* 10 (1978): 313.

8. Another notable modernist typeface that integrates shapes from both the upper and lowercases is A. M. Cassandre's Peignot (1937). Though this face has two separate cases, the lowercase is a unique combination of traditionally upper and lowercase characters, as well as unusually tall ascenders. This makes Peignot a sort of modern equivalent of Francesco Griffo's Bembo (1496)—an attempt to better integrate the upper and lowercases by adjusting the heights of the lowercase to meet the height of the upper. Cassandre's combination of cases here, as well as his single-case typeface Bifur (1929), are notable for being built at the expense of the lowercase rather than the uppercase as other modernists were doing.

9. Audrey Bennett and Bridget Rice, "Bradbury Thompson's Alphabet 26: A Font System for Early Readers?" *AIGA*, December 20, 2005. See also Susan Merritt, "Bradbury Thompson," *AIGA*, August 14, 2017. https://www.aiga.org/medalist-bradbury-thompson.

10. Though Christian Boer is dyslexic himself, and so his design is based in first-hand experience, there is no definitive evidence so far that his typeface reliably helps dyslexic readers.

11. S. B. Telingater, "The Standardization of Alphabetic Graphemes," *Journal of Typographic Research* 2, no. 3 (July 1968): 233–240.

12. This lettering does not appear to have a name. See Blackwell, *20th Century Type*, 23.

13. See, for instance, Wim Crouwel, "Type Design for the Computer Age," *Journal of Typographic Research* 4, no. 1 (Winter 1970): 51–58; Adrian Frutiger, "Letterforms in Photo-typography," *Journal of Typographic Research* 4, no. 4 (Autumn 1970): 327–335; and Hermann Zapf, "The Changes in Letterforms Due to Technical Developments," *Journal of Typographic Research* 2, no. 4 (Oct. 1968): 351–368.

14. Wim Crouwel, *New Alphabet: A Possibility for the New Development, An Introduction for a Programmed Typography* (Hilversum: Steendrukkerij de Jong, 1967), inside cover.

15. Crouwel, "Type Design for the Computer Age," 54–57.

16. While a student at the Rhode Island School of Design (ca. 1988–1992), Tobias Frere-Jones reportedly designed a typeface named Sum of the Parts (or alternately Some of the Parts), which was intended to illustrate this importance of context in our ability to read a typeface. He used handwriting in order to blur the identities of individual characters, isolating eleven ambiguous shapes that could function, thanks to context, in place of the twenty-six distinct letters we are used to. See Tobias Frere-Jones, "Experiments in Type Design," *Texts on Type: Critical Writings on Typography*, ed. Steven Heller and Philip B. Meggs (New York: Allworth Press, 2001), 233–234.

17. Crouwel, *New Alphabet*, n.p.

18. Timothy Epps, *Alphabet* (Hilversum: Steendrukkerij de Jong, 1969).

19. Some OCR typefaces were designed for specific machines; for instance, Viafont (1969) was an OCR typeface designed for the short-lived Viatron.

20. Adrian Frutiger, "OCR-B: A Standardized Character for Optical Recognition," *Journal of Typographic Research* 1, no. 2 (April 1967), 139. OCR-B was intended to be a more aesthetically pleasing alternative to the already extant OCR-A, being used in America.

21. Frutiger, "OCR-B," 143.

22. Frutiger, "OCR-B," 142.

23. Heidrun Osterer and Philipp Stamm, eds., *Adrian Frutiger—Typefaces: The Complete Works* (Boston: Birkhäuser, 2009), 179.

24. Osterer and Stamm, *Adrian Frutiger—Typefaces*, 183.

25. Zuzana Licko, "Interview by Rudy VanderLans," *Emigre* 15 (1990), https://www.emigre.com/Essays/ZuzanaLicko/Emigre15.

26. In this way Variex is similar to Meander, discussed in the Introduction.

27. Licko, "Interview by Rudy VanderLans."

28. Recall from chapter 2 that Beatrice Warde argued that type should not attract attention to itself, while Stanley Morison argued that the type designer should not upset the reader's expectations. See Warde, "The Crystal Goblet," and Morison, "First Principles."

29. See, for instance, Weingart's typographic work in *TM/RSI* (*Typografische Monatsblätter/ Revue Suisse de L'Imprimerie*) in 1972.

30. Chuck Byrne and Martha Witte, "Brave New World: Understanding Deconstruction," in *Looking Closer*, ed. Michael Bierut, William Drenttel, and Steven Heller (New York: Allworth Press, 1994), 116.

31. Quoted in Rick Poynor, "Type and Deconstruction in the Digital Era," in *Looking Closer*, 87.

32. Robin Kinross has written rather disparagingly about this period of design (he's not alone in that; many critics have decried what took place in 1980s and 1990s typographic design). While he recognizes the influence of continental theory (deconstruction, semiotics), he also characterizes this period as having a "peculiarly Protestant-American interpretation of the post-structuralist theory of 'difference,' which lapsed back into a simple espousal of the liberty of the individual" (Kinross, *Modern Typography*, 173). This is a fascinating point, nicely capturing the complicated politics (or mere appearance of politics) in this movement. Designers like Mr. Keedy did disregard the politics of thinkers like Barthes and Foucault, and Kinross's characterization of this depoliticization might serve as a snapshot of the larger trend by which the neoliberal thinking championed by the enemies of these designers (Reagan, Thatcher) nonetheless became internalized by left-wing politics in the United States and the UK.

33. Rick Poynor, "Conceptual Hybrids: Type in the 1990s," *Artifact* 3, no. 1 (2013): 2.2.

34. Poynor, "Conceptual Hybrids," 2.6.

35. Gerard Unger, "All My Type Designs: Decoder (1992)," http://www.gerardunger.com/allmytypedesigns/allmytypedesigns13.html.

36. Tracy, *Letters of Credit: A View of Type Design*, 31. See also Ellen Lupton, "Cold Eye: An Exact Science," *Print* 57, no. 5 (Sept.–Oct. 2003), 22.

37. According to Lee, the typeface is partly motivated by the desire to reintroduce the joyful experience of learning to read to adults who are already proficient. Ji Lee, email to the author, July 11, 2019.

38. Given the curve of the U, it is easiest to tell it apart from the H if viewed from underneath.

39. Ji Lee, *Univers Revolved* (New York: Harry N. Abrams, 2004).

40. The inclusion of symbol sets like Dingbats or Webdings within the set of typographic shapes will inevitably raise the question of whether emoji should similarly be included within that set. As Lisa Gitelman notes, there are important differences between emoji and printed text—the latter including both alphanumerical and nonalphanumerical characters. Emoticons would certainly exist in the set of typographic shapes—as these are made up of existing typographic characters ;). However, emoji are pictographic symbols that are not part of typography. One can note significant differences in a number of realms—linguistically, they do not signify in the same way alphanumerical characters do (Gitelman nicely elaborates this point). Legally, they enjoy intellectual property protections that are withheld from typefaces in the United States. Practically, they are produced by two different kinds of artist. And relationally, while some emoji include typographic forms within them, they do not generally share forms with other typographic shapes. The existence of things like chess fonts, and typefaces like Rattera (which we will discuss in the chapter 7) do raise challenges to this line between typography and emoji, but at the present date, I believe the distinction between typographic shapes and emoji is worth maintaining. See Gitelman, "*Emoji Dick* and the Eponymous Whale: An Essay in Four Parts," *Post 45*, July 8, 2018, http://post45.org/2018/07/emoji-dick-and-the-eponymous-whale-an-essay-in-four-parts/.

41. See Carson interviewed in Hustwit, dir., *Helvetica*; and Lewis Blackwell, *The End of Print*, 2nd ed. (London: Laurence King, 2000), n.p.

Chapter 6

1. Muriel Cooper, quoted in David Reinfurt and Robert Wiesenberger, *Muriel Cooper* (Cambridg, MA: MIT Press, 2017), n.p.

2. Saussure, *Course in General Linguistics*, 67–68.

3. This is not surprising, given his disregard for the materiality of the signifier.

4. Dehaene, *Reading in the Brain*, 47.

5. Hofstadter, "Metafont, Metamathematics, and Metaphysics," 331. Robin Kinross has argued that something relational (or at least something more than the individual/isolated form) was at the heart of Anthony Froshaug's thinking on typography as well. In order to create isomorphic representations of their ideas (that is, representations that share the same structure as the

things they're representing), poets like William Blake and Guillaume Apollinaire composed their own configurations of graphic elements, breaking with the conventions of poetry. See Anthony Froshaug, "The Book as a Means of Communicating Ideas," in *Anthony Froshaug Texts & Type*, ed. Robin Kinross (London: Hyphen Press, 2000), 106; and Robin Kinross, "Technics and Ethics: The Work of Anthony Froshaug," *Octavo* 86.1 (1986): 4.

6. A use-theory of language recognizes that we use language in ways that are messier, more creative, more vague (and yet still operational) than a strict logical understanding of language will be able to capture. So rather than constructing an understanding of language upon a series of logical propositions, use theory seeks to study how language actually operates (not unlike Wolfgang Ernst's media archaeology).

7. Wittgenstein, *Philosophical Investigations*, 31e–34e.

8. Wittgenstein, *Philosophical Investigations*, 31e.

9. Wittgenstein, *Philosophical Investigations*, 32e.

10. Wittgenstein, *Philosophical Investigations*, 32e.

11. Ideo, "Font Map," http://fontmap.ideo.com/.

12. Kevin Ho, "Organizing the World of Fonts with AI," *Medium*, April 19, 2017, https://medium.com/ideo-stories/organizing-the-world-of-fonts-with-ai -7d9e49ff2b25; Katharine Schwab, "A Map of the Typographic Universe Drawn By AI," *Fast Company*, April 25, 2017, https://www.fastcompany.com/90111599 /a-map-of-the-typographic-universe-drawn-by-ai.

13. Quoted in Schwab, "A Map of the Typographic Universe Drawn By AI." The square bracket text appears in Schwab's article; it does not indicate a change I've made.

14. Thibaudeau's classification system calls unusual typefaces Fantasies; both Vox and British Standards 2961 call them Graphic; and Alan Bartram, Alexander Lawson, and Lewis Blackwell call them Decorated or Decorative. See Bartram, *Typeforms: A History*; Blackwell, *20th Century Type*; British Standards Institution, BS 2961: 1967 Typeface Nomenclature and Classification (London, 1967); Alexander Lawson, *Printing Types: An Introduction* (Boston: Beacon Press, 1971); Francis Thibaudeau, *La lettre d'imprimerie* (Paris: Bureau de l'édition, 1921); Maximilien Vox, *Défense and Illustration de la lettre* (Paris: Monotype, 1955).

15. Wittgenstein, *Philosophical Investigations*, 33e. Wittgenstein makes this claim about the utility of even undefined concepts in response to Gottlob Frege, who argued that a concept is like an area: it needs clear definition if it is to be called an area at all. In Wittgenstein's refusal of this point, and in his denial that there is one common feature of all *language* (or of all *games*), his philosophy is rejecting both of the types of definition that the previous pages of this book has dealt with—the skeletal definition and the outer limit definition.

16. Nietzsche, "On Truth and Lies in a Non-Moral Sense," 15–49. He argues that the concept (an equation of unequal things) is problematic because we are supplanting truth with convenience. He would argue that there is no such

thing as a *leaf*, only a vast diversity of tens of thousands of variants of leafy vegetation.

17. Henry Glassie. *Pattern in the Material Folk Culture of the Eastern United States* (Philadelphia: University of Pennsylvania Press, 1968), 32. I'm indebted to Lisa Gitelman for bringing this book to my attention.

18. Ellen Lupton and J. Abbott Miller, "A Natural History of Typography," in *Looking Closer*, ed. Michael Bierut, William Drenttel, and Steven Heller (New York: Allworth Press, 1994), 19–25.

19. Lupton and Miller, "A Natural History of Typography," 20.

20. Lupton and Miller, "A Natural History of Typography," 19.

21. Lupton and Miller, "A Natural History of Typography," 19.

22. Mullaney, "The Moveable Typewriter," 784–789. Ido Ramati has found similar forces at play in Hebrew text production. In "The Mechanization of Modern Hebrew Writing" (presentation at the Before and Beyond Typography Online Conference, June 5, 2020), he shows how the difficulty of including diacritical marks in typewritten text influenced the preferred means of spelling in Hebrew writing—favoring the so-called plene spelling, using no diacritical marks to indicate vowels.

23. Charles Darwin, *The Origin of Species* (New York: Signet, 2003), 6. See also chapter 3 of the same work, "Struggle for Existence," in which Darwin provides numerous examples of these kinds of relationships.

24. Jane Jacobs, *The Death and Life of Great American Cities* (New York: Random House, 1961), 15.

25. This is not to ignore dominant influences, such as the influence of a supremely popular typeface like Helvetica on other faces; or the dominant force of the Latin script in the history of typographic design.

26. Marcel Duchamp's sculpture *Fountain*, for instance, was a factory-produced urinal set on its side, signed, and placed on a pedestal in gallery exhibits. By its inclusion within the conventions of the art world, and because Duchamp was an artist, this urinal was transformed into a work of art.

27. Woody Leslie's book *Understanding Molecular Typography* (Chicago: One Page Productions, 2015) is an art book, published as though it is the rediscovered work of the fictional H. F. Henderson, and is passed off as a primer, for novices, of an emerging field of scientific study. I'm indebted to Jacob Ford for bringing this book to my attention—Ford produced a pop-up book that animates the binding of these typographic elements. That pop-up book can be seen in action in "The Molecular Typography Pop-Up Book," at https://vimeo.com/173524096.

28. The k, z, and x suggest there are more than two parts, as there's a diagonal block that appears in these characters that are not present in any others.

29. Gerard Unger, "All My Type Designs: Decoder (1992)."

30. This is also reminiscent of the definition the US House of Representatives came up with in their consideration of the extension of copyright to typefaces. Recall the discussion in chapter 2. See Kastenmeier, "Copyright Law Revision."

31. Noordzij, *The Stroke*, 13–15.

32. "Superunion Helps Elliptic Find the Truth behind Crypto-crimes with New Identity," *Superunion*, June 13, 2018.

33. Antimatter was first published in *Fuse 20*. See Neville Brody and Jon Wozencroft, eds., *Fuse 1–20: From Invention to Antimatter* (Cologne: Taschen, 2012).

34. Hofstadter, "Metafont, Metamathematics, and Metaphysics," 310.

35. Harald Geisler has designed Sigmund Freud (2013), Albert Einstein (2015), Martin Luther (2017), and Martin Luther King, Jr. (forthcoming).

36. Jon Wozencroft, "Why Fuse?" in *Fuse 1–20: From Invention to Antimatter*, ed. Neville Brody and Jon Wozencroft (Cologne: Taschen, 2012), 22.

37. Perhaps the most notable example of this revivalist spirit can be found in the Arts and Crafts or private press movement. Inspired by the work of William Morris, Venetian typefaces (such as Jenson's Roman from 1470) were revived in the midst of industrial modernism. Thoroughly resisting the efficiency of the mechanical engineer, this revival valorized the calligrapher's pen.

38. Also referred to as faux or faux-foreign typefaces, this kind of typeface seems to emerge first in the nineteenth century and to correspond to that period's racism and stereotyping. For instance, pseudo-Chinese typefaces, like Mikita (George Bruce type foundry, 1867) or Mikado (Hamilton Type Foundry, ca. 1887), were designed at a time when the US was institutionalizing its anti-Chinese racism in laws like the Chinese Exclusion Act of 1882. See Rob Giampetro, "New Black Face: Neuland and Lithos as Stereotypograph," *Lined & Unlined*, 2004, https://linedandunlined.com/archive/new-black-face/; Paul Shaw, "Stereo Types," *Print* (June 17, 2009), https://www.printmag.com/article/stereo_types/. Thanks to Whei Hsin Lujan for giving me cause to look into the history of these typefaces.

Chapter 7

1. Ruder, *Typographie: Manual of Typographic Design*, 76.

2. Crouwel has noted that New Alphabet was never intended to be used in a number of different places. See for instance McNeil, *The Visual History of Type*, 377; MoMA, "Wim Crouwel, New Alphabet, 1967," https://www.moma.org/collection/works/139322.

3. Matthew Mirapaul, "Is It about to Rain? Check the Typeface," *New York Times*, July 24, 2003. This typeface replaces a "weatherball" that used to change color according to the weather, sitting on the rooftop of the Northwestern National Bank building.

4. It's worth noting that I haven't found much evidence of Rattera having existed (outside of projects related to Barnbrook's typeface, and nothing that appears offline). Certain elements of his biography also make his existence unbelievable (according to Barnbrook's brief biography of him, Rattera was in the car when Ted Kennedy crashed in Chappaquiddick, killing Mary Jo Kopechne. And as a result of the injuries he sustained, and the legal and political desire

to get him out of the country as quickly as possible, he was unable to attend Woodstock . . .). I've found no newspaper reports in the UK of any Alfred Rattera; and there are no scholarly works on him, even though he's characterized as a child prodigy who performed music publicly, an outsider artist, and genius of sorts. If Rattera is merely a figment of Jonathan Barnbrook's imagination, it's an impressive amount of work for the sake of a typeface.

5. Jonathan Barnbrook, "Rattera Font," in *Fuse 1–20: From Invention to Antimatter*, ed. Neville Brody and Jon Wozencroft (Cologne: Taschen, 2012), supplemental digital material.

6. Jonathan Barnbrook, Rattera poster, in *Fuse 1–20*, supplemental digital material.

7. I identify decoding as the "most immediate" end of human reading because, as Stuart Hall argued, decoding often takes in information and then encodes that into new messages, continuing the cycle of communication. See Hall, "Encoding and Decoding in the Television Discourse"; and figure 1.9 of this book.

8. And while typography may be used to influence people's opinion of a brand, product, resumé, etc., while typefaces may conjure up certain psychological impressions in individual readers, these are not the primary concern of the medium. These are specialist cases, not the medium's general operation.

9. Hochuli, *Detail in Typography*, 10. To be fair to Hochuli, he offers this definition as the primary way in which reading takes place; as the secondary way, he acknowledges the associations we then make with those letters—more of the linguistic/literary sense of reading.

10. One exception to the fact that we don't read character by character is when we encounter unfamiliar words, or non-words; in these cases, we do read that word character-by-character. Dehaene, *Reading in the Brain*, 39–40.

11. See Dehaene, *Reading in the Brain*, 15–17; and for more on fixation points and eye movements in reading Chinese, see Jie-Li Tsai and George W. McConkie, "Where Do Chinese Readers Send Their Eyes?" in *The Mind's Eye: Cognitive and Applied Aspects of Eye Movement Research*, ed. J. Hyönä, R. Radach, and H. Deubel (New York: Elsevier, 2003), 159–176.

12. George W. McConkie and Keith Rayner, "The Span of the Effective Stimulus During a Fixation in Reading," *Perception & Psychophysics* 17, no. 6 (1975): 583. Earlier studies found that other information like capital letters and punctuation is perceivable at a greater distance from the fixation point (and is used by the eye to prepare its next steps). See same article, 578.

13. Hochuli, *Detail in Typography*, 32.

14. Bringhurst, *Elements of Typographic Style*, 27.

15. Hochuli, *Detail in Typography*, 47. See also Giambattista Bodoni's *Manual of Typography*, ed. Stephan Füssel (Cologne: Taschen, 2016).

16. For instance, an uneven distribution of ink is one of many reasons that Comic Sans is such a derided typeface.

17. The difference between sans and serif is generally only an issue in special cases such as at small sizes, on low-resolution screens, or on signs meant to be read while moving at high speeds.

18. The effect of x-height on character recognition is not settled science, but examples of claims can be found historically in Zachrisson, *Studies in the Legibility of Printed Text*, 39. Myra Thiessen et al. briefly address the lack of definitive science on x-height in "Brainy Type: A Look at How the Brain Processes Typographic Information," *Visible Language* 49, nos. 1–2 (Apr. 2015): 174–189. As Richard Pyke notes in his collection of findings in *The Legibility of Print* (London: His Majesty's Stationery Office, 1926), numerous early scholars on the legibility of type studied legibility at the level of individual characters. This suggests that while there are general features that may aid legibility (like a tall x-height), different characters require different kinds of features. Based on a series of studies from 1885 to 1925, the five most legible characters were said to be A, L, W, D, and P in the uppercase, and m, w, d and q (tied), p, and j in the lowercase.

19. Dehaene, *Reading in the Brain*, 4. See also Maryanne Wolf, *Proust and the Squid* (New York: HarperCollins, 2007), 169–170. This is because humans have had writing for only about 5,400 years, with alphabetic writing only 3,800 years old.

20. Laurent Cohen, Stanislas Dehaene, Lionel Naccache, and Stéphane Lehéricy, "The Visual Word Form Area," *Brain* 123 (2000): 291–307. Gordon E. Legge has noted that "word form" is distinct from "word shape." The visual word form area processes the identity and spatial relation of letters, but not details like typeface, size, case, etc. See Legge's *Psychophysics of Reading in Normal and Low Vision* (Mahwah, NJ: Lawrence Erlbaum, 2007), 96.

21. Cathy J. Price and Joseph T. Devlin, "The Myth of the Visual Word Form Area," *NeuroImage* 19 (2003): 473–481.

22. Dehaene, *Reading in the Brain*, 64.

23. Dehaene, *Reading in the Brain*, 70, 97–100; Abubaker A. A. Almabruk, Kevin B. Paterson, Victoria McGowan, and Timothy R. Jordan, in "Evaluating Effects of Divided Hemispheric Processing on Word Recognition in Foveal and Extrafoveal Displays: The Evidence from Arabic," *PLOS ONE* 6, no. 4 (Apr. 2011): 6, find that the specialization in the left hemisphere in Latin reading also applies to Arabic; Uri Hasson, Ifat Levy, Marlene Behrmann, Talma Hendler, and Rafael Malach, in "Eccentricity Bias as an Organizing Principle for Human High-Order Object Areas," *Neuron* 34, no. 3 (Apr. 25, 2002): 479–490, find activation in the left occipito-temporal area among Hebrew readers (reading right to left, as in Arabic); and Kimihiro Nakamura, Stanislas Dehaene, Antoinette Jobert, Denis Le Bihan, and Sid Kouider, in "Subliminal Convergence of Kanji and Kana Words," *Journal of Cognitive Neuroscience* 17, no. 6 (2005): 954–968, find that while there are some small differences between the processing of Kanji and Kana scripts in Japanese, both make use of neural pathways found in Latin readers as well.

24. This aesthetic universality would be distinct from a linguistic "Universal Grammar" that Noam Chomsky proposed. Given the ease with which children learn language, Chomsky proposed that humans must have an innate language faculty. If such a faculty is species-wide, this would mean that all languages must have some quality in common, which makes it compatible with this faculty despite whatever other differences exist between languages. He proposed that this Universal Grammar was the phenomenon of recursion—our ability to efficiently

nest ideas one within another (so that a statement like "A brown owl is perched on the oak tree" does not need to be expressed as "There is an owl. The owl is brown. The owl is perched on a tree. The tree is oak"). However, languages that do not have recursion (e.g., Pirahã) have brought Chomsky's proposals into question. See Marc D. Hauser, Noam Chomsky, and W. Tecumseh Fitch, "The Faculty of Language," *Science* 298, no. 5598 (Nov. 22, 2002): 1569–1579; and, on this debate in linguistics and Daniel Everett's work on the Pirahã language, see John Colapinto, "The Interpreter," *New Yorker*, April 16, 2007, 118–137.

25. Jacques Rancière, *The Future of the Image*, trans. Gregory Elliott (New York: Verso, 2007), 99.

26. Ellen Lupton, "A Post-Mortem on Deconstruction?" in *Texts on Type: Critical Writings on Typography*, ed. Steven Heller and Philip B. Meggs (New York: Allworth Press, 2001), 47.

27. Mark A. Changizi and Shinsuke Shimojo, "Character Complexity and Redundancy in Writing Systems over Human History," *Proceedings of the Royal Society B* 272 (2005): 267–275.

28. Changizi, and Shimojo, "Character Complexity and Redundancy in Writing Systems," 271. Changizi refers to this as the *invariant-length approach* to building characters.

29. Mark A. Changizi, Qiong Zhang, Hao Ye, and Shinsuke Shimojo, "The Structures of Letters and Symbols throughout Human History Are Selected to Match Those Found in Objects in Natural Scenes," *American Naturalist* 167, no. 5 (May 2006): E117–E139. Changizi and Shimojo introduce both of these ideas at the end of their 2005 study as well ("Character Complexity and Redundancy in Writing Systems," 273–274).

30. Changizi et al., "The Structures of Letters and Symbols throughout Human History," E121–E123.

31. Changizi et al., "The Structures of Letters and Symbols throughout Human History," E123–E125, E129.

32. Dehaene, *Reading in the Brain*, 137.

33. Irving Biederman, "Recognition-by-Components: A Theory of Human Image Understanding." *Psychological Review* 94, no. 2 (1987), 135–139.

34. Changizi and Shimojo, "Character Complexity and Redundancy in Writing Systems," 272.

35. McNeil, "Minuscule," in *The Visual History of Type*, 612–613.

36. Chris Calori, *Signage and Wayfinding Design* (Hoboken, NJ: Wiley, 2015), 166–167. The equation for highway signage is $((N+6)S/100) + (D/10) = H$, where N is the number of messages that will appear on the sign, S is the speed limit, D is the horizontal distance the sign is set back from the road, and H is the height of the letters.

37. Dehaene, *Reading in the Brain*, 19. According to Almabruk et al., "Evaluating Effects of Divided Hemispheric Processing on Word Recognition," reading Arabic requires the fixation point of the fovea be centered in the word.

38. McConkie and Rayner, "The Span of the Effective Stimulus during a Fixation in Reading," 578.

39. Dehaene, *Reading in the Brain*, 20–21. It should be noted that some characters are easier to recognize across cases—for instance, O and o versus r and R.

40. Matt Davis, "Aoccdrnig to a Rscheerach at Cmabrigde Uinervtisy, It Deosn't Mttaer in Waht Oredr the Ltteers in a Wrod Are," *University of Cambridge: MRC Cognition and Brain Sciences Unit*, Oct. 30, 2003, http://www.mrc-cbu.cam .ac.uk/people/matt.davis/Cmabrigde/.

41. Jonathan Grainger and Carol Whitney, "Does the Huamn Mnid Raed Wrods as a Wlohe?" *Trends in Cognitive Sciences* 8, no. 2 (Feb. 2004): 58–59.

42. This discussion of Grainger and Whitney's work comes from Dehaene's *Reading in the Brain*, 155–156.

43. Dehaene, *Reading in the Brain*, 157–158.

44. Gerard Unger, *While You're Reading* (New York: Mark Batty, 2007), 71.

45. Andrew Tobin, "Can You Read 'Aravrit,' the Typography of Peace?" *Times of Israel*, June 1, 2017, http://www.timesofisrael.com/can-you-read-aravrit-the-typog raphy-of-peace/.

46. Dehaene, *Reading in the Brain*, 54–65. As neuroscience has built much of its knowledge about how the healthy brain functions by studying cases where this healthy functioning breaks down, this case was key to advancing our understanding of where reading takes place in the brain.

47. Dehaene, *Reading in the Brain*, 56–57.

48. Laurent Cohen and Stanislas Dehaene, "Calculating without Reading: Unsuspected Residual Abilities in Pure Alexia," *Cognitive Neuropsychology* 17, no. 6 (2000): 563–583.

49. Stanislas Dehaene, *Number Sense* (New York: Oxford University Press, 2011), 180–181.

50. Cohen and Dehaene, "Calculating without Reading," 563–583.

51. Dehaene, *Number Sense*, 62.

52. Tobias Dantzig, *Number: The Language of Science* (New York: Pi Press, 2005).

53. Georges Ifrah, *The Universal History of Numbers* (New York: John Wiley & Sons, 2000).

54. Tobias Dantzig estimates there was about 5,000 years between the development of tally sticks for keeping records, and the full development of positional numeration. See Dantzig, *Number*, 29.

55. Cardinal number systems use representations of quantities for numbers 1–9, and then special symbols for 10, 100, 1,000, etc. Ordinal number systems, on the other hand, rely on the existing order of the symbols they use. For instance, both Greek and Phoenician used letters for their numerals, so a number would be indicated by the order of the letters ($\alpha' = 1$, $\beta' = 2$, $\gamma' = 3$, etc.). These number systems were sufficient for counting, but not for calculating. See Dantzig, *Number*, 21–25.

56. Sofie Beier made this point in a talk at ATypI 2017, "The Legibility of Numer-als." In this talk, she indicates the lack of research into the legibility of nu-merals, and takes the audience through a number of experiments she has carried out with Jean-Baptiste Bernard. Their findings concerning numeral shape are that open counters increase legibility, and that added details (dis-tinguishing one numeral from another) don't actually aid legibility. Beyond this they tested whether lining or nonlining numerals are more legible, and do not seem to have arrived at a single conclusion on this. Beier's conclusion of this talk was, somewhat disappointingly, that readers read best what they're used to, so designers shouldn't rock the boat.

57. Dehaene, *Reading in the Brain*, 95.

58. Numerous authors who early on set standards for typographic legibility have expressed a preference for serifs (e.g., Émile Javal, Theodore L. De Vinne, Bar-bara Roethlein, Luciene Legros, the Mergenthaler Linotype company—see Pyke's *The Legibility of Print*; and Mergenthaler Linotype Company, *The Legi-bility of Type* [Brooklyn, NY, 1935]). However, no measurable difference in read-ing speed between serif and sans-serif type has been found; see Miles Tinker, *Legibility of Print* (Ames: Iowa State University Press, 1963); and for more con-temporary studies, see Aries Arditi and Jianna Cho, "Serifs and Font Legibil-ity," *Vision Research* 45 (2005): 2926–2933; Daniel Boyarski, Christine Neuwirth, Jodi Forlizzi, and Susan Harkness Regli, "A Study of Fonts Designed for Screen Display," *CHI '98: Proceedings of the SIGCHI Conference on Human Factors in Computing Systems* (New York: ACM Press, 1998), 87–94.

59. Andrew J. Manley, Tina Lavender, and Debbie M. Smith, "Processing Fluency Effects," *Patient Education and Counseling* 98 (2015): 391–394.

60. Norbert Schwartz, Lawrence J. Sanna, Ian Skurnik, and Carolyn Yoon, "Meta-cognitive Experiences and the Intricacies of Setting People Straight: Im-plications for Debiasing and Public Information Campaigns," *Advances in Experimental Social Psychology* 39 (2007): 127–161; Hyunjin Song and Norbert Schwarz, "Fluency and the Detection of Misleading Questions: Low Process-ing Fluency Attenuates the Moses Illusion," *Social Cognition* 26, no. 6 (2008): 791–799.

61. Alter et al., "Overcoming Intuition." The two levels in William James's the-ory find parallels in philosophy of the mind, e.g., in Searle's distinction be-tween functional experience and conscious understanding in his Chinese room thought experiment (see Searle's *Minds, Brains and Science*, 32–41), and in David Chalmers's distinction between the functional and the conscious in *The Conscious Mind* (New York: Oxford University Press, 1996). In behavioral economics, see Daniel Kahneman's *Thinking, Fast and Slow* (New York: Farrar, Straus and Giroux, 2011).

62. Alter et al., "Overcoming Intuition," 570–571.

63. Diemand-Yauman, Oppenheimer, and Vaughan, "Fortune Favors the **Bold** (*and the Italicized*)," 111–115.

64. Diemand-Yauman, Oppenheimer, and Vaughan, "Fortune Favors the **Bold** (*and the Italicized*)," 114.

65. In *Thinking, Fast and Slow*, Daniel Kahneman claims that studies have found a statement in bold is more likely to be perceived as true than one set in regular type (see p. 63). He does not identify which studies he is referring to, but if studies on disfluency suggest a deeper level of analytical thought, it would seem text set in bold is less likely to be taken simply at face value, that is, is less likely to be believed, until the reader has given it some thought.

66. Sara Margolin, "Can Bold Typeface Improve Readers' Comprehension and Metacomprehension of Negation?" *Reading Psychology* 34 (2013): 85–99. For more on the benefits of disfluency, see Ivan Hernandez and Jesse Lee Preston, "Disfluency Disrupts the Confirmation Bias," *Journal of Experimental Social Psychology* 49 (2013): 178–182.

67. Errol Morris, "Are You an Optimist or a Pessimist?" *New York Times*, July 9, 2012.

68. Errol Morris, "Hear, All Ye People; Hearken, O Earth (Part 1)," *New York Times*, August 8, 2012. Morris's collaborator (and numbers cruncher), David Dunning, expresses surprise that the experiment worked given its uncontrolled environment.

69. Baskerville and Computer Modern's levels of weighted disagreement were 9693 and 9745, respectively. The three sans serifs were all around the same range (Comic Sans, 10258; Trebuchet, 10293; and Helvetica, 10322). Georgia was not much higher than this, at 10439.

70. For more on how typography might aid the education of dyslexic readers, see the British Dyslexia Association's "Dyslexia Style Guide," 2018, https://www.bdadyslexia.org.uk/employer/dyslexia-style-guide-2018-creating-dyslexia-friendly-content; and Lindsay Evett and David Broan, "Text Formats and Web Design for Visually Impaired and Dyslexic Readers—Clear Text for All," *Interacting with Computers* 17 (2005): 453–472.

71. In a never-trust-anyone-over-the-age-of-thirty sort of indictment, graphic designer Paula Scher associated Helvetica with the Vietnam War and corrupt politicians when she was a design student. Asked, in Gary Hustwit's documentary *Helvetica*, what the typeface of the Iraq War was, she laughed and again said it is Helvetica. It is worth noting, however, that NASA—presumably one of the government agencies that would be on the front line in defending Earth against a meteor strike—also uses Helvetica.

72. Morris follows up his first two articles in this series with a third that suggests it will explain why Baskerville stood out in his experiment's results. However, that third article is largely a biography of John Baskerville. While he does have a quirky, fascinating life (and afterlife), it doesn't serve as an explanation of the typeface itself. See Morris, "Hear, All Ye People; Hearken, O Earth (Part 2)."

73. The eleven core web fonts were selected in 1996 by the World Wide Web Consortium with the intention of ensuring that web pages would be able to load on any given computer. By setting out a set of core fonts for web design that were also commonly found on personal computers, they hoped to ensure that content on the web would be supported by any user's hardware. As a result of being enshrined as core fonts, these typefaces will have a higher level of familiarity than those faces that haven't been established as core (the same principle applies to default typefaces in word processing software).

74. Licko, "Interview by Rudy VanderLans." As the study of fluency suggests, it's also worth asking—as Licko's contemporaries Erik van Blokland and Just van Rossum do—whether "best is really better." Though they are questioning aesthetics rather than reading, their question can be seen as an echo of Stuart Hall's challenge to exact communication (discussed in the introduction of this book). See Erik Van Blokland and Just van Rossum, "Is Best Really Better?" *Letterror*, https://letterror.com/articles/is-best-really-better.html.

75. Herbert Bayer, "On Typography," in *Texts on Type*, ed. Steven Heller and Philip B. Meggs (New York: Allworth Press, 2001), 112.

76. Goudy v. Hansen, 247 Fed. 782, 1264 (1st Cir. 1917).

77. Charles Babbage carried out studies of legibility using different colored paper as early as 1827. See Spencer, *The Visible Word*, 13.

78. Unger, *While You're Reading*, 87.

79. Herbert Spencer, ed., *The Liberated Page: A Typographica Anthology* (San Francisco: Bedford Press, 1987). On the book's influence on deconstructivist design, see Byrne and Witte, "Brave New World."

80. Spencer, *The Visible Word*, 7.

81. Abraham Flexner, *The Usefulness of Useless Knowledge* (Princeton: Princeton University Press, 2017).

82. Arendt, *The Origins of Totalitarianism*, viii. See also the discussion of this passage in the introduction to this book.

83. See Burk, "Expression, Selection, Abstraction," 615. Burk argues that we protect collections of bricks, not the bricks themselves, because bricks are fungible. And he implies, mistakenly, that type is similarly fungible. Worryingly, it would seem that in the development of nanotechnology this IP logic is no longer being followed, as basic units for future development of biotechnology have been patented, likely limiting the development of that field's research. See Siva Vaidhyanathan, "Nanotechnologies and the Law of Patents: A Collision Course," in *Nanotechnology*, ed. Geoffrey Hunt and Michael Mehta (London: Earthscan, 2006).

84. See chapter 3 for discussion of Qandus and divisible Chinese type.

85. Knuth, "The Concept of a Meta-Font," 303. See also the discussion of this idea in chapter 4.

86. Byung-Chul Han, *Shanzhai: Deconstruction in Chinese*, trans. Philippa Hurd (Cambridge, MA: MIT Press, 2017), 72.

87. For earlier discussions of these theories, see chapter 4 for Hofstadter and the introduction for Shannon and Hall.

88. Han, *Shanzhai*, 78.

89. Hannah Arendt, "Interview with Roger Errera," in *Thinking without Banisters*, ed. Jerome Kohn (New York: Shocken Books, 2018), 498.

Bibliography

AbiFares, Huda Smitshuijzen. *Arabic Typography: A Comprehensive Sourcebook.* London: Saqi Books, 2001.

Almabruk, Abubaker A. A., Kevin B. Paterson, Victoria McGowan, and Timothy R. Jordan. "Evaluating Effects of Divided Hemispheric Processing on Word Recognition in Foveal and Extrafoveal Displays: The Evidence from Arabic." *PLOS ONE* 6, no. 4 (Apr. 2011): 1–9.

Alter, Adam, Daniel M. Oppenheimer, Nicholas Epley, and Rebecca N. Eyre. "Overcoming Intuition: Metacognitive Difficulty Activates Analytic Reasoning." *Journal of Experimental Psychology: General* 136, no. 4 (2007): 569–576.

Anderson, Benedict. *Imagined Communities.* New York: Verso, 2003.

Arditi, Aries, and Jianna Cho. "Serifs and Font Legibility." *Vision Research* 45 (2005): 2926–2933.

Arendt, Hannah. *Eichmann in Jerusalem: A Report on the Banality of Evil.* New York: Penguin, 1964.

Arendt, Hannah. "Interview with Roger Errera." In *Thinking without Banisters*, edited by Jerome Kohn, 489–505. New York: Shocken Books, 2018.

Arendt, Hannah. *The Origins of Totalitarianism.* New York: Harcourt Brace, 1973.

Armstrong, Isobel. *Victorian Glassworlds: Glass Culture and the Imagination 1830–1880.* New York: Oxford University Press, 2008.

Atrissi, Tarek. "Arabic Type Design." *Tarek Atrissi Design*, Nov. 19, 2006, https://www.atrissi.com/arabic-type-design/.

Babbage, Charles. *The Works of Charles Babbage*, vol. 8: *The Economy of Machinery and Manufactures.* Edited by Martin Campbell-Kelly. New York: NYU Press, 1989.

Bailey, Francis. Forming punches. US Patent X-4, January 1791.

Bain, Peter, and Paul Shaw, eds. *Blackletter: Type and National Identity.* New York: Princeton Architectural Press, 1998.

Baines, Phil, and Andrew Haslam. *Type and Typography.* New York: Weston-Guptill Publications, 2005.

Ball, Philip. *Invisible: The Dangerous Allure of the Unseen.* Chicago: University of Chicago Press, 2015.

Ballinger, Raymond A. *Lettering in Modern Use*. New York: Reinhold, 1952.

Barnbrook, Jonathan. "Rattera Font." In *Fuse 1–20: From Invention to Antimatter*, edited by Neville Brody and Jon Wozencroft, supplemental digital material. Cologne: Taschen, 2012.

Barnbrook, Jonathan. Rattera poster. In *Fuse 1–20: From Invention to Antimatter*, edited by Neville Brody and Jon Wozencroft, supplemental digital material. Cologne: Taschen, 2012.

Barthes, Roland. *Mythologies*. Translated by Annette Lavers. New York: Hill & Wang, 1972.

Barthes, Roland. "Rhetoric of the Image." In *Image, Music, Text*, translated by Stephen Heath, 32–51. New York: Hill & Wang, 1977.

Bartram, Alan. *Typeforms: A History*. New Castle, DE: Oak Knoll Press, 2007.

Bayer, Herbert. "On Typography." In *Texts on Type: Critical Writings on Typography*, edited by Steven Heller and Philip B. Meggs, 110–114. New York: Allworth Press, 2001.

Bayer, Herbert. "Toward a Universal Type." In *Looking Closer 3*, edited by Michael Bierut, Jessica Helfand, and Steven Heller, 60–62. New York: Allworth Press, 1999.

Beier, Sofie. "The Legibility of Numerals." Lecture presented at ATypI, Montreal, September 2017. https://www.youtube.com/watch?v=k67hqPFXj1Q.

Bennett, Audrey, and Bridget Rice. "Bradbury Thompson's Alphabet 26: A Font System for Early Readers?" *AIGA*, December 20, 2005.

Benton, Josiah Henry. *John Baskerville: Type-founder and Printer, 1706–1775*. Boston: Marymount Press, 1914.

Biederman, Irving. "Recognition-by-Components: A Theory of Human Image Understanding." *Psychological Review* 94, no. 2 (1987): 115–147.

Bigelow, Charles. "Other Replies to Donald E. Knuth's Article 'The Concept of A Meta-Font.'" *Visible Language* 16, 4 (Fall 1982): 339–343.

Bigelow, Charles, and Donald Day. "Digital Typography." *Scientific American* (August 1983): 106–119.

Blackwell, Lewis. *The End of Print: The Grafik Design of David Carson*. 2nd ed. London: Laurence King Publishing, 2000.

Blackwell, Lewis. *20th Century Type*. New Haven: Yale University Press, 2004.

Blakinger, John R. *Gyorgy Kepes: Undreaming the Bauhaus*. Cambridge, MA: MIT Press, 2019.

Boardley, John. "History of Typography: Transitional. Part 3: Siècle des Lumières." *I Love Typography*. January 17, 2008. http://ilovetypography.com/2008/01/17/type-terms-transitional-type/.

Bodoni, Giambattista. *Manual of Typography*, edited by Stephan Füssel. Köln: Taschen, 2016.

Bolz, Norbert. "Farewell to the Gutenberg-Galaxy." Translated by Michelle Mattson. *New German Critique*, no. 78, Special Issue on German Media Studies (Autumn 1999): 109–131.

Boutros, Mourad. *Arabic for Designers*. New York: Mark Batty Publisher, 2006.

Boyarski, Daniel, Christine Neuwirth, Jodi Forlizzi, and Susan Harkness Regli. "A Study of Fonts Designed for Screen Display." In *CHI '98: Proceedings of the SIGCHI Conference on Human Factors in Computing Systems* (New York: ACM Press, 1998), 87–94.

Boyle, James. "Fencing Off Ideas: Enclosure and the Disappearance of the Public Domain." *Daedalus* 131, no. 2 (Spring 2002): 13–25.

Bringhurst, Robert. *Elements of Typographic Style*. Point Roberts, WA: Hartley & Marks, 2004.

British Dyslexia Association. "Dyslexia Style Guide," 2018. https://www.bdadyslexia .org.uk/employer/dyslexia-style-guide-2018-creating-dyslexia-friendly-content.

British Standards Institution. BS 2961: 1967 Typeface Nomenclature and Classification. London, 1967.

Brody, Neville, and Jon Wozencroft, eds. *Fuse 1–20: From Invention to Antimatter*. Cologne: Taschen, 2012.

Bronsard, Henri-Paul. "Other Replies to Donald E. Knuth's Article 'The Concept of A Meta-Font.'" *Visible Language* 16, no. 4 (Fall 1982): 341–344.

Bruce, George. Letters Patent No. 1. US Design Patent 1, November 19, 1842.

Buck-Morss, Susan. "Envisioning Capital." *Critical Inquiry* 21 (Winter 1995): 434–467.

Bullen, Henry Lewis. "Notes Toward the Study of Types: 1. The Power of the Serif; Evolution of Type Faces by Change of Serifs." *Graphic Arts* 1, no. 1 (Jan. 1911): 33–37.

Burk, Dan L. "Expression, Selection, Abstraction: Copyright's Golden Braid." *Syracuse Law Review* 55, no. 3 (2005): 593–618.

Burke, Christopher. *Paul Renner: The Art of Typography*. New York: Princeton Architectural Press, 1998.

Byrne, Chuck, and Martha Witte. "Brave New World: Understanding Deconstruction." In *Looking Closer: Critical Writings on Graphic Design*, edited by Michael Bierut, William Drenttel, and Steven Heller, 115–121. New York: Allworth Press, 1994.

Calori, Chris. *Signage and Wayfinding Design*. Hoboken, NJ: Wiley, 2015.

Carroll, Terrence J. "Protection for Typeface Designs: A Copyright Proposal." *Computer & High Technology Law Journal* 10 (1994): 139–194.

Carter, Thomas Francis. *The Invention of Printing in China, and Its Spread Westward*. 2nd ed. Revised by L. Carrington Goodrich. New York: The Ronald Press Company, 1955.

Catich, Edward M. *The Origin of the Serif: Brush Writing and Roman Letters*. Davenport, IA: St. Ambrose University Press, 1991.

Chalmers, David. *The Conscious Mind*. New York: Oxford University Press, 1996.

Changizi, Mark A., and Shinsuke Shimojo. "Character Complexity and Redundancy in Writing Systems over Human History." *Proceedings of the Royal Society B* 272 (2005): 267–275.

Changizi, Mark A., Qiong Zhang, Hao Ye, and Shinsuke Shimojo. "The Structures of Letters and Symbols throughout Human History Are Selected to Match Those Found in Objects in Natural Scenes." *American Naturalist* 167, no. 5 (May 2006): E117–E139.

Chappell, Warren. *The Anatomy of Lettering*. Pelham, NY: Bridgeman, 1940.

Chappell, Warren, and Robert Bringhurst. *A Short History of the Printed Word*. 2nd ed. Point Roberts, WA: Hartley & Marks, 1999.

Cheng, Karen. *Designing Type*. New Haven: Yale University Press, 2005.

Chia, Lucille. *Printing for Profit: The Commercial Publishers of Jianyang, Fujian (11th–17th Centuries)*. Cambridge, MA: Harvard University Press, 2002.

Cohen, Laurent, and Stanislas Dehaene. "Calculating without Reading: Unsuspected Residual Abilities in Pure Alexia." *Cognitive Neuropsychology* 17, no. 6 (2000): 563–583.

Cohen, Laurent, Stanislas Dehaene, Lionel Naccache, and Stéphane Lehéricy. "The Visual Word Form Area: Spatial and Temporal Characterization of an Initial Stage of Reading in Normal Subjects and Posterior Split-Brain Patients." *Brain* 123 (2000): 291–307.

Colapinto, John. "The Interpreter: Has a Remote Amazon Tribe Upended Our Understanding of Language?" *New Yorker*, April 16, 2007, 118–137.

Cooke, Rachel. "Eric Gill: Can We Separate the Artist from the Abuser?" *Guardian*, April 9, 2017. https://www.theguardian.com/artanddesign/2017/apr/09/eric-gill-the-body-ditchling-exhibition-rachel-cooke.

Coueignoux, Philippe. "Approche Structurelle De La Lettre." *Langue Française*, no. 59 (Sept. 1983): 45–67.

Cox, C. H., P. Coueignoux, B. Blesser, and M. Eden. "Skeletons: A Link between Theoretical and Physical Letter Descriptions." *Pattern Recognition* 15, no. 1 (1982): 11–22.

Craig, James. *Phototypesetting: A Design Manual*. New York: Watson-Guptill Publications, 1978.

Crain, Patricia. *The Story of A: The Alphabetization of America from "The New England Primer" to "The Scarlet Letter."* Stanford: Stanford University Press, 2000.

Crouwel, Wim. *New Alphabet: A Possibility for the New Development, An Introduction for a Programmed Typography*. Hilversum: Steendrukkerij de Jong, 1967.

Crouwel, Wim. "Type Design for the Computer Age." *Journal of Typographic Research* 4, no. 1 (Winter 1970): 51–58.

Dantzig, Tobias. *Number: The Language of Science*. New York: Pi Press, 2005.

Darling, Kate, and Aaron Perzanowski, eds. *Creativity without Law: Challenging the Assumptions of Intellectual Property*. New York: NYU Press, 2017.

Darwin, Charles. *The Origin of Species*. New York: Signet, 2003.

Davis, Matt. "Aoccdrnig to a Rscheerach at Cmabrigde Uinervtisy, It Deosn't Mttaer in Waht Oredr the Ltteers in a Wrod Are." *University of Cambridge: MRC Cognition and Brain Sciences Unit*, Oct. 30, 2003. http://www.mrc-cbu.cam.ac.uk/people/matt .davis/Cmabrigde/.

De Vinne, Theodore L. *The Invention of Printing*. New York: Francis Hart, 1876.

Dehaene, Stanislas. "Natural Born Readers." *New Scientist*, July 5, 2003, 30–33.

Dehaene, Stanislas. *Number Sense: How the Mind Creates Mathematics*. New York: Oxford University Press, 2011.

Dehaene, Stanislas. *Reading in the Brain: The Science and Evolution of a Human Invention*. New York: Viking, 2009.

Denicola, Robert C. "Applied Art and Industrial Design: A Suggested Approach to Copyright in Useful Articles." *Minnesota Law Review* 67 (1983): 707-748.

Derrida, Jacques. *Of Grammatology*. Translated by Gayatri Chakravorty Spivak. Baltimore: Johns Hopkins University Press, 1997.

Diemand-Yauman, Connor, Daniel M. Oppenheimer, and Erikka B. Vaughan. "Fortune Favors the **Bold** (*and the Italicized*): Effects of Disfluency on Educational Outcomes." *Cognition* 118 (2011): 111–115.

DiFolco, C. Letter to Frank Martinez. August 8, 2018. http://luc.devroye.org/fonts-95584 .html.

Drier, Thomas. *The Power of Print and Man*. New York: Mergenthaler Linotype, 1936.

Drucker, Johanna. *The Alphabetic Labyrinth: The Letters in History and Imagination*. London: Thames & Hudson, 1995.

Drucker, Johanna. *Graphesis: Visual Forms of Knowledge Production*. Cambridge, MA: Harvard University Press, 2014.

Drucker, Johanna. *The Visible Word: Experimental Typography and Modern Art*. Chicago: University of Chicago Press, 1994.

Du Bois, W. E. B. *The Souls of Black Folk*. New York: Signet Classic, 1995.

Du Bois, W. E. B. *W. E. B. Du Bois's Data Portraits: Visualizing Black America*. Edited by Whitney Battle-Baptiste and Britt Rusert. New York: Princeton Architectural Press, 2018.

Dürer, Albrecht. *Of the Just Shaping of Letters: From the Applied Geometry of Albrecht Dürer*. New York: Dover, 1965.

Eisenstein, Elizabeth. *The Printing Revolution in Early Modern Europe*. New York: Cambridge University Press, 1983.

Ellison, Ralph. *Invisible Man*. New York: Vintage, 1995.

Epps, Timothy. *Alphabet*. Hilversum: Steendrukkerij de Jong, 1969.

Ernst, Wolfgang. "Experimenting with Media Temporality: Pythagoras, Hertz, Turing." In *Digital Memory and the Archive*, edited by Jussi Parikka, 184–191. Minneapolis: University of Minnesota Press, 2013.

Ernst, Wolfgang. "Media Archaeography: Method and Machine versus Narrative of Media." In *Media Archaeology: Approaches, Applications & Implications*, edited by Jussi Parikka and Erkki Huhtamo, 239–255. Berkeley: University of California Press, 2011.

Ernst, Wolfgang. "Media Archaeology—Method and Machine." Lecture given at Anglia Ruskin University, Cambridge, UK, November 18, 2009.

Ernst, Wolfgang. "Signals versus Symbols." Extended version of lecture given at Post Script: After Textuality/On Media, Yale University, March 29, 2012.

Ernst, Wolfgang. "Telling versus Counting? A Media-Archaeological Point of View." *Intermédialités* 2 (Autumn 2003): 31–44.

Eteraz, Ali. "The Death of the Urdu Script." *Medium*. October 7, 2013. https://medium.com/@eteraz/the-death-of-the-urdu-script-9ce935435d90.

Evett, Lindsay, and David Broan. "Text Formats and Web Design for Visually Impaired and Dyslexic Readers—Clear Text for All." *Interacting with Computers* 17 (2005): 453–472.

"Ex Parte Schmohl," *Official Gazette of the United States Patent Office* 140 (Mar. 7–Apr. 25, 1905): 505.

Fawcett, Waldon. "Is There Need for More Protection for Type-Faces?" *Inland Printer* 60, no. 6 (Mar. 1918): 798–800.

Flexner, Abraham. *The Usefulness of Useless Knowledge*. Princeton: Princeton University Press, 2017.

Flusser, Vilém. "The Gesture of Writing." *Flusser Studies* 8 (May 2009): 1–18. http://www.flusserstudies.net/pag/archive08.htm.

Flusser, Vilém. *Into the Universe of the Technical Image*. Translated by Nancy Ann Roth. Minneapolis, MN: University of Minnesota Press, 2011.

Flusser, Vilém. "On Memory (Electronic or Otherwise)." *Leonardo* 23, no. 4 (1990): 397–399.

Flusser, Vilém. "On Typography." Unpublished essay, n.d. Flusser Archiv, Universität der Künste, Berlin.

Flusser, Vilém. *Writings*. Edited by Andreas Ströhl. Minneapolis: University of Minnesota Press, 2002.

Flusser, Vilém. "Why Do Typewriters Go 'Click'?" In *The Shape of Things: A Philosophy of Design*, translated by Anthony Mathews, 62–65. London: Reaktion Books, 1999.

Ford, Jacob. "The Molecular Typography Pop-Up Book." *Vimeo*, n.d. Accessed Nov. 9, 2020. https://vimeo.com/173524096.

Franklin, Benjamin. "From Benjamin Franklin to John Baskerville [ca. 1760]." *National Archives*. https://founders.archives.gov/documents/Franklin/01-09-02-0085.

Frere-Jones, Tobias. "Experiments in Type Design." In *Texts on Type: Critical Writings on Typography*, edited by Steven Heller and Philip B. Meggs, 228–234. New York: Allworth Press, 2001.

Frege, Gottlob. "Sense and Reference." *Philosophical Review* 57, no. 3 (May, 1948): 209–230.

Frege, Gottlob. "Über Sinn und Bedeutung." In *Funktion, Begriff, Bedeutung: Fünf logische Studien*, edited by Günther Patzig. Göttingen: Vandenhoeck & Ruprecht, 2008.

Froshaug, Anthony. "The Book as a Means of Communicating Ideas." In *Anthony Froshaug Texts & Type*, edited by Robin Kinross, 104–106. London: Hyphen Press, 2000.

Froshaug, Anthony. "Typographic Norms." In *Anthony Froshaug Texts & Type*, edited by Robin Kinross, 179–182. London: Hyphen Press, 2000.

Froshaug, Anthony. "Typography Is a Grid." In *Anthony Froshaug Texts & Type*, edited by Robin Kinross, 187–190. London: Hyphen Press, 2000.

Frutiger, Adrian. "Letterforms in Photo-typography." *Journal of Typographic Research* 4, no. 4 (Autumn 1970): 327–335.

Frutiger, Adrian. "OCR-B: A Standardized Character for Optical Recognition." *Journal of Typographic Research* 1, no. 2 (April 1967): 137–146.

Frutiger, Adrian. *Type, Sign, Symbol*. Translated by Andrew Bluhm. Zurich: ABC Edition, 1980.

Fry, Blake. "Why Typefaces Proliferate Without Copyright Protection." *Journal on Telecommunication and High Technology Law* 8, no. 2 (2010): 425–490.

Garfield, Simon. *Just My Type*. New York: Gotham Books, 2011.

Gaskell, Philip. *A New Introduction to Bibliography*. New Castle, DE: Oak Knoll Press, 1995.

Giampetro, Rob. "New Black Face: Neuland and Lithos as Stereotypograph." *Lined & Unlined*, 2004. https://linedandunlined.com/archive/new-black-face/.

Gill, Eric. *Autobiography*. New York: Devin-Adair, 1941.

Gill, Eric. *An Essay on Typography*. Boston: David R. Godine, 1988.

Gitelman, Lisa. "*Emoji Dick* and the Eponymous Whale, An Essay in Four Parts." *Post 45*, July 8, 2018. http://post45.org/2018/07/emoji-dick-and-the-eponymous-whale-an-essay-in-four-parts/.

Glassie, Henry. *Pattern in the Material Folk Culture of the Eastern United States*. Philadelphia: University of Pennsylvania Press, 1968.

Google. "Google Noto Fonts: FAQ." Accessed April 15, 2018. https://www.google.com/get/noto/help/faq/.

Gottschall, Edward. "The State of the Art in Typeface Design Protection." *Visible Language* 19, no. 1 (Winter 1985): 149–156.

Goudy, Frederic W. "I Am Type." In *Texts on Type*, edited by Stephen Heller and Philip B. Meggs, 218. New York: Allworth Press, 2001.

Grainger, Jonathan, and Carol Whitney. "Does the Huamn Mnid Raed Wrods as a Wlohe?" *Trends in Cognitive Sciences* 8, no. 2 (Feb. 2004): 58–59.

Gropius, Walter. "The Theory and Organization of the Bauhaus." In *Art in Theory 1900–1990: An Anthology of Changing Ideas*, edited by Charles Harrison and Paul Wood, 338–343. New York: Blackwell, 1999.

Gros, Frédéric. *A Philosophy of Walking*. Translated by John Howe. New York: Verso, 2014.

Hall, Stuart. "Encoding and Decoding in the Television Discourse." *CCCS Stencilled Occasional Papers*, no. 7 (1973). https://www.birmingham.ac.uk/Documents /college-artslaw/history/cccs/stencilled-occasional-papers/1to8and11to24and38to48 /SOP07.pdf.

Han, Byung-Chul. *In the Swarn: Digital Prospects*. Translated by Erik Butler. Cambridge, MA: MIT Press, 2017.

Han, Byung-Chul. *Shanzhai: Deconstruction in Chinese*. Translated by Philippa Hurd. Cambridge, MA: MIT Press, 2017.

Hasson, Uri, Ifat Levy, Marlene Behrmann, Talma Hendler, and Rafael Malach. "Eccentricity Bias as an Organizing Principle for Human High-Order Object Areas." *Neuron* 34, no. 3 (Apr. 25, 2002): 479–490.

Hauser, Marc D., Noam Chomsky, and W. Tecumseh Fitch. "The Faculty of Language: What Is It, Who Has It, and How Did It Evolve?" *Science* 298, no. 5598 (Nov. 22, 2002): 1569–1579.

Hayles, N. Katherine. "Hyper and Deep Attention: The Generational Divide in Cognitive Modes." *Profession* (2007): 187–199.

Henderson, Linda Dalrymple. *The Fourth Dimension and Non-Euclidean Geometry in Modern Art*. Cambridge, MA: MIT Press, 2013.

Henkin, David M. *City Reading: Written Words and Public Spaces in Antebellum New York*. New York: Columbia University Press, 1998.

Hernandez, Ivan, and Jesse Lee Preston. "Disfluency Disrupts the Confirmation Bias." *Journal of Experimental Social Psychology* 49 (2013): 178–182.

Ho, Kevin. "Organizing the World of Fonts with AI." *Medium*. April 19, 2017. https:// medium.com/ideo-stories/organizing-the-world-of-fonts-with-ai-7d9e49ff2b25.

Hochuli, Jost. *Detail in Typography*. London: Hyphen Press, 2008.

Hofstadter, Douglas R. "Metafont, Metamathematics, and Metaphysics: Comments on Donald Knuth's Article 'The Concept of a Meta-Font.'" *Visible Language* 16, no. 4 (Fall 1982): 309–338.

Husserl, Edmund. *General Introduction to Pure Phenomenology*. Translated by F. Kersten. Dordrecht: Springer Netherlands, 1982.

Husserl, Edmund. *Logical Investigations*, vol. 2. Translated by J. N. Findlay, edited by Dermot Moran. New York: Routledge, 2001.

Hustwit, Gary, dir. *Helvetica*. 2007; Brooklyn, NY: Plexifilm, 2010. DVD.

Hyndman, Sarah. *Why Fonts Matter*. Berkeley, CA: Gingko Press, 2016.

"Hypnopaedia." *Emigre Fonts*. Accessed Nov. 9, 2020. https://www.emigre.com/Fonts /Hypnopaedia.

Ideo. "Font Map." Accessed Nov. 9, 2020. http://fontmap.ideo.com/.

Ifrah, Georges. *The Universal History of Numbers: From Prehistory to the Invention of the Computer*. Translated by David Bellos, et al. New York: John Wiley & Sons, 2000.

Innis, Harold. *Empire and Communications*. Toronto: Dundum, 2014.

Jacobs, Jane. *The Death and Life of Great American Cities*. New York: Random House, 1961.

Johnston, Edward. *Writing & Illuminating, & Lettering*. New York: Pitman Publishing, 1954.

Judge, Elizabeth F., and Daniel Gervais. "Of Silos and Constellations: Comparing Notions of Originality in Copyright Law." *Cardozo Arts & Entertainment* 27 (2009): 375–408.

Jury, David. *Reinventing Print: Technology and Craft in Typography*. New York: Bloomsbury, 2018.

Kahneman, Daniel. *Thinking, Fast and Slow*. New York: Farrar, Straus and Giroux, 2011.

Karjala Dennis S., and Keiji Sugiyama. "Fundamental Concepts in Japanese and American Copyright Law." *American Journal of Comparative Law* 36, no. 4 (Autumn 1988): 613–679.

Kastenmeier, Rep. Robert. "Copyright Law Revision." US House of Representatives Report No. 94-1476, September 3, 1976.

Kepes, György. *Language of Vision*. Chicago: Paul Theobald, 1964.

Kinross, Robin. *Modern Typography: An Essay in Critical History*. London: Hyphen Press, 2004.

Kinross, Robin. "Technics and Ethics: The Work of Anthony Froshaug." *Octavo* 86, no. 1 (1986): 4–9.

Kittler, Friedrich. *Gramophone, Film, Typewriter*. Translated by Geofrey Winthrop-Young and Michael Wutz. Stanford, CA: Stanford University Press, 1999.

Knuth, Donald. "The Concept of a Meta-Font." In *Digital Typography*, 289–313. Stanford, CA: CSLI Publications, 1999.

Knuth, Donald. "Conversations, 1996: Printing." In *Companion to the Papers of Donald Knuth*, 55–72. Stanford, CA: CSLI Publications, 2011.

Knuth, Donald. "Digital Typography." In *Digital Typography*, 1–18. Stanford, CA: CSLI Publications, 1999.

Knuth, Donald. "Donald Knuth Interviewed by Donald J. Albers and Lynn A Steen." In *Mathematical People: Profiles and Interviews*, edited by D. J. Albers and G. L. Alexanderson, 183–203. Boston: Birkhäuser, 1985.

Knuth, Donald. "Lessons Learned from Metafont." *Visible Language* 19, no. 1 (Winter 1985): 35–54.

Knuth, Donald. "The Letter S." In *Digital Typography*, 263–284. Stanford, CA: CSLI Publications, 1999.

Knuth, Donald. "Mathematical Typography." *Bulletin (New Series) of the American Mathematical Society* 1, no. 2 (Mar. 1979): 337–372.

Kripke, Saul. *Naming and Necessity*. Cambridge, MA: Harvard University Press, 1980.

Kuskin, William, ed. *Caxton's Trace: Studies in the History of English Printing*. Notre Dame: University of Notre Dame Press, 2006.

Lawson, Alexander. *Anatomy of a Typeface*. Boston: David R. Godine, 1990.

Lawson, Alexander. *Printing Types: An Introduction*. Boston: Beacon Press, 1971.

Lee, Ji. *Univers Revolved: A Three Dimensional Alphabet*. New York: Harry N. Abrams, 2004.

Legge, Gordon E. *Psychophysics of Reading in Normal and Low Vision*. Mahwah, NJ: Lawrence Erlbaum, 2007.

Legros, Luciene Alphonse, and John Cameron Grant. *Typographical Printing-Surfaces: The Technology and Mechanism of Their Production*. London: Longmans, Green, 1916.

Leslie, Woody. *Understanding Molecular Typography*. Chicago: One Page Production, 2015.

Levit, Briar, dir. *Graphic Means: A History of Graphic Design Production*. Austin, TX: Tugg, 2018. DVD.

Licko, Zuzana. "Interview by Rhonda Rubenstein." *Eye* 11, no. 43 (Spring 2002). http://www.eyemagazine.com/feature/article/reputations-zuzana-licko.

Licko, Zuzana. "Interview by Rudy VanderLans." *Emigre* 15 (1990). https://www.emigre.com/Essays/ZuzanaLicko/Emigre15.

Licko, Zuzana. "Zuzana Licko Answers Frequently Asked Questions." *Emigre Fonts*, 2000, https://www.emigre.com/Essays/ZuzanaLicko/FAQ.

Lipton, Jacqueline. "To © or Not to ©? Copyright and Innovation in the Digital Typeface Industry." *University of California, Davis Law Review* 43 (2009): 143–192.

List, Larry. *The Imagery of Chess Revisited*. New York: Noguchi Museum, 2005.

Loos, Adolf. "Ornament and Crime." In *Programs and Manifestoes on 20th-Century Architecture*, edited by Ulrich Comrads, 19–24. Cambridge, MA: MIT Press, 1970.

Loxley, Simon. *Type: The Secret History of Letters.* New York: I. B. Tauris, 2004.

Lupton, Ellen. "Cold Eye: An Exact Science." *Print* 57, no. 5 (Sept./Oct. 2003): 22; 185.

Lupton, Ellen. "A Post-Mortem on Deconstruction?" In *Texts on Type: Critical Writings on Typography*, edited by Steven Heller and Philip B. Meggs, 45–47. New York: Allworth Press, 2001.

Lupton, Ellen, and J. Abbott Miller. *Design Writing Research.* New York: Phaidon, 2006.

Lupton, Ellen, and J. Abbott Miller, "A Natural History of Typography." In *Looking Closer: Critical Writings on Graphic Design*, edited by Michael Bierut, William Drenttel, and Steven Heller, 19–25. New York: Allworth Press, 1994.

MacCarthy, Fiona. *Eric Gill: A Lover's Quest for Art and God.* New York: Dutton, 1989.

Manfredi, Travis L. "Sans Protection: Typeface Design and Copyright in the Twenty-First Century." *University of San Francisco Law Review* 45, no. 3 (Winter 2011): 841–871.

Manley, Andrew J., Tina Lavender, and Debbie M. Smith. "Processing Fluency Effects: Can the Content and Presentation of Participant Information Sheets Influence Recruitment and Participation for an Antenatal Intervention?" *Patient Education and Counseling* 98 (2015): 391–394.

Marcel, J. J. *Leçons de langue Arabe.* Paris: Éberhart, Imprimeur du Collége Royal de France, 1819.

Margolin, Sara. "Can Bold Typeface Improve Readers' Comprehension and Meta-comprehension of Negation?" *Reading Psychology* 34 (2013): 85–99.

McConkie, George W., and Keith Rayner. "The Span of the Effective Stimulus During a Fixation in Reading." *Perception & Psychophysics* 17, no. 6 (1975): 578–586.

McGann, Jerome J. *Black Riders: The Visible Language of Modernism.* Princeton: Princeton University Press, 1993.

McGann, Jerome J. *The Textual Condition.* Princeton: Princeton University Press, 1991.

McKenzie, D.F. *Bibliography and the Sociology of Texts.* New York: Cambridge University Press, 1999.

McLuhan, Marshall. *The Gutenberg Galaxy.* Toronto: University of Toronto Press, 2011.

McNeil, Paul. *The Visual History of Type.* London: Laurence King Publishing, 2017.

Meggs, Philip B. *A History of Graphic Design.* 5th ed. Hoboken, NJ: Wiley, 2012.

Meiss, Millard. "The First Alphabetical Treatises in the Renaissance." *Journal of Typographic Research* 3, no. 1 (Jan. 1, 1969): 3–30.

Mendelsberg, Martin. "Alef-Beit: A Typographic Journey." In *The Education of a Typographer*, edited by Steven Heller, 142–145. New York: Allworth Press, 2004.

Mendelsohn, Richard L., trans. "Diary: Written by Professor Dr Gottlob Frege in the Time from 10 March to 9 April 1924." *Inquiry* 39, no. 3–4 (1996): 303–342.

Mergenthaler Linotype Company. *The Legibility of Type.* Brooklyn, NY: Mergenthaler Linotype, 1935.

Mergler, H. W., and P. M. Vargo. "One Approach to Computer Assisted Letter Design." *Journal of Typographic Research* 2, no. 4 (Oct. 1968): 299–322.

Merritt, Susan. "Bradbury Thompson." *AIGA*. August 14, 2017. https://www.aiga.org /medalist-bradbury-thompson.

Meseguer, Laura. "Qandus, a Triscript Typeface Family." *Laura Meseguer*, 2018, http:// www.laurameseguer.com/project/qandus.

Mezrich, Jonathan L. "Extension of Copyright to Fonts—Can the Alphabet Be Far Behind?" *Computer Law Review and Technology Journal* (Summer 1998): 61–67.

Middleton, Michael. *Soldiers of Lead: An Introduction to Layout and Typography for Use in the Labour Party*. London: Pelican Press, 1943.

Mirapaul, Matthew. "Is It about to Rain? Check the Typeface." *New York Times*, July 24, 2003.

Misra, Tanvi. "Can Google Build a Typeface to Support Every Written Language?" *NPR: Codeswitch*, August 3, 2014. https://www.npr.org/sections/codeswitch/2014/08 /03/337168933/-no-tofu-doesn-t-equate-to-no-problem-for-google-universal-typeface.

Moholy-Nagy, Laszlo. "The New Typography." In *Texts on Type: Critical Writings on Typography*, edited by Steven Heller and Philip B. Meggs, 108–109. New York: Allworth Press, 2001.

Moholy-Nagy, Laszlo. "Typophoto." In *Looking Closer 3: Classic Writings on Graphic Design*, edited by Michael Bierut, Jessica Helfand, and Steven Heller, 24–26. New York: Allworth Press, 1999.

MoMA. "Wim Crouwel, New Alphabet, 1967." https://www.moma.org/collection/works /139322.

Moran, James. *Printing Presses: History and Development from the Fifteenth Century to Modern Times*. Berkeley, CA: University of California Press, 1973.

Morison, Stanley. "First Principles of Typography." In *Typographers on Type*, edited by Ruari McLean, 61–67. New York: W. W. Norton, 1995.

Morison, Stanley. *Politics and Script: Aspects of authority and freedom in the development of Graeco-Latin script from the sixth century B.C. to the twentieth century A.D.* Oxford: Clarendon Press, 1972.

Morris, Errol. "Are You an Optimist or a Pessimist?" *New York Times*, July 9, 2012.

Morris, Errol. "Hear, All Ye People; Hearken, O Earth (Part 1)." *New York Times*, August 8, 2012.

Morris, Errol. "Hear, All Ye People; Hearken, O Earth (Part 2)." *New York Times*, Aug. 9, 2012.

Mullaney, Thomas. *The Chinese Typewriter: A History*. Cambridge, MA: MIT Press, 2017.

Mullaney, Thomas. "The Moveable Typewriter: How Chinese Typists Developed Predictive Text During the Height of Maoism." *Technology and Culture* 53 (Oct. 2012): 777–814.

Mumford, Lewis. *Technics and Civilization*. New York: Harcourt, Brace & World, 1962.

Nakamura, Kimihiro, Stanislas Dehaene, Antoinette Jobert, Denis Le Bihan, and Sid Kouider. "Subliminal Convergence of Kanji and Kana Words: Further Evidence for Functional Parcellation of the Posterior Temporal Cortex in Visual Word Perception." *Journal of Cognitive Neuroscience* 17, no. 6 (2005): 954–968.

Nasr, Seyyed Hossein. *Islamic Art and Spirituality*. Albany: SUNY Press, 1987.

Nietzsche, Friedrich. "On Truth and Lie in a Nonmoral Sense." In *On Truth and Untruth: Selected Writings*, edited and translated by Taylor Carman, 15–49. New York: HarperCollins, 2010.

Noordzij, Gerrit. *Letterletter: An Inconsistent Collection of Tentative Theories That Do Not Claim Any Other Authority Than That of Common Sense*. Point Roberts, WA: Hartley & Marks Publishers, 2000.

Noordzij, Gerrit. *The Stroke Theory of Writing*. Translated by Peter Enneson. London: Hyphen, 2005.

Oman, Ralph, and Daniel J. Boorstin. "Notice of Inquiry: Copyrightability of Digitized Typefaces." *Announcement from the Copyright Office, Library of Congress, Washington, D.C. 20559*. Excerpt from *Federal Register* 51, no. 197 (Oct. 10, 1986): 36410–36412.

Oman, Ralph, and James H. Billington. "Final Regulation; Registrability of Computer Programs That Generate Typefaces." *Announcement from the Copyright Office, Library of Congress, Washington, D.C. 20559*. Excerpt from *Federal Register* 57, no. 35 (Feb. 21, 1992): 6201.

Ong, Walter. *Orality and Literacy: The Technologizing of the Word*. London: Routledge, 2000.

Orwell, George. "In Front of Your Nose." In *Facing Unpleasant Facts: Narrative Essays*, compiled by George Packer, 209–213. New York: Mariner Books, 2009.

Orwell, George. "Politics and the English Language." In *Why I Write*, 102–120. New York: Penguin, 2004.

Osterer, Heidrun, and Philipp Stamm, eds. *Adrian Frutiger—Typefaces: The Complete Works*. Boston: Birkhäuser, 2009.

Papanek, Victor. *Design for the Real World: Human Ecology and Social Change*. 2nd ed. Chicago: Academy Chicago Publishers, 2000.

Peirce, Charles Sanders. "What Is A Sign?" In *The Essential Peirce*, vol. 2 *(1893–1913)*. Bloomington, IN: Indiana University Press, 1998.

Peters, John Durham. *Speaking into the Air: A History of the Idea of Communication*. Chicago: University of Chicago Press, 1999.

Phares, Gloria C. "An Approach to Why Typography Should Be Copyrightable." *Columbia Journal of Law & The Arts* 39, no. 3 (2016): 417–420.

Plato. "Phaedrus." In *The Collected Dialogues of Plato*. Translated by R. Hackforth and edited by Edith Hamilton and Huntington Cairns. Princeton, NJ: Princeton University Press, 1989.

Poynor, Rick. "Conceptual Hybrids: Type in the 1990s." *Artifact* 3, no. 1 (2013): 2.1–2.6.

Poynor, Rick. "Type and Deconstruction in the Digital Era." In *Looking Closer: Critical Writings on Graphic Design*, edited by Michael Bierut, William Drenttel, and Steven Heller, 83–87. New York: Allworth Press, 1994.

Price, Cathy J., and Joseph T. Devlin. "The Myth of the Visual Word Form Area." *NeuroImage* 19 (2003): 473–481.

Pyke, Richard Lionel. *The Legibility of Print*. London: His Majesty's Stationery Office, 1926.

Ramati, Ido. "The Mechanization of Modern Hebrew Writing." Paper presented at Before and Beyond Typography Online Conference, June 5, 2020.

Rancière, Jacques. *The Future of the Image*. Translated by Gregory Elliott. New York: Verso, 2007.

Reed, Talbot Baines. *A History of the Old English Letter Foundries: With Notes Historical and Biographical*. London: Elliot Stock, 1887.

Reinfurt, David, and Robert Wiesenberger. *Muriel Cooper*. Cambridge, MA: MIT Press, 2017.

Rider, Robin. "Shaping Information: Mathematics, Computing & Typography." In *Inscribing Science: Scientific Texts and the Materiality of Communication*, edited by Timothy Lenoir, 39–54. Stanford, CA: Stanford University Press, 1998.

Ringer, Barbara. "Letter to Representative Kastenmeier, June 6, 1975." Reprinted in "Registration of Original Typeface Designs, Legislative Consideration," *Announcement from the Copyright Office, Library of Congress, Washington, D.C. 20559.*

Ringer, Barbara, and L. Quincy Mumford. "Registration of Original Typeface Designs." *Announcement from the Copyright Office, Library of Congress, Washington, D.C. 20559.* Excerpt from *Federal Register* 39, no. 176 (Sept. 10, 1974).

Roberts, Jennifer. "The Power of Patience." *Harvard Magazine*, Nov.–Dec. 2013. https://www.harvardmagazine.com/2013/11/the-power-of-patience.

Rose, Mark. *Authors and Owners: The Invention of Copyright*. Cambridge, MA: Harvard University Press, 1993.

Rosenblatt, Elizabeth L. "A Theory of IP's Negative Space." *Columbia Journal of Law & the Arts* 34, no. 3 (2011): 317–365.

Ruder, Emil. *Typographie: Manual of Typographic Design*. New York: Visual Communications Books, 1981.

Saussure, Ferdinand de. *Course in General Linguistics*. Translated by Roy Harris. Chicago: Open Court, 2008.

Schafroth, Colleen. *The Art of Chess*. New York: Harry N. Abrams, 2002.

Schwab, Katharine. "A Map of the Typographic Universe Drawn By AI." *Fast Company*. April 25, 2017. https://www.fastcompany.com/90111599/a-map-of-the-typographic-universe-drawn-by-ai.

Schwartz, Kathryn A. "Did Ottoman Sultans Ban Print?" *Book History* 20 (2017): 1–39.

Schwartz, Norbert, Lawrence J. Sanna, Ian Skurnik, and Carolyn Yoon. "Metacognitive Experiences and the Intricacies of Setting People Straight: Implications for Debiasing and Public Information Campaigns." *Advances in Experimental Social Psychology* 39 (2007): 127–161.

Schwitters, Kurt. "Proposal for a Systemschrift (Anregungen zur Erlangung einer Systemschrift)." *International Revue 1927–1929*, 10 (1978): 312–316.

Searle, John. *Minds, Brains and Science*. Cambridge, MA: Harvard University Press, 1984.

Shannon, Claude. "A Mathematical Theory of Communication." *Bell System Technical Journal* 27 (July 1948): 379–423.

Shaw, Paul. "Stereo Types." *Print* (June 17, 2009). https://www.printmag.com/article/stereo_types/.

Simpson, Nicola. *Notes from the Cosmic Typewriter: The Life and Work of Dom Sylvester Houédard*. London: Occasional Papers, 2012.

Solt, Mary Ellen, ed. *Concrete Poetry: A World View*. Bloomington: Indiana University Press, 1970.

Song, Hyunjin, and Norbert Schwarz. "Fluency and the Detection of Misleading Questions: Low Processing Fluency Attenuates the Moses Illusion." *Social Cognition* 26, no. 6 (2008): 791–799.

Spencer, Herbert, ed. *The Liberated Page: A Typographica Anthology*. San Francisco: Bedford Press, 1987.

Spencer, Herbert. *The Visible Word: Problems of Legibility*. London: Lund Humphries, 1968.

Spiekermann, Erik, and E. M. Ginger. *Stop Stealing Sheep and Find Out How Type Works*. Berkeley, CA: Adobe Press, 2003.

Stinson, Liz. "Two Legends Dish on How to Design a Typeface." *Wired*. June 5, 2013. https://www.wired.com/2013/06/typefaces/.

Sullivan, Louis. "The Tall Office Building Artistically Considered." *Lippincott's Monthly Magazine* (March 1896): 403–409.

"Superunion Helps Elliptic Find the Truth behind Crypto-Crimes with New Identity." *Superunion*. June 13, 2018.

Taan, Yasmine Nachabe. *Abdulkader Arnaout: Designing as Visual Poetry*. Amsterdam: Khatt Books, 2017.

Telingater, S. B. "The Standardization of Alphabetic Graphemes." *Journal of Typographic Research* 2, no. 3 (July 1968): 233–240.

Themerson, Stefan. "Idéogrammes Lyriques." In *The Liberated Page: A Typographica Anthology*, edited by Herbert Spencer, 68–90. San Francisco: Bedford Press, 1987.

Thibaudeau, Francis. *La lettre d'imprimerie*. Paris: Bureau de l'édition, 1921.

Thiessen, Mary, et al. "Brainy Type: A Look at How the Brain Processes Typographic Information." *Visible Language* 49.1–2 (Apr. 2015): 174–189.

Thompson, D'Arcy. *On Growth and Form*. Cambridge: Cambridge University Press, 1952.

Tinker, Miles A. *The Legibility of Type*. Ames, IA: Iowa University Press, 1963.

"Tobias Frere-Jones: Fibonacci." In *Fuse 1–20: From Invention to Antimatter*, edited by Neville Brody and Jon Wozencroft, 186. Cologne: Taschen, 2012.

Tobin, Andrew. "Can You Read 'Aravrit,' the Typography of Peace?" *Times of Israel*, June 1, 2017, http://www.timesofisrael.com/can-you-read-aravrit-the-typography-of-peace/.

Torres, Julio. "Papyrus." *Saturday Night Live*, Sept. 30, 2017.

Tory, Geofroy. *Champ Fleury*. Translated by George B. Ives. Mineola, NY: Dover, 1967.

Tracy, Walter. *Letters of Credit: A View of Type Design*. Boston: David R. Godine, 1986.

Tsai, Jie-Li, and George W. McConkie. "Where Do Chinese Readers Send Their Eyes?" In *The Mind's Eye: Cognitive and Applied Aspects of Eye Movement Research*, edited by J. Hyönä, R. Radach, and H. Deubel, 159–176. New York: Elsevier, 2003.

Tschichold, Jan. *The New Typography: A Handbook for Modern Designers*. Translated by Ruari McLean. Berkeley: University of California Press, 1995.

Tullett, Barrie. *Typewriter Art: A Modern Anthology*. London: Laurence King, 2014.

Unger, Gerard. "All My Type Designs: Decoder (1992)." *Gerard Unger*. http://www.gerard unger.com/allmytypedesigns/allmytypedesigns13.html.

Unger, Gerard. "Other Replies to Donald E. Knuth's Article 'The Concept of a Meta-Font.'" *Visible Language* 16, no. 4 (Fall 1982): 353–356.

Unger, Gerard. *While You're Reading*. New York: Mark Batty Publisher, 2007.

Updike, Daniel Berkeley. *Printing Types: Their History, Forms, and Use*. New Castle, DE: Oak Knoll Press, 2001.

Usher, Abbott Payson. *A History of Mechanical Inventions, Revised edition*. Cambridge, MA: Harvard University Press, 1954.

Vaidhyanathan, Siva. "Nanotechnologies and the Law of Patents: A Collision Course." In *Nanotechnology*, edited by Geoffrey Hunt and Michael Mehta. London: Earthscan, 2006.

Van Blokland, Erik, and Just van Rossum. "Is Best Really Better?" *Letterror*. https://letterror.com/articles/is-best-really-better.html.

VanderLans, Rudy. "The Trouble with Type." In *Texts on Type: Critical Writings on Typography*, edited by Steven Heller and Philip B. Meggs, 223–227. New York: Allworth Press, 2001.

Vox, Maximilien. *Défense and Illustration de la lettre*. Paris: Monotype, 1955.

Walter, Gerard O. "Typesetting." *Scientific American* 220, no. 5 (May 1969), 60–69.

Warde, Beatrice. "The Crystal Goblet or Printing Should Be Invisible." In *Looking Closer 3: Classic Writings on Graphic Design*, edited by Michael Bierut, Jessica Helfand, and Steven Heller. New York: Allworth Press, 1999.

Williams, Raymond. "Base and Superstructure in Marxist Cultural Theory." In *Media and Cultural Studies*, edited by Meenakshi Gigi Durham and Douglas M. Kellner. Malden, MA: Blackwell, 2006, 131–143.

Wilson, Doug, dir. *Linotype: The Film*. Colorado Springs, CO: Ikonik Media, 2012. DVD.

Wittgenstein, Ludwig. *Philosophical Investigations*. Translated by G. E. M. Anscombe. Oxford: Blackwells, 2001.

Wolf, Maryanne. *Proust and the Squid: The Story and Science of the Reading Brain*. New York: HarperCollins, 2007.

Wozencroft, Jon. "Why Fuse?" In *Fuse 1–20: From Invention to Antimatter*, 21–22. Cologne: Taschen, 2012.

Zachrisson, Bror. *Studies in the Legibility of Printed Text*. Stockholm: Almqvist & Wiksell, 1965.

Zapf, Hermann. "The Changes in Letterforms Due to Technical Developments." *Journal of Typographic Research* 2, no. 4 (Oct. 1968): 351–368.

Zapf, Hermann. "Is Creativity in Alphabet Design Still Wanted?" *Visible Language* 24, no. 3 (Summer 1990): 254–261.

Zapf, Hermann. "New Typeface Designs in the Shadow of Protection." In *Hermann Zapf & His Design Philosophy*, 78–84. Chicago: Society of Typographic Arts, 1987.

Zapf, Hermann. "A Plea for Authentic Type Design." In *Texts on Type: Critical Writings on Typography*, edited by Steven Heller and Philip B. Meggs, 34–35. New York: Allworth Press, 2001.

Index

separability in copyright, 38–41
  technological function obscuring
    form, 32–35
  variety of functions, 155–158
Frege, Gottlob, 12–14, 250n15. *See also*
    Mode of presentation
  sense and reference, 224n31, 225n32
Fregio Mecano (typeface), 142–143, 200
Frere-Jones, Tobias, 65, 88, 141, 199,
    224n24, 247n16
  and Jonathan Hoefler, 88
Froshaug, Anthony, 65–66, 249n5
Frutiger, Adrian, 61–62, 112, 116–118, 127,
    210, 217
Fuse magazine, 41, 122, 124, 142, 149–150
Futura (typeface), 63, 81, 83, 101–102, 200

Geometric ideals, 76–82, 85, 96, 95–96,
    101, 111, 141, 155, 158
Georgia (typeface), 177–178, 200
Gill, Eric, 51, 103, 211, 216, 239n1
Google, 69–72, 148, 183, 209, 221n7
  Noto (type family), 69–72, 209
Goudy, Frederic W., 32–33, 37, 53,
    201, 231n25
Goudy Old Style (typeface), 151, 201
Goudy v. Hansen, 32–33, 37, 178
Grandjean, Philippe, 78, 158, 212, 232n32
Greek type, 67, 109–110, 228n2
Grid, 9–10, 65–66, 77–78, 200, 205
  digital, 62, 96, 112–113, 115, 151,
    208, 209

Habit, 4, 82–84, 149, 174–176, 178–181. *See
    also* Arendt, Hannah; Disfluency
Hall, Stuart, 19–21, 132, 184–185,
    253n7, 259n74
Han, Byung-Chul, 184, 229n12
Hebrew type, 67, 88, 171–172, 188, 251n22
Helvetica (typeface), 97, 139, 177–178, 183,
    202, 213, 227n45, 246n55, 258n71
  and Arial, 42–43, 188, 233n43
  and transparency, 229n11
  and wayfinding, 244n17
Hochuli, Jost, 158–161
Hofstadter, Douglas, 97–98, 133, 144,
    184, 206

Husserl, Edmund, 16–17
Hybrid typefaces, 40, 123, 128, 195,
    204, 211
Hypnopaedia (typeface), 43–44, 127, 148,
    155, 202

Information visualization, 22–23, 26, 30
Intellectual property. *See* Copyright;
    Patents
Invisibility. *See* Transparency
Ionic (typeface), 42, 203
ITSYLF (type program), 86–87, 203

Javal, Émile, 169, 244n19, 257n58
Jenson's Roman (typeface), 6, 58, 203,
    252n37

Kabel (typeface), 81, 83, 204
Keedy Sans (typeface), 122, 204
Kepes, Gyorgy, 26, 44, 48
*Keystone Type Foundry v. Portland
    Publishing Co.*, 34, 192
Knuth, Donald, 94–98, 128, 133, 142, 177,
    194, 206, 213
Kombinationsschrift (typeface),
    142–143, 204
Korean type, 4, 53, 57, 67, 71,
    222n10, 237n9

Latin alphabet, 27, 52, 138, 148, 165–167,
    171–172, 174
  alphabetic reforms, 102–110, 156–157
  and copyright, 32, 33, 35, 37–39,
    41, 43–44
  and technology, 71
Leaden Army, 53–54
Lee, Ji, 127–217
Legibility, 27, 114–115, 119–124, 137,
    179–180, 237n4, 254n18. *See
    also* Reading
  and readability, 27, 108, 124–128,
    162, 176
  serif vs. sans serif, 174–175, 244n19
Letter, 5, 51–53, 55, 87, 91, 94, 133, 148,
    183. *See also* Latin alphabet
  basic unit of Latin script, 65
  character and, 3–4, 34